Content Delivery Networks

Content Delivery Networks

Fundamentals, Design, and Evolution

By Dom Robinson

Co-Founder, Director and Creative Fire-Starter
id3as-company ltd.

This edition first published 2017
© 2017 John Wiley & Sons, Inc.

The right of Dom Robinson to be identified as the author(s) of this work has been asserted in accordance with law.

Registered Offices
John Wiley & Sons, Inc., 111 River Street, Hoboken, NJ 07030, USA

Editorial Office
111 River Street, Hoboken, NJ 07030, USA

For details of our global editorial offices, customer services, and more information about Wiley products visit us at www.wiley.com.

Wiley also publishes its books in a variety of electronic formats and by print-on-demand. Some content that appears in standard print versions of this book may not be available in other formats.

Library of Congress Cataloguing-in-Publication Data

Names: Robinson, Dom, author.
Title: Content delivery networks : fundamentals, design, and evolution / Dom Robinson.
Description: Hoboken, NJ : John Wiley & Sons, 2017. | Includes bibliographical references and index. |
Identifiers: LCCN 2017009407 (print) | LCCN 2017014475 (ebook) | ISBN 9781119249887 (pdf) | ISBN 9781119249894 (epub) | ISBN 9781119249870 (cloth)
Subjects: LCSH: Computer networks. | Internetworking (Telecommunication)
Classification: LCC TK5105.5 (ebook) | LCC TK5105.5 .R6255 2017 (print) | DDC 004.6–dc23
LC record available at https://lccn.loc.gov/2017009407

Cover Design: Wiley
Cover Image: © MickeyCZ/Gettyimages

Set in 10/12pt Warnock by SPi Global, Pondicherry, India

Printed in the United States of America

10 9 8 7 6 5 4 3 2 1

So family had my credit last time: this time it's professional!

Thanks and credits:

To those who inspire and allow me the honor to work with them: Adrian Roe and Steve Strong.

To those who have travelled much of the journey with me: Steve Miller-Jones, Tim Thompson, Tim Gebbett, Dane Streeter, Dom Pates, and Michael O'Rourke

To those who set me on key paths in life but themselves are no longer with us: Chris Daniels and Brian Smith (my Godfather) - RIP both.

To those who gave me a place in the industry: Eric Schumacher-Rasmussen, Dan Rayburn, Tim Siglin, Jan Ozer, Sjoerd Vogt, Jose Castillo and Joel Unickow and the Streamingmedia.com extended family.

To some of our clients for allowing us to address some very big complicated technical challenges for them: Andreas Heidoetting, Simon Ball, Osman Sen Chadun and Jon Holden-Dye, Ken Takagi and Mark Myslinski

To these guys who have shepherded my meanderings in various ways over the years: Steve Hatch, Richard Trimble, Tony Ballardie, John Riordan, Eric Van Der Kleij, Harvi Bains, Nick Lansman, Donald Miller-Jones, Daniel Montuschi, Steve Woolcock, Elle Todd, and John Enser.

To these industry figures who have made key contributions to the sector over the years: Ben Waggoner, Greg Shepherd, Jon Crowcroft, Steve Deering, Kon Wilms, Mark East, Richard Lindsay-Davis, Lee Atkinson and Stef van der Ziel.

To Mukaddim Pathan - whose nudge ultimately made this book happen (and of course to the entire Wiley team for just being absolutely great!)

To the cast of thousands who have been part of this story (which includes all my readers!)

..and finally to Vint Cerf for both, inventing the Internet, and for taking the time to help me with personal projects on a number of occasions over the years.

Contents

Frontispiece

Provides the reader with comprehensive insight into the structural decisions that can to be made when architecting a content distribution system that uses IP-based networks

The narrative of this book draws on a wealth of real-world and practical experience that the author has accrued through two decades of coalface experience architecting and delivering large, mission critical live video, webcasts, and radio streaming online, over both the Internet and private IP networks.

From this loosely defined "tradeperson's" standpoint, rather than the often explored tightly academic or business-sales point of view, this book takes a broad, humored, and at times pencil-sucking look at the art of building content delivery workflows.

Topics Include

- Delivery of live, catch-up, scheduled, on-demand, TVOD and SVOD
- CDN topologies including edge-caching, stream-splitting, Pureplay, Operator, Satellite, and Hybrid
- Computation hosting and orchestration in models such as dedicated appliances and virtualization
- Format considerations and achieving adaptive, format resilient operator networks and backbone infrastructure
- General comments on market forces over cycles and eras of evolution of these technologies

This book aims to talk in backroom engineers' English about the challenges faced in the real world, and to stimulate the reader to think extremely broadly about the options and problem spaces, and how to ensure that delivery is always, at the least, "good enough" for the operator's and consumers' commercial objectives.

As we enter what the author calls the "third generation of CDN," architects who are new to the area can use this text to draw on the author's own practical experience over the first two generations.

The book will also be an interesting read for those who have themselves built large infrastructure, providing a moment to reflect on other ways around problems. It will be a useful quick-start tool for those who are trying to understand the complex challenges of large-scale content delivery.

Not one for hiding opinion, the author also throws a number of challenging "what if" scenarios into the discussion to highlight some possible long-term design architectures that today may be a little fantastical but tomorrow may evolve based on the clear demand that such architectures could reach, should the commercial model evolve in line.

This discussion zooms in on the recent evolution of software-defined networking and the changes that this schism will bring as capabilities for many players in the network stack become unlimited, and infrastructure allocated to a particular task can be repurposed at the flick of a bit.

About the Book

While content delivery network architecture texts typically focus on current and forthcoming best practice, few take a deep retrospective view and embrace the cycles in the sector. CDNs also typically comprise 20% of their engineering work on video despite its being 80% of their traffic overhead. The author has focused on live video and audio transmission because the problems span so many layers of the network stack. There are, of course, many application-specific challenges, with particularly gaming and conferencing and to a lesser extent dynamic website acceleration and small object or large file delivery. Some of these do cause network layer issues, but generally the traffic is not impacting to a network operator – it is impacting to the Software as a Service provider or the application user. There are many complex issues that can be explored, and many are touched on in this book; however, for the main part, the core focus of this book is on live (and to a lesser extent on-demand) video delivery – TV, radio, video, and live audio over IP networks.

Synposis

Starting in 1973, streaming audio and subsequently video have been baked into the IP protocols. With the web making the quick discovery of content near ubiquitous, the demand for not only huge volumes of text but also for web apps, and significantly for high-quality video, has exploded.

The likes of the BBC, YouTube, Netflix, and countless other online publishers, have lit up the information highway with literally inconceivable amounts of information conveyed in huge quantities of bytes. Those data have to be delivered to destinations by someone, and the dark art these people practice is called content delivery networking.

Over the past 20 years we have seen several trends emerge, and these exist at both the micro level, where we are encoding pixels of video into a streaming format, and the macro level, where millions of users are able to consume content from hundreds of thousands of servers, reliably and with a great deal of resilience.

Trends in GPUs are changing how encoding resources are deployed. Evolutions in distributed computing are bringing about a macro change in the architecture of these types of services.

This evolution promises greater service levels, more flexibility to meet the customers' exact requirements, and new security challenges as infrastructure becomes increasingly shared in multi-tenant public cloud models.

Telecoms network operators are now seeing IP services as a core part of their businesses, and their understanding of their own internal content delivery architecture requirements is a key driver for their rapid adoption of a software operating model. Soon operators will, at-will, be able to deliver the CDN as an SaaS model on their own infrastructure, and additionally offer other SaaS models in the same infrastructure, providing risk mitigation as they try to underpin services for an ever more divergent target market.

Unique Perspective

The book describes the historical context of the streaming media and content delivery market from the unique perspective of the author who is a true native to the sector. It draws heavily on personal experience and hands-on examples from 20 years of live webcast production through to public company infrastructure architecture. There are few in the industry who can boast such a rich and varied practical experience across the sector, and this unique insight is fundamental to the narrative.

Aside from the anecdotal and practical commentary, the book takes the implementer through a wide range of design considerations for different network topologies, starting with the author's own requirement filtration processes through to initial sketches, through to roles and responsibilities, and to the complexity of managing change in established teams, agile as opposed to waterfall considerations, in the context of large blue chips, security and commercial models, and value chain alignment.

This widely embracing viewpoint, supported by examples ranging from IETF discussions, regulatory considerations, policy formation, coders, hardware vendors network operators, and more, is rarely available from one author. The author draws on conversations with peers in the industry, and in the course of writing, he gathers their comments and input too.

While many books on these topic slice and dice these seemingly unrelated schools of thinking into their constituent parts of commercial, technical, operational (etc.), this book can help service designers embrace the world-view of influences that need to be considered when architecting a robust and high-quality content delivery service for today's online consumers and business users.

Market Need

Today's market is just about to fully enter what the author call its third generation.

- The first – which spanned until around 2005 – was the appliance era dedicated hardware and software
- The second – which spanned from 2005 until around 2014 – was the virtual machine era when software could be moved machine to machine
- The third – which started in 2014 – is the emerging container era characterized by software that is highly componentized and is deployed to the resource best suited to the task as the capability is required

As the SDN/NFV models stimulate understanding across the Telco sector, there is about to be a tech refresh like no other: all the hardware that has traditionally been dedicated to task is going to become software driven in entirety. The Telco operators who were about to deploy Gen2 CDNs are holding back to see how the underlying infrastructure is going to evolve, to then deploy their CDN as a gen3 model using the network's built in resources to deploy the CDN as an SaaS and when a client needs it.

That cycle is going to take a further three to five years.

As it happens, service architects are going to be planning more against customer requirement than against "productizability," and this requires a breadth of thinking at the COO / CTO level from every engineer and commercial participant too.

Designing a CDN for tomorrow is a broad challenge – and this book strives to get the reader thinking like a content delivery network designer.

Audience

Target: Streaming media readership, IP / cable/ satellite / Telco / mobile and TV operators, content producers, ISPs, policy and regulatory (net neutrality and content rights), and all stakeholders in networks that may deliver large quantities of video or audio (and data / applications too).

The book is intended to start with a basic introduction, and while it will expect to push the limits of even advanced academics at times, the narrative will attempt to keep even nontechnical readers immersed in the commentary.

1

Welcome

1.1   A Few Words of Introduction

I am literally buzzing from the past few days. When the team at Wiley got me involved in the previous title I worked on with them (*Advanced Content Delivery, Streaming, and Cloud Services,* 2014), I was feeling some way out of my comfort zone. I normally write extensive commentary around the streaming media and content delivery network sector for a variety of trade presses, and very much with a hands-on tradeperson's view. This was the first time I was to contribute some writing to the community among recognized academics: a notably different focus to the engineers in enterprises who read the trade press that has been my writing home for two decades.

While I am no academic, I was bought up at the knees of academics. My godfather was head of Maths and Physics at Sussex University for many years, and he was my favorite babysitter! The opportunity to build the first Mac network at the university in the mid-1980s (unboxing the gift from Apple was a way to occupy a 9-year-old during a holiday), through to, at 17 in 1991, having a log-in (including an email and remote access to the William Herschel Telescope) to Starlink, which was one of the early global IP networks, my teenage years were spent as a geek.

However, I left two different degree courses (Astrophysics and Artificial Intelligence) to pursue commercial ventures. I was typically always naturally more entrepreneurial and impatient more than patient and academic, so I wanted to get to the place where the interesting changes could be made by applying the right technology at the right time. And I believe I have been lucky enough to be in a sufficient number of good places at the right time, and – importantly – with the right people, to have achieved some interesting things, both in delivery of that new technology but, more importantly, achieving the end goal that the technology was underpinning.

The academic world has, to an extent, caught up with the front line of practical implementations of the types of solutions, architectures, and services that

Content Delivery Networks: Fundamentals, Design, and Evolution, First Edition. Dom Robinson.
© 2017 by John Wiley & Sons, Inc. Published 2017 by John Wiley & Sons, Inc.

I am familiar with, and the previous title was exciting, in part for its success and recognition but also, for me, to write for a wider audience than those who read trade magazines!

My style was welcomed by Wiley, and the team felt that my perspective added a lot of context. Immediately after publication there was a hint that, should I have some ideas that could commit to paper, there may be interest in another publication.

Over the summer this past year I came to the conclusion that there may be some use not in trying to define an empirical best practice, but to impart a more general range of insights and to write more gutturally about the overall experience and insights I have gained from the front lines in evolving many CDN architectures, and using many others.

While my idea was being discussed with the Wiley team during these last weeks, I chaired the Content Delivery World 2015 conference (a regular "gig" for me). A speaker couldn't show, so I was asked to fill a 30 minute slot at short notice. With discussion about this book fresh in my head, I filled the 30 minute slot by talking from the top of my head about many of the topics in these pages. The room filled up to about 300 people – many CTOs and chief architects of large global blue chip Telcos, mobile networks, and broadcasters – and afterward I had a rain of business cards inviting me in to follow up. For me, this was some validation of the relevance of a sector-tradesperson's experience to the community, and reinforced my feelings that this book would have some value to readers.

The Wiley team contacted me literally as I returned from that conference and said "let's do the book," sent me the contract, and I returned it within a few minutes.

Well, you only live once. So if this isn't the right time to record some of my insights and experience, I have no idea when it will be!

I hope you find the book fun, enlightening, at times challenging, and, if nothing else, stimulating to your thought processes as you develop your content delivery strategy.

1.2   The "Why" of this Book

Today there is a wealth of excellent documentation available to the CDN architect that defines best practices. Be that for the core technical services architectures, compute paradigms, CoDec configurations, hardware setups or any other aspect, there is generally speaking both a "For Dummies" guide and a "Master Engineer" pool of literature.

There is, however, a complete lack of middle ground material. Most people who engage with streaming media, video delivery, and scaling large service platforms tend to pass through the space, and their interest is part of a specific project or role they have taken for a while in a larger corporation. They require deep understanding to address the problem space they are in, but once they acquire or develop those insights, they may move on to a new role with different responsibilities or even a completely different focus. This means that as each generation passes through some of the niche, their specific learning is then diffused away. To use an analogy, the "aural" tradition of the "bush hunter" is lost to the anthropologist's archive, and the practical tips and tricks that are only learned on the job, or spoken about at 2 am during the drive home from an event, fail to get passed on in any formal text. I aim to capture some of this and share it with you.

There is an intentional levity in my writing. I have been writing about deeply technical subjects for years, and in trade press if you don't instantly engage the reader, the reader will turn the page. My style is to develop a sense of backroom chat, and so from that perspective I hope you will allow me some creative scope and license – particularly on the analogies, which quite often are not supposed to microscopically represent the accurate details of a story but aim to help contextualize the next part of the voyage.

Do feel free to jump around: you will for sure have your own focus and reasons to pick up the book. While I try to take the reader on a voyage from start to finish, some of you will want to go head deep into my opinions on a certain scope. Do it! I am not a linear person, and I myself tend to read books in many directions! Don't be hesitant! Make it work for you.

... And do email me dom@id3as.co.uk if you want to throw virtual eggs or discuss any of the finer points!

1.3   Relevant Milestones of the Personal Voyage

So at the risk of writing what could become a CV – and no, I am not looking for a job (as you will see I have rather an awesome job) – let me give you a little potted history of some of my key milestones that will form the spine of the coming journey.

As mentioned, I was brought up on a university campus and was essentially computer conversant by the time I was squeezing pimples. In my generation that was unusual: the nerds were the ones who would get bullied by the "jocks" at school, unless they were me and large enough to give as good as I got. So I was largely left alone to geek-out, building radio telescopes and working out how to do wireless telemetry between early personal computers (BBC Micro/ ZX81 being my early platforms of choice!). You got the picture. I am assuming I am among company.

However, as university loomed, and girls got more interesting, I became more interested in music. In fact I got more interested in music and production than in astrophysics and computers. While computers were becoming more dominant, I was drawn extensively to event production/PAs/sound engineering/video production/VJing, and so on. After a few months working at Raves, and a longer spell putting on drum and bass and "chill out" club nights I left university to one side.

Two key things happened at this time.

The first, I was encouraged by a friend, Chris Daniels, to focus not on club promotion but on the promotion of micro-billing systems.

In 1994 and 1995 the UK Premium Rate Information Services and Paging Services were all the rage, and I essentially had an idea to give pagers to all the students at a very large local university for free. The plan was to allow the university to message the students with email headers if they had something in their university email (saving the poor students traveling in for email to the university network, as 90% did at the time in the pre-laptop era), and all the while charging a premium tariff to friends and family for messages sent to the students pager. The idea was well received by a variety of key people and with the support of not just the vice chancellor but also the government committee that had just published a report about how critical it was to "wire up" the students. So I – and a friend, Steve Miller-Jones, who will feature again later in the book – managed to raise £250,000 for the pager CAPEX from a wealthy venture capitalist, who himself ran a large cable network operation across Europe called UPC.

The second major thing that happened was that while the club promotion was still ongoing, I was invited to bring our Brighton club night to the Ministry of Sound in London for that year's London Institute Student Union's freshers' night festivities.

And so it was in 1996 that we wired a Real Audio encoder stream from the decks at the Ministry of Sound to an online-hosted server and then relayed it to our "normal" club in Brighton in "stereo" over a phone line. Yes, it was a 48 kbps audio feed. Yes, it was impressive that we managed to make it work at all, and yes, it was life changing.

Through that single event I saw quite how much the Internet was about to change the "music industry." The disintermediation of the record company's Vinyl monopoly was only a matter of time.

In what was *so nearly* my sharpest move, I missed registering the domain mp3.com by two weeks but managed to grab m3u.com – which was the streaming meta-file that was universally associated with mp3 and enabled instant playback through what is called progressive download.

Meanwhile my pager project had hit some issues in its test. We had a sample of 30 pagers and a class of computer science students. They were to help us measure if the revenue from their friends and family messages would help show significant enough return for us to commit the £250k investment and launch the business across the university. The test was scheduled to run for one month.

We failed to allow for the fact that the "meme" of a student's pager number needed to propagate to many places and have enough opportunity to be used before a sufficient volume of friends and family would call back and generate the level of income we required.

In the 30 days of our 30-person trial, of course, that did not happen. There was only one thing to do – to take that £250k cheque back to its owner intact. That I did.

At once that decision put me out of pocket, but in a place of deep regard with the venture capitalist. The VC then in turn asked what else I was working on, and I explained about mp3.com and m3u.com.

He instantly invested in "me," providing me expenses for R&D, travel and a living salary. Within a few months I was in the full throes of the late 1990s dot-com boom. I was in a plane every other day traveling Europe, East Coast US, and West Coast, meeting some of the folks from companies that then became internationally known. We helped get the download mp3.com functioning with its "listen now" feature, replacing the.mp3s with.m3us that pointed to the mp3s in their charts – simple but an instant effect. I recall being seated in their facilities as the my.mp3.com furore hit, and as their valuation went into the billions, and at the same time became the pre-Napster hot potato.

I knew Napster and Scour as they kicked off – having met them at early Streaming Media Conferences (one at which Bill Gates gave the keynote), although was in practice closer to mp3.com myself. I also engaged with Real Networks and Microsoft Netshow Theatre as it became Windows Media.

It was an awesome, electric time.

However, in 2000 the bubble was already showing severe signs of deflation, and it was time to come back to focus on the UK and establish my own base and business, rather than continue to work in an Incubator that itself was struggling to turn out some big wins in a turning tide.

So I set up as a streaming media and IPTV consultant and webcaster, and went about getting my first major client. Thanks to another crazy, but close friend – known as Timmy or "TT" – who is one of the more fearless sales guys I have ever met, we essentially walked up to the UK Prime Minister's office and engaged the webmaster there in a discussion about improving the PMO's communications using video (and a demo of streaming live drum and bass to an HP Jornada over a 9.6 band infrared modem on a Nokia phone!).

From there I was put forward to help a small company, Westminster Digital, with their deployments of video workflows for both the PMO and for Parliament; in particular, I helped develop the workflow that brought the weekly Prime Minister's questions to the web.

With that on my CV, establishing engagements with interesting broadcasters and Internet companies proved much easier, and my freelance consulting and webcasting managed to keep me fed, while the stability of regular article writing for the ISP *World and Streaming Media* helped with both marketing and cash flow. I managed to hook into most of the London-based former DVD authoring – now webcasting – companies as their ad hoc live encoding engineer. This allowed me to get involved with literally hundreds, if not thousands, of live events – ranging from simple audio conferences through to the Glastonbury Festival, FatBoySlim, and many others.

I have worked with three heads of state, royalty on two occasions, many pop stars and CEOs, and some downright dirty and dodgy people too, both public sector and private! It gave me pragmatism about the real "honesty" of media, although my impartial addiction to the technical was what kept me fed. I recall producing the conference league soccer for BT and Talkpoint over a couple of years: what kept me directing the production was an absolute lack of interest in the sport. I could always be relied on to be watching the kit over and above the game, although did on occasion confuse the audiences by putting up scores on the displays for the wrong teams ....

However, I grew increasingly frustrated by the lack of UK-based CDNs and the limitations that working with US CDNs always carried. They typically sought minimum monthly commitments for 6 to 18 months even if you only wanted to do a single event. They had maximum throughput on long contribution feeds into US servers maxing me at 400 Kbps with no UK entry points, etc.

I was also increasingly fascinated with IP multicast – an amazing technology that I saw has the potency to disintermediate broadcast networks in the same way that mp3 disintermediated the monopoly of the record industry.

I could use it on my own LANs and my clients' privately run Enterprise networks, but I couldn't multicast on the Internet. It took me a significant amount of deep reading to understand why. I subsequently tracked down those few academics – mostly huddled around Professor Jon Crowcroft, then of UCL and now at Cambridge – who understood the problem, and had some solutions technically, but as I was to discover, the academics had not really focused on the real-world business case that would drive the technological adoption ...

... and that was where I realized I had something, perhaps entrepreneurial, to add to that community.

I rounded on Dr. Tony Ballardie. He had, as part of his academic career, pioneered key multicast protocols CBT, PIM-SM/SSM, and MBGP, and later, after a project we worked on together, he introduced AMT at a BOF in the IETF .... And if you didn't follow that, then be ready to Google some of those terms when you see them appear again later on!

He and I met when I arrived at a tennis match he was competing in, in 2001, and I convinced him to sit down for a coffee, whereupon I explained my vision for how multicast eventually would have to be scaled up to deliver content to large audiences, as the evolution of TV online would demand it.

Remember, this was at a time when the FT had published a report for the recording industry saying that the Internet would never be capable of delivering multicast in a consumer friendly way, and they should focus on using it for DVD e-Commerce sales ....

It was then I realized that while there were many things multicast was developed for, TV being one of them, which the Multicast pioneers had foreseen for their technology, it was also clear that none of them came from or knew the broadcast and production world …

… which was generally where a "webcaster" hung out. I could see the real-world commercial arrival of this disruptive technology. Tony knew how it worked.

With the huge dot-com crashes happening around us, it was a complicated time. However, in the midst of the Enron crisis (also accompanied by the Global-Crossing collapse that directly affected Global-MIX) a sudden beam of business broke through and gave the online video sector validity, and that was something called "Fair Disclosure" – which, in short, means that public companies suddenly had to webcast their annual and quarterly analyst briefings to their shareholders. I will deep dive more on this later, particularly in the case studies around NASDAQ OMX.

So Tony and went to ground together for some time, and in early 2003 we took an architecture to Keith Mitchell, one of the founders of the London Internet eXchange, who gave us some nominal resources to build the world's first Multicast Interconnect eXchange, Global-MIX.

Come 2004 we were in service acquiring live video feeds from dozens of TV channels, and using Windows Media services' multicast capabilities, we were forwarding multicast live streams onto the MIX where anyone at the exchange could take on direct delivery of the IP multicasts.

Naturally, because we were trying to seed something, the adoption was patchy, and it took us a further year or two, and a large commercial content delivery project or two, to really understand that the insurance-stream unicast, which was essentially a low-SLA backup that most of our clients actually used – since their ISP was not MIX / MBGP peered – was increasingly our best weapon.

As an ISP, we would point out to our peers where large quantities of the same traffic were impacting their general peering, and we would work with them to establish a single multicast peering, and sometimes reduce many Gbps of traffic to a few Mbps. We gauged that at peak we managed to reach 15% of our audience with a multicast, and for a decade this was the largest such peak with public ISP delivery. The biggest problem was the churn of the ISPs we peered. Even when we managed to get multicast peering, and flow right through to the ISP subscribers with a particular ISP, we were such an anomaly to normal ISP operations that we would often find that the multicast would be switched off overnight across a large multicast peer as part of some other service deployment, or network policy, would seep in and prevent the flow.

The amount of saving it was making was relatively small – video was in its infancy – and even if it had represented a significant saving, there was another critical problem. As we increased our unicast fallback volumes, our buying power put us in a position where we could compete well in the same market as other unicast providers – however, if we optimized our network and our traffic volumes on the unicast side dropped, then our price on the 85% of our traffic that was unicast jumped up. Our own efficiency became a thorn in our side. While multicast is great for an operator, the commercial model had problems for an OTT player such as Global-MIX a decade ago, and indeed persists for most CDNs today.

Additionally operational overhead of managing OTT multicast was considerable for those ISPs we peered with, and as 2008 cut in, and as the advertising market, and YouTube pushed everyone to Adobe's Flash (which could not be multicast), we could see the writing on the wall for Windows Media.

Worse in that climate, we had just developed a first of its type virtual encoder ourselves, and yet we were still running our core business on an appliance-built infrastructure. So we didn't have agility when we needed it most.

Along the way I have also built a dozen or so small start-ups in and around (and occasionally miles away from) the online media space – particularly live TV or webcasting online. Most of these were rolled into Global-MIX between 2007 and 2009, and individually they had degrees of success ranging from "not very interesting," either to this audience or to anyone focused on financial opportunities, through to ones that created jobs and were recognized on international stages. I will give examples of these where they become relevant in the text.

At the end of 2009 I dissolved Global-MIX, and we handed the business to peers in the sector in a very controlled way – allowing us to maintain the professional relationships with our long-standing clients. This meant that the team became almost universally embedded in key roles in some of the up and coming online video companies, including Limelight, Origin Digital, and Sharp-Stream.

For my part, I teamed up with Dr. Adrian Roe and Steve Strong, who I had been considering working with to implement our AMT Gateway suite as Global-MIX was in its zenith a short while before.

These guys were something different; they had a deep background in Fintech and Retail software at scale, virtualized, with stringent regulatory and service level frame works, and yet, after 20 years building several companies up to three-figure headcounts, they wanted a break from Fintech and Retail and wanted to come to deploy some of their skill, insights, and experience to the online media space.

I had a list of problems in the sector needing solutions, and Adrian and Steve were no mere systems integrators; they were pure code alchemists. This meant we could (nearly) always solve the problems; the decision was which to do first and which would show the best return.

Since then we have never been short of id3as ("ideas") – there will be plenty of discussion about our outlook, approach, and projects in the next pages.

2

Context and Orientation

OK. With that preamble and personal contextualization complete, let me now take you through a little deep dive into the broad history of the industry and its technologies. Much of the content relating to live streaming (in particular) here was also covered in my chapter in *Advanced Content Delivery, Streaming, and Cloud Services*, and I have bought forward some of the key points from there verbatim. However, I have re-hashed that content somewhat, since it was heavily focused only on live and linear streaming, to include more insights into streaming of on-demand content too.

While I have a particular personal fascination with, and interest in the challenges live linear distribution presents, I am also strongly aware that the larger part of the market is focused on the immediacy of on-demand delivery – so much so that still to this day I hear broadcasters and large content service providers describe the Internet as if it was only able to deliver on-demand content. Interestingly they often view the Internet content models as if they were junior brothers, and simply not going to be able to participate in the live linear distribution that has traditionally been the preserve of broadcasters.

I am well known on the conference circuit for challenging such views. I will discuss my challenges a little as we go, but for now just take it as spoken that I believe all "broadcast" will be simulcast online as "the norm" within just a few years, and with time the commoditization in the IP technologies and pressure on spectrum will show traditional DTH and DTV broadcast to be ineffective commercially, despite not being "broken" or limited in any functional way. The challenge for broadcast will be to increase its value proposition by factors such as increasing the quality of the content production (and story) and secondarily the quality of images broadcast ... why do you think it is that 4k and UHD are so popular at the time of writing! Yes, the fastest way to roll out such capability may be via broadcast – and no, it doesn't matter that the end user cannot even perceive the benefit; people will buy in herds anyway, if for nothing else than to feel social inclusion with the neighbors ...

... but I digress into opinion. Let us go back to some basics.

Content Delivery Networks: Fundamentals, Design, and Evolution, First Edition. Dom Robinson.
© 2017 by John Wiley & Sons, Inc. Published 2017 by John Wiley & Sons, Inc.

2.1   History of Streaming

While there are many isolated events and micro steps that have converged to evolve today's rich and versatile range of live streaming applications and technologies, there are a few milestones that demark clear step-changes of note.

The live streaming systems in use today are all derived from voice conferencing technologies. Largely because audio requires less bandwidth to transmit over a network than video does, it is also worth noting that voice and audio streaming pre-dates video streaming and in fact the birthdate of live streaming within an Internet Protocol context is arguably the date of introduction of the Network Voice Protocol[1] on ARPANET.

While the formal RFC741 was not published until November 22, 1977, NVP was, according to that RFC, first tested in December 1973, a mere two months after TCP for "Internetworking Protocols" was introduced to the world by Vint Cerf and Robert Kahn in Sussex University (September 1973). Here is an excerpt from that RFC:

> The Network Voice Protocol (NVP), implemented first in December 1973, and has been in use since then for local and trans-net real-time voice communication over the ARPANET at the following sites:
>
> - Information Sciences Institute, for LPC and CVSD, with a PDP-11/45 and an SPS-41
> - Lincoln Laboratory, for LPC and CVSD, with a TX2 and the Lincoln FDP, and with a PDP-11/45 and the LDVT
> - Culler-Harrison, Inc., for LPC, with the Culler-Harrison MP32A and AP-90
> - Stanford Research Institute, for LPC, with a PDP-11/40 and an SPS-41

An unpublished memorandum from USC /ISI in April 1, 1981, by Danny Cohen is widely referenced as adding extensions to the Network Voice Protocol called the NVP-II or "Packet Video Protocol," and this seems to mark a clear starting point for the formalization of combined real-time audio and video delivery over Internet-worked networks.

In the process of compiling this history Vint Cerf was referenced for his views on who the pioneers were when specifically looking for who did the first webcasts, and he in turn pointed us to both Danny Cohen and also to Stephen Casner of ISI. Though they were part of multiple teams, it is clear that Cohen and Casner had key insights to the creation of the first audio streaming over what was then the ARPANET.

---

1 http://en.wikipedia.org/wiki/Network_Voice_Protocol

Here is the history as communicated in an email to me by Stephen Casner:

> Danny and I, along with others at ISI and at several other cooperating institutions, worked on transmission of packet voice over the ARPAnet starting in 1974. It was specific to voice rather than any audio signal because we needed significant bandwidth compression using voice coding (vocoding) to fit in the capacity of the ARPAnet. This was not voice over IP because IP did not exist yet, but it was packet voice using ARPAnet protocols.
>
> It was not until the early 1980's that we expanded to video when a higher capacity packet satellite network called Wideband Net was installed. The first video was, indeed, crackling black & white with variable frame rate depending upon how much of the image was changing. Later we adapted commercial videoconferencing CoDecs that had been designed to work over synchronous circuits to instead work over the packet network. These provided colour and higher fidelity.
>
> While work on developing our packet video system occurred during the first half of the 1980s, the packet video system wasn't completed and operational until 1986. The following is an excerpt from the Internet Monthly Report for March, 1986:
>
> Multimedia Conferencing Demo
>
> On April 1, a real-time multimedia teleconference was held between ISI and BBN using packet video and packet voice over the Wideband Net, along with the presentation of text and graphics on Sun workstations at each end. This was the first use of packet video for a working conference. Participants included BBN, ISI and SRI, plus sponsors from DARPA and NOSC.
>
> The teleconference was the culmination of several efforts during March. Our packet video installation at Lincoln Lab was moved to BBN for ready access by the multimedia conferencing researchers there. Performance of the Voice Funnel and Packet Video software was tuned to allow maximum throughput and to coordinate the simultaneous use of packet voice with packet video. And last but certainly not least, the Wideband Net stream service and QPSK modulation were made available to provide the high bandwidth and low delay required for good packet video.
>
> – *Steve Casner*

So, for the purposes of live video streaming over the Internet Protocols, the *definitive* birthdate of live streaming is April 1, 1986 – the day the ARPANET was turned off leaving only the Internet – although it is clear that in the context of the ARPANET a very similar range of streaming had been pioneered some years before.

It is also interesting to note that these technologies took at least 10 years to evolve into the media players and production tools that have since become increasingly familiar to today's Internet browser and connected TV users.

So what of on-demand content delivery? Well, to understand the drivers and technologies that turned file delivery into streaming content delivery, we should take a moment to think about what streaming really means.

2.1.1 Foundations – What does "Streaming" Really Mean?

Just as there are many histories of the origins of live streaming, there are many interpretations of what the term means!

Live streaming typically has four key stages that align to form a "workflow."

As Figure 2.1 shows, the encoding stage converts the video feed into a suitable form for streaming (typically compressing it to "fit" within the bandwidth of the available network), and "contributes" it to the network, sending it to the publishing server. Once "acquired," the publishing server prepares the audio or video for distribution and forwards it to a network of relays that forms the content distribution network (CDN). Each client then uses a directory or schedule such as a webpage or electronic program guide (EPG) to discover the content they want to consume, and metadata is passed to the decoding media player. The decoding media player connects to the distribution network, requests and receives the stream, and subsequently decodes the encoded video or audio, presenting it to the user's display.

For most people, the experience of using a simple webcam-based videoconference system, such as those that Apple Facetime or Skype can provide, has become a common experience of live streaming. The real-time facility of being able to hold a conversation in a natural way between two remote locations is a solid starting point for understanding what we mean, in common language, when we talk about video being "live." But, while it seems obvious at first, "live" is not a simple term in the context of data delivery.

In the context of data delivered electronically or digitally, the speed of light alone determines a small delay between the moment an action occurs (or a sound is made) and when the recipient experiences it. This delay is a combination of two effects: propagation delay and latency. Propagation delay is a simple physical effect, specific to the length of network link that the transmission occurs over and caused by the time the electrons or photons carrying the signal take to traverse that length, where latency also includes delays caused by

Figure 2.1 Classic live streaming workflow.

intermediate processes within the network. We will explore latency and these contributory intermediate processes later in this chapter; however, it is worth noting that latency is often used as a single term including propagation delay, since with the exception of satellite transmission, propagation delay is usually relatively insignificant in comparison to the latency effects of processing.

Typically in telephony and real-time conversation a maximum end-to-end latency of 150 ms is thought to be acceptable (Telecommunication Standarization Sector of ITU, 2013). This is an important starting point for the understanding of what can be considered to be live in the context of networked audio visual content delivery. If 150 ms latency is acceptable for two humans to hold a natural conversation, then this can most certainly be considered to be real-time live conversation. This synchronicity of communication gives the users of the system a sense that they are both with each other in "real life" despite the separation caused by the telecommunications (note *tele* = "far" in Greek).

Now, although this form of video is two way, obviously the key here is that events happening at either location are percieved to be seen "live" at the other remote location. Interestingly, if we now turn off one of the two-way channels, we might assume that we are watching the same live content. However, we would actually have no frame of reference should that video from the remote location be delayed by a further few tens of milliseconds, or even minutes or hours. For a viewer at a remote location with no other way to know when the remote events occur, they are still perceived to be live.

This can cause some confusion when talking about live video transmission. Indeed it is possible for a viewer to, for example, make a phone call to the source and discover that the phone call has lower latency – in a "real-time" experience, where the video may take considerably longer to transmit back – resulting in the caller hearing the source on the phone say hello some moments before they are seen to say hello on the video signal.

Strictly speaking it would be better to use a slightly different term to describe what is commonly called "live video." Often the term "linear video" is used for televisual content that is transmitted to its receiver synchronously as it is created by its origin or source, while "nonlinear video" is used to describe content that is accessed "randomly" by the receiver asynchronously, or some time after it has been created – for example, an on-demand movie viewing.

Incidentally, while the concepts are similar the terms "linear video" and "nonlinear video" are not to be confused with linear and nonlinear editing – while they are similar and in many ways related, they are different, and refer to techniques of editing video content.

2.1.2 Streaming

Despite the term having entered common vernacular, "streaming" remains a distinctly difficult term to accurately and clearly define. By understanding why a "live" stream may lag behind "real life," we begin to appreciate that in the context of digital televisual communications "things must happen" to enable the communication. These "things" can be one or a series of continuous, synchronous processes all working together to bring the subject of the video to the receiver as fast as possible, or these "things" can be a sequence of asynchronous processes that occur over a much wider timespan, sometimes occurring a long time after the event that is the subject of the video is over, and where the audience can access the content at a later time, be that of their choosing or of the video service providers scheduling.

In a packet network, such as the Internet, whatever the underlying processes that contribute to a communication of data, that "item" of data will, by definition, be broken up into a series of constituent packets that must be sent in a coordinated way over the network, sequenced by the receiver, usually having any missing packets "re-ordered and re-delivered," and then the receiver must process those packets to reconstitute the item and restore it to being a usable communication.

Typically, when we think about these "items" of data being sent over the Internet, we think of messages, files, images, or pages. This thinking persists for most people when they think about video, not least because most people make extensive use of on-demand services such as YouTube and Netflix, and the impression is that some entire "film" is being downloaded in the same way an email is downloaded when you wish to read it. Our traditional perception of obtaining such data in the nonvirtual world is filled with content in the form of letters, books, photographs, and so on, and we have a tradition of understanding the content being preserved as discrete items in some form of medium – Intellectual Property lawyers call these "fixations."

Streaming changes that.

One of the first things to be understood when trying to understand streaming is what it tries to achieve. Let's take a look at mp3 audio as an example. In the early 1990s when the Internet was expanding into the domestic environment, users typically could access via dial up over standard telephone lines, and the typical access speed was 14.4 kbps. Today domestic broadband speeds are usually faster than 1Mbps – so over a thousand times faster than in the mid-1990s – and many are over 100Mbps. In this new age a single 5 MB mp3 file may only take a few seconds to download – noticeably less time than it takes to play that mp3 file – however, in the mid-1990s, when mp3 first emerged, it could take at least as long as the play duration of the file to download – so a 5 minute long piece of music would take often more than 5 minutes between the point of choosing to listen to it, and the point it could be heard. This is was far from satisfactory from the user's point of view.

One of the problems was that once a download of the mp3 was started, even though much of the audio data was available on the local computer, the computer itself could not make sense of the file – it was not a discrete item.

Because computer data files typically needed to accurately convey information, files needed to have a clear structure, and this not only included the title and the first information about the file (the "file headers") at the front (called the Front of File data) to configure the software that would handle the incoming file as its processing began, but it also needed the last bit of data, the so-called End of File (EOF), which often included error-checking information at the very least. Only when the EOF was received, and error checking was complete, was the downloaded file "released" to the operating system as a complete data item for use in applications such as media players. Among other things, this protected the computer from endlessly downloading data and filling up its local memory, which ultimately would have brought the computer to a standstill.

Engineers noted that *during the file transfer,* the data already received by the computer could potentially be used by the "media player application," even though there was more being delivered by the download process. The logic was: if this were possible, then the listener need not wait until the download of an mp3 completed in entirety before their player could begin to process the incoming data and play the music "as it arrived"....

Note that while the file was still in mid-transfer, it was being transferred by being broken into small "chunks" by the underlying packet network process. Each chunk was in its own right a small file – it just happened that the data it contained made little sense in isolation as a single "item" to the application layer technologies such as the media players. However, by accruing enough of these chunks in a buffer between the source and the point of processing, a media player application could be set up so that it really made no difference if the chunks were being retrieved from disc or from a buffer. The result was that playback of the mp3 became possible despite no EOF being present, and for as long as the buffer contained "the next" chunk that the player requested.

This continuous flow of chunks of data derived from a larger file and delivered over a packet network became known as a "stream." It is important to note here that a continuously updated source of a stream could potentially be configured to play forever. This configuration or model is the starting point for understanding what a live stream is.

In summary: A series of chunks of audio or video data that are being continuously generated by a source or origin (now usually called an "encoder"), and transferred (by a network of distribution servers) to a recipient (the "decoder").

Live streaming is a linear process, synchronous in nature. The EOF may or may not be part of the story – some modern models have evolved so the "chunks" may actually have many EOFs, but for the purposes of common understanding a key difference between a "live stream" and an "on-demand" stream is that, in the case of a live stream at least, the EOF will never be transferred while the transmission is "live."

2.1.3 Related Network Models

Earlier we briefly looked at propagation delay and latency and the effect these have on perceptions of what "live" means. While the propagation delay is a physical effect, as described above, other factors cause delays, and these are more widely embraced under the description of latency. It is important to understand the OSI Network (Telecommunication Standarization Sector of ITU, 1994) and TCPIP network stacks.[2]

For convenience let us consider a summary diagram of the two in Figure 2.2.

The TCPIP model is not explicitly defined in the same detail as the OSI model, since the Internet Engineering Taskforce strives to be a consensual group rather than a standards organization, but the diagram shows a common interpretation of the equivalence of the two stacks. Network engineers will talk about these layers from the bottom up, commonly referring to the physical layer (common to both) as layer 1, but the application layer is referred to as layer 4 in the TCPIP model, and layer 7 in the OSI model. For the purpose of the rest of this section, I will refer only to the layering in the TCPIP model.

2.1.4 Physical Network Considerations

The propagation delay occurs in the Network Interface layer 1. This is where light passes through fiber, and electric current flows through Ethernet (etc.). Internet networks consist of a variety of mixed forms of physical point-to-point

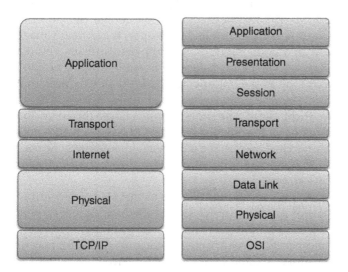

Figure 2.2 TCP/IP and OSI network layer models compared.

---

2 http://tools.ietf.org/html/rfc1122

links terminated by various telecommunications and networking systems that then interface with each other at junctions called routers. The computational processing in the terminations usually, but not always, happens as part of an electrical process or a photoelectric process with little computed logic – so, for example, fiber multiplexers operate optically based on wavelength of light, and Ethernet switches work electrically based on the sequence of bits in the header of the datagram. There may be some delay introduced, but at this stage the latency is largely affected by propagation delay more than any other form of delay.

2.1.5 Internet Layer Considerations

Once the packets are handed to the router – the Internet layer 2 – things start to change. The router must have a degree of "intelligence" to decide which of the multiple possible "other connected network links" that router should forward each packet. The first time a stream of data is routed, this forwarding path must be discovered, and this can take a few milliseconds – possibly more. This adds latency to the time it takes these packet to reach the recipient.

Once the route is discovered, the router will make a note and will store that routing in a local "directory" called a "routing table." This minimizes the processing that the router must do. However, any changes to the networks condition will cause a "re-evaluation" of the route over which the router can forward packets. Again, this will add some latency to the packets that are being throughput.

Routing is typically an optimized process and uses dedicated technology that can function by introducing minimal latency.

It is important to understand the effects of the network layer in introducing propagation. When streaming live, the variety of options one is presented with along the workflow can indeed critically affect the overall process.

If the original signal is delivered over a network link that is prone to varied propagation delay or other contributing latency factors, then no matter how well constructed the onward distribution network is, it can only distribute a varied and delayed source image or sound.

2.1.6 Transport Layer Considerations

Planning the contribution feed is of *utmost importance* to the creation of a stable and high-quality user experience in the live streaming environment. While layer-1 and layer-2 network services are typically bought in from a network services operator, there are many choices that the live streaming engineer (often called a "webcaster" in the context of streaming purely on the Internet) can autonomously make in the use of the layer-3 IP network services that he or she buys.

Continuing our journey "up the stack," we move up from the simple IP routing on layer 2 into the transport layer (layer 3), and we find the Transmission Control Protocol (TCP) and its twin the User Datagram Protocol (UDP).

UDP has a variety of good uses in audio and video streaming, and for many years UDP-based transport protocols for audio and video streaming were developed on the assumption that UDP would become the standard way to transmit audio and video.

UDP has no automatic retransmission process. So, if a packet fails to make it over the network link, it is up to the programmer to define when (or indeed *if*) this should be corrected. In the case of a large quantity of data sent in an audio or video transmission, a few lost packets in a stream are generally not missed. The end user does not notice a few pixels of data not shown in a moving image – the eye and brain work together to correct this (known as "perceptual" audio and video encoding).

For many years the early streaming protocols were thus engineered with UDP transport in mind, and this led to a range of custom servers, called "media servers," appearing that specialized in packetizing encoded video into UDP datagrams. Often these media servers had separate control protocols that enabled client applications to communicate with the media servers to establish unique user sessions and subsequently control which video or audio stream is played. These application control protocols offered features such as pause, stop, rewind, and play.

2.1.7 Applications – Transport Protocols

The best example of a media server is RTSP, the Real Time Streaming Protocol, which acts as a control protocol for an RTP (Real Time Protocol) stream, and is almost invariably (although not exclusively, as we will see below) transported on UDP. RTP essentially sequences the packets and sends them onto the network, and the recipient client, the "media player," reassembles all the packets into sequence in a buffer before playing it to the user. Missing packets are ignored, and timestamps in the packets allow for the correct timing of the playback, even if packets are missing. RTSP also allows the user to request a live stream from the server or to seek various places in the stream if the stream is a playback of an on-demand file.

While common internally on private networks, and still used today for many IPTV installations, RTSP (which collectively refers to RTP too) has a few shortcomings. Natural address translation (NAT), which allows a router with a single public IP address to then provide gateway access to multiple machines, is a common way to put enterprises or groups of computers online with a shared single Internet connection.

For a number of reasons, however, UDP is quite complex to route into a NATted LAN. The router receives the UDP from the offsite server, but without an additional application controlling the UDP packet forwarding, the router doesn't know where (on the LAN) to forward the packet. For this reason RTSP struggled for many years in scenarios where publishers wanted to deliver that content into enterprises and homes with more than one computer.

The two major vendors during this era (1996 to 2004), Real Networks and Microsoft, had to implement "fallback" strategies so that when the "optimal" UDP-based RTSP streams could not be received by media players inside NATted LANs the media players could then explicitly request the stream over RTSP using the "reliable" Transport Control Protocol (TCP). RTSP also requires fairly specific firewall configurations, allowing RTSP requests and responses in and out of the LAN, and the resulting stream (be it TCP or UDP) to "flow" into the LAN on ports, which, by default, were often closed.

To receive the stream inside the LAN, home users would then be required to open up such firewalls – something that was usually beyond their expertise. For enterprise administrators, this made streaming using RTSP very much an "opt-in" process, which then meant building a business case for allowing streaming video and audio into the enterprise. Anecdotally this was, in the late 1990s, akin to "building a business case to bring a TV to work" – and was blocked by most network administrators.

Interestingly, streaming was, in the culture of engineers of the era, seen to be something that *needed* its own transports. Because network bandwidth was a relatively scarce commodity, optimization was required, and retransmission of lost video packets was one of the fundamental "waste of bandwidth" elements that contributed to that culture. UDP-based streaming protocols such as RTSP PNA and even MPEG-TS (over IP) were refined to ensure that in controlled network conditions the bare minimum network utilization occurred, ensuring that one user's use of a video impacted other users on the network as little as possible.

Despite this collective work, there were some interesting external factors that eventually meant that by the end of the first decade of this century, less optimal methods for streaming have become the dominant players in the market.

2.1.8 Protocol Evolution

Adobe's RTMP protocol, while close to RTSP, supported TCP only, thus losing all the advantages of RTP's UDP support in terms of network optimization but also gaining simplicity and, firewall issues aside, removing the complexity of NAT forwarding.

Initially the proprietary RTMP locked users into the Flash ecosystem – it was the only way for audio and video stream publishers to reach the widely distributed (and free) Flash Media Player, which had gained its ubiquity as a cross-platform browser plug-in that simplified the presentation for graphics and animations in webpages, and included audio and video presentation capabilities. The only way to generate RTMP streams was with the Flash Media encoder/ server combination, and at first the video enCOding and DECoding (CoDec) video compression choice was limited and was very low quality. However, the simple fact that when the player opened it would reliably open a video stream was a "magic bullet" and meant that the Flash ecosystem had a key economic driver that the other "more optimized" formats didn't: principally it worked for *advertisers.*

Very quickly it became interesting for publishers to add video to their sites because the Flash Player brought with it pre-roll adverts that played as soon as the webpage opened, and each advert brought the publisher money. Regardless of any other technology advantages under the hood, the owners of the publishing companies were enthused, so Flash video gained rapid adoption. This wasn't without exception – the enterprises still had to make the same "opt-in" policy decisions to allow Flash Media Player to install, and in fact even today many enterprises prefer the IP multicast enabled Windows Media Player model to ensure low impact of traffic during live webcasts on their LANs. However, the vast majority of streaming – both live and on demand – has rapidly moved to the TCP-based RTMP.

2.1.8.1 Platform Divergence and CoDec Convergence

One would think that this would be the end of the story – but at this stage some other factors began to come into force. The proprietary nature of RTMP increasingly locked in some publishers to the Adobe format, but it also "locked out" others: and many of these were the major broadcasters who, seeing online video "coming of age" wanted to add Internet and IP-networked video to their workflow outputs. The problem with RTMP and the Flash Media ecosystem and format is that it had a number of shortcomings. First and foremost Adobe was slow to adopt the increasingly popular h.264 video compression standard. Other technologies were faster to market with h.264, which was both undeniably better quality than Adobe's own choice of VP6 CoDec and presented a reduced risk for broadcasters looking at their long-term storage strategies for their video archives. h.264 is an international standard, while Adobe's widespread VP6 was not, so risk-assessors within in broadcasters preferred the vendor independence that h.264 offered.

In 2007 Wowza introduced their media server. It was the first independent commercially supported server that could acquire a live stream from Adobe's Flash Media live encoder and distribute that stream to Flash Media Player – and it came with a price ticket that was roughly a quarter of the Flash Media server. Historically there has been a risk of a legal case between Adobe and Wowza concerning patents and use of "proprietary" variations of the RTMP standards, but aside from that, the critical step forward here was that Wowza's media server also supported other transport protocols, including RTSP, the Internet radio streaming protocols Shoutcast and Icecast, and critically MPEG transport streams (MPEG-TS).

Once the Flash ecosystem updated to include decode capabilities for h.264, the native support for MPEG-TS in Wowza was of particular significance to the Broadcast industry since it enabled their traditional TV and Satellite workflows, which already used MPEG-TS for their "traditional" broadcasting systems, to "ingest" the live signals which had been encoded in h.264, into Wowza and, by "trans-muxing" the stream from MPEG-TS to RTMP through the Wowza server, they could, in one step, simply distribute the live signals over the Internet to the ubiquitous Flash Media Players.

While Wowza was still proprietary, its relatively open integration with many third party encoders, and reach to Flash Media Player, encouraged more and more organizations to publish to the Internet.

2.1.8.2 Adaptive Bitrate Arrives

Despite this convergence on the h.264 CoDec, and widespread success of Flash Player underpinned by both Adobe and Wowza, there were still some significant innovations to come. While the fundamental concept was initiated in 2002 as part of the DVD Forum,[3] a range of technologies, collectively known as "adaptive bitrate streaming" technologies, took several years to reach mainstream adoption as common Internet streaming formats. The runaway successes of these commercial implementations, which have emerged are Microsoft's Smooth Streaming ("Smooth") and Apple's HTTP Live Streaming (HLS). Adobe have tried to keep up by introducing Adobe's HTTP Dynamic Streaming, although arguably it has not seen nearly as much adoption as both Smooth (which was first to market) and HLS (which enjoyed a strong piggyback on the success of the iOS-based iPhone and iPad and so pretty much forced HLS into the market as the only option to live stream to those devices).

The principle aim of adaptive bitrate streaming technology is to allow the publisher to produce several quality streams at the same time – perhaps one for mobile streaming at 300 kbps, one for domestic SD streaming over WiFi at 750Kbps, and one for HD streaming at 1.4Mbps, for example – and to synchronize the publishing of each of these streams in such a way that if a recipient decoder wishes to switch from one bitrate to another (perhaps because the network conditions are varying), then the client player simply requests the "next" packets from the lower or higher bitrate stream, and these are sequenced seamlessly in the player's buffer. This means that while the quality of the image may pixelate or increase mid-playback, there is no transport layer interruption of the flow of the streaming – and so the changing quality is not accompanied by a break in the continuity of the stream. This provides a much better quality

---

3 http://en.wikipedia.org/wiki/Adaptive_bitrate_streaming

of experience (QoE) for the viewer. This smooth transition from one bitrate to another was precisely why Microsoft named their technology Smooth Streaming.

Such technologies almost invariably require discrete layer-3 connections between each player and the server and so invariably use TCP as the control protocol. This comes with significant network overhead, as discussed above, and in fact the nature of creating a buffer to manage the bitrate switching, and the decision-making processes involved in that, combine to add significant latency. While there were one or two very early approaches to try to adapt traditional media servers to support distribution of adaptive bitrate streaming technologies, the role of these servers was almost universally to act as a termination point of the source contribution feed, and to "chunk" or "fragment" the different bitrates into synchronized blocks of video – usually split at the video key frames along the lines of the MPEG "groups of pictures" (GoPs) – and then to packetize these in wrappers of HTTP transport protocol packets.

Accordingly the distribution technology of choice quickly became relatively common HTTP servers, with modifications appearing for Microsoft's IIS, and Apache, among others. Again, from a purist's point of view, while there were many network-optimization reasons not to use HTTP (which has, for example, no flow control and simply uses all available network bandwidth to transfer any given datagram), there were some critical advantages that this method of streaming introduced.

2.1.8.3 Adaptive Bitrate – Enterprise

The first of these concerned enterprise networks. HTTP traffic is Worldwide Web traffic. To "block" this type of streaming from a corporate network requires intelligent firewalling – and so suddenly the policy decision to block streaming in the enterprise moved from "opt-in" to "opt-out." Accordingly the argument behind the business case for streaming in the enterprise moved from "what is the business case for streaming" to "what is the business case for turning it off?"

The second advantage was also a critical issue for enterprises. Windows Media's own protocol (MMS), Flash's RTMP, and the "standard" RTSP were all complex protocols to forward into the enterprise. Each essentially required a proxy server between the LAN and the WAN, which would acquire the stream from the Internet source and then handle all subsequent requests from within the LAN.

For video-on-demand systems this caching required custom technology to set up, but this was not expressly complex.

However, when the CEO of the enterprise made a live announcement to all the staff, it became critical that the live stream was pre-configured on the proxy/gateway technology so that only a single stream would be delivered over the WAN to the thousands of recipients potentially wanting to "tune in" – and this severely limited the ability of enterprises to deploy live streaming in an ad hoc fashion.

Commercial solutions were almost invariably developed from the basic Windows or Adobe media server SDKs, and either came as part of wider proxy server solutions (often simply as a virtual machine image running on board the proxy using a common interface) or was delivered as custom-built implementations of the same SDKs. This meant there were no cheap options, and again, this inhibited enterprise live streaming adoption.

It is worth noting here that live traffic in enterprises is often concentrated around live "events" rather than 24/7 television-like streaming, and this causes very specific congestion issues on the networks involved. In a corporate LAN, the typical network is 100Mbps or even 1Gbps, so 100 users streaming at 500 kbps use a significant amount of the overall network capacity. While 30 minute on-demand files may take hours or event days or weeks to circulate an office, the number of simultaneous users will always be limited and so congestion on the network will be limited.

When the CEO makes a live announcement about forthcoming redundancies (for example) on the corporate network, the entire community may want to watch the stream, and this may saturate the networks in many ways – particularly in the absence of an IP multicast (which, again, always takes a specific and manual configuration). In the case of a modern 1Gbps LAN, it is possible that the internal network can handle most users' requests, but it is unusual for a corporate office to have a 1Gbps WAN connection between sites. This WAN connection, when it becomes saturated by the CEO's live stream, also prevents all other traffic from using the inter-site WAN resources, and given these other reasons are usually the main reason for the network existing in the first place, this makes streaming unpopular with network administrators. (The author had to help a bank pick up the pieces after a badly configured "multicast" became an unplanned unicast and the 2000 or so viewers saturated the corporate network, which also supplied the trading floor, resulting in several millions pounds of lost trades).

Adaptive bitrate HTTP streaming not only found its way through the firewall by essentially being web traffic but also critically added another benefit. Even in the case of a live stream, adaptive bitrate HTTP video is broken into small individual fragments of video transported on HTTP. These fragments can be cached by standard web proxy servers and served again to any number of users who are also requesting those streams.

While it can mean that these proxy server caches become full of chunks of video data very quickly for the duration of a live stream, this actually significantly addresses the WAN link saturation problem – only one copy of each video fragment (for each bitrate) will be copied into the proxy server. The proxy server may still serve many separate copies of that stream out over the 1Gbps

LAN, but if that LAN is only connected to a 10Mbps WAN, then most of that WAN link will still be available for all the other applications that that network is used for – so banking/web access/database referencing/VoIP, and so on, would all be relatively unaffected by the CEO's live stream, since the proxy server would be doing all the serving within the LAN and requesting just a single stream over the smaller WAN link.

2.1.8.4 Adaptive Bitrate in the CDN and ISP

Moving up the distribution chain into the ISPs and the content delivery networks (which are topics covered in depth elsewhere in this book) HTTP presents a simplification of the distribution paradigm, and while it introduces significant latency – perhaps two or three GoP lengths (typically 8 to 12 seconds) – and while HTTP traffic itself is bursty, and cannot be managed in the same way that the superior live streaming protocols can, its very simplicity has left HTTP as the de facto way to transport streams. Incidentally RTMP now, only a few years after adaptive bitrate became commercially available, only dominates where low latency to the largest media player "reach" is the key performance indicator (KPI) for a video stream – such as for sports-betting video to web applications.

2.1.8.5 Internet Radio and HTTP

Interestingly the success of HTTP takes us back to one of the early streaming methods: HTTP progressive download. HTTP progressive download was not originally considered to be a live streaming protocol by many webcasters. This is arguably no longer the case. Referring back to the mp3 streaming example at the start of this chapter, and seeing HTTP-based adaptive bitrate streaming come to dominate today's modern delivery strategies, it is useful to highlight that the HTTP transport is not limited to streaming adaptive bitrate "chunked" or "fragmented" formats – HTTP is now widely accepted, and with that the older Shoutcast and Icecast protocols used for Internet radio streaming have seen a strong resurgence in the past few years.

These are important formats – many times as much mp3 and aac (described in Section 2.5) encoded music and radio is streamed by HTTP progressive download to many more different technologies and devices than any form of IP streaming video – not least because the 256 kbps Internet still exhibits significantly wider reach than the 10Mbps Internet!

Streaming radio does not make up such significant volumes of bandwidth and traffic online as streaming video, but the audience sizes can be staggering. A single video server may break sweat when it is serving a thousand clients – and even the best server clusters may manage only ten thousand before they need to offload to a distributed CDN.

A basic Icecast server on a domestic PC can comfortably serve 20,000 streams given suitable network interface cards and connectivity. It is important not to dismiss these technologies!

2.1.9   Format Evolution

The ARPANET NVP variants and the early packet video protocols were pioneering. But as we have seen with many formats over the years, it's not always the pioneering solutions that mature to be the market leaders.

We have all spoken about VHS vs. Betamax video formats – and the success of (widely considered to be inferior) VHS. But what is a format?

While the term "format" is sometimes used in very specific contexts, it is also used as a general term for groups of vertically integrated technologies that together provide an end-to-end delivery solutions, and so a "format" may refer to everything from compression/decompression algorithms (CoDecs) and encryption technologies, to packetization and containers, transport streams, and even the delivery servers and consumer players. Examples could include end-to-end ecosystems such as Windows Media or Adobe Flash, or they may include references to just one part of such an ecosystem as specifically the CoDec or specifically the MPEG-TS. However, the term as applied there refers typically to three or four things that come together to make a format successful:

- "Good-enough" technology
- Positioning
- A commercial vehicle that can drive adoption, by making something widely (the 'content') available in a joined up economic way

In 20 years I have seen many organizations present a format with clever solution to a specific problem, but often it is a problem that that too few people have (or care about). I have also all seen many formats flare up, have a season, and then drop away forgotten as their moment comes and goes, often as a result of over-acceleration through financial stimulus, or again, because ultimately there was a sense of "so what" to the problem they solve. (Need I mention the 3DTV format!)

2.2   Industry Evolution

While the pure software companies such as Microsoft and Adobe, and those that blur the line a little like Google and Apple, are all extremely present in the overall narrative of the evolution of streaming media formats, in order to broaden our perspective, it is important to understand both the telecoms and the content sectors to some extent.

2.2.1 "Stack Creep"

In 2010 I penned a widely read article, which was titled "The State of the Stack."[4]

In the IT and many other sectors, we all often talk about "horizontal and vertical integration," and I believe this article was successful because it clearly explained those vectors – at least as far as our niche of the industry was concerned. In it I took a focus on the OSI network stack, drawing attention to how companies often "creep" around the stack, venturing out from their natural home positioning, and that can be highly disruptive. This is particularly the case if that venturing company ends up creating competition with their own existing client base or suppliers through vertical "creep" up or down the stack.

2.2.2 Real World – Blue Chips and Video Delivery Networks

There are many "creep" examples that come to mind. While the immediately obvious one is the relationship of a company called Brightcove with its CDNs, I will return to this example later in the book when we specifically look at the online video publishing (OVP) space. For now Cisco is an interesting case in point.

While ostensibly a router and related switchgear "appliance" vendor, over the past 20 years Cisco have tinkered (by which I mean "acquired, looked at, and then put down") many video systems. Among those, they have notably bought three very different companies with a close focus on Internet video:

- Inlet, which was mainly notable for an early implementation of multi-machine Microsoft Smooth Streaming, was acquired ($95 m). Cisco Digital Media Encoders, as the unit became branded, must have some customers somewhere, but I have personally not come across a customer with a live one in production for a few years now. I am sure figures will show that Cisco have made strides forward with these technologies, but in practice, no one talks about their technology, so, if nothing else, by becoming part of Cisco, Inlet's capabilities have been diluted into a much larger marketing campaign, and I am not convinced that Cisco know how to market video technology. It is a classic "stack creep" that hasn't worked in my opinion.
- Another company that Cisco bought were FlipCam ($590 m). Now FlipCam were an explosive fad. Cisco acquired the company and it literally disappeared overnight, leaving only its brand as a generic term for the millions of me-too products that have since flooded the market. In fact Cisco shuttered the project only a few months after the acquisition. Despite the rumor that there may be some intellectual property or patents of value to Cisco,

---

4 http://www.streamingmedia.com/Articles/Editorial/Featured-Articles/The-State-of-the-Stack-70623.aspx

there has certainly not been clearly shown any great value commensurate with that $590m spend. I should imagine someone lost his or her job over that. On a personal note, my mum still finds her FlipCam much easier to use than a smartphone video UI. A real shame they were torn down by this acquisition.

- The last company they acquired was Tandberg ($3bn). Once a broadcasting technology giant, but again, since the Cisco acquisition, the company has not maintained its presence. The aura and profile it once had is essentially being relegated to a niche video conferencing play in ever more Skype-enabled enterprise markets now.

While interesting, I don't mention Cisco as an example to highlight anything particular about what happens to small companies when the "big guys" acquire them to enter a sector. Instead, I want to highlight that while the large vendors frequently "dabble" in the sector, there is yet to be a large blue chip technology vendor to really break into the streaming sector.

While many have tried, the big software houses Apple, Google, Amazon, Microsoft, and to an extent Adobe have, by and large, been very successful at making the Internet streaming and OS-based access technology "their" space. You only have to use an AppleTV or a Roku for a few minutes and you will never want to use the clumsy and ugly UI on a broadcast/traditional TV Set-Top Box again.

The traditional technology vendors such as, on the IT side, Ericsson and Cisco, and on the broadcast side, Tandberg, PACE, and most interestingly Sony, all do their best to appear to be in the "game," but among engineers they are perceived to always be playing "catch-up" (at best).

Ericsson has had a go at positioning itself as a strong technology partner to broadcasters over the past couple of years – and their recent acquisition of streaming media giant Envivio was notable, stepping into a utility-broadcast-OTT and streaming service provider role that hitherto fore had been dominated by players such as Siemens and Accenture (both of which are great at showing the revenue they take from their clients but, to be frank, have shown the technical prowess of complete beginners on many occasions).

Still more and more broadcasters are moving to a virtual space, and Ericsson and Cisco both face the challenge of keeping up with a virtualizing world, something particularly challenging from their recognized role as purveyors of "boxed" appliances.

The traditional telecoms targeted vendors have labored for years on the model that their appliances were more reliable than virtual- or software-based alternatives, but the fact is that now software in a cloud models can provide far greater resilience with very nearly equal performance. And ultimately the commoditization of the underlying compute resource to a common "commercially off-the-shelf" (COTS) architecture means that the same or better resilience and availability can now be achieved in a software-only model with better financial options – when you don't use a cloud, you typically don't pay.

This means that these traditional vendors face an identity crisis. They all currently sell appliances or leverage fixed infrastructure. They need to become software companies, without letting on to their existing customers that the appliance world is ... frankly ... over.

Big acquisitions are always interesting, but the acquiring company's vision (or lack thereof) once the deal is done is often very apparent. Nearly always a smart radical upstart company is bought by a conservative blue chip, and the very essence of the smart upstart's opportunity is hammered out of it, and tempered by a mode of "well you are part of a much bigger company now," meaning that while the founders of the smaller company are made wealthy, the vision does not become shared and the bigger company fails to realize the potential of that vision.

At the time of writing, there is still a significant amount of rumor around the recent Amazon Web Services $296m acquisition of Elemental, which is this season's "in flavor" encoding vendor. By the time we reach print, that deal might have become a little clearer, but at this point, most in the industry agree that it cannot have been a purchase for technical reasons. Quarter of a billion dollars will buy you a lot of technical development, and considering Elemental is almost entirely integrating third party software internally, it is inconceivable that the acquisition has been for technical reasons. It is much more likely that some of its recent client deals give lock in to a wider strategic relationship between AWS and some of Elemental's many broadcast clients – the BBC being a kingpin example.

In the midterm, however, the AWS partners that have been competing with Elemental may now take their business away from AWS to other infrastructures where the infrastructure provider has no clear interest in competing. This is a classic "stack-creep" problem.

Admittedly, while baffling today, there is a reasonable chance that a valid model may emerge from that acquisition. Until it does emerge, Elemental's acquisition is generally viewed by the peers I speak with as "a significant player in the sector has been taken off the market." Elemental may, at some point in the future, appear as part of AWS' ever-increasing portfolio of SaaS technologies. In the meanwhile the acquisition opens a considerably larger space in the market for other operators (including my own company, id3as), and it broadly makes the sector's environment financially fertile for acceleration by companies with a similar capability.

To wrap up this quick comment on industry evolution – of which there will be more references throughout the text – let us be careful not to stack-creep in an uncontrolled way, nor over-accelerate where we are not *really* solving problems at a large enough scale.

2.3   Consumer Adoption

Let us turn our attention now to the end users and consumers.

I will begin by scoping out the audiences to which the networks reach, and the typical audiences that demand content from these networks, and through this attempt to examine a little about what "audience" means in various different contexts.

We must talk about the traditional ratings companies and audience measurement as it has existed throughout the history of – in particular – radio and television for many years. I have some pretty challenging views about this – some may consider them to be potentially into the realms of "conspiracy theory" – but I also think it is critically important to consider those potential counters to the common thinking to, if nothing else, validate the value of the status quo – should you maintain that the status quo is valid.

I will explain why this audience measurement is a complex beast, and why that complexity has caused problems for widespread adoption of streaming, and why that has led to my "conspiracy theory"!

We will look at various sets of data, and explore the schisms and niches that divide the audiences. I will introduce some small but real examples that caused me to challenge some of the current belief, and also look at some predictions of others, particularly with regard to new adoption among the so-called millennials and native Internet users.

I will also explore the "device effect," returning to the topic of formats and the impact video formats (in particular) are having on network architecture from core to device.

Finally I will touch on social media influences, curation, and discovery and make a short comment about piracy.

2.3.1   The Audience

So let us try to establish a common understanding of what the "audience" actually is. I want to start with an analogue real-world model: let's picture a crowd pressing into a full room, with a public address (PA) system and a man (or woman) speaker on the stage.

The speaker on stage is our transmitter, equivalent to our broadcast head-end, or our point of media origination. What (s)he says is the "media," the content itself. The medium is the PA and the air that transfers the sound. The audience in this context COULD be considered to include all those in the room. However, some audience members are not listening to the speaker; they are waiting for the next act to take the stage, and they are disengaged, perhaps talking to each other, listening to music on their portable music player and headphones, or reading something else distractedly. Some ARE listening intently, and others are simply in the wrong room, or managing the PA or the door, or serving drinks.

The walls of the room are notionally the defining scope of the intended audience reach – although some people are standing outside the door and can hear, and yet others are cheekily standing on a chair and listening through an open window. Still more are recording the talk on their handheld devices and will take it home to play to other people later on.

As we can see, it is possible for the speaker to count all those in the room, and all those outside the room but within earshot, and even those who might hear the recordings sometime later as his "audience." However, that would be stretching the truth somewhat. The reality is that only a subset of the total "audience" is really engaged as the speaker's potential audience, and an even smaller number are *fully* engaged as far as his message is concerned, since they actively want to hear, and are *actually* listening when he speaks. We also have subsets that paid to get into the room to hear the speaker, and others who paid to get into the room to hear others, but remain seated enduring his speech as they wait.

It should be fairly apparent that when we translate our model to a broadcast network, the speaker is likely the television announcer, the PA is the radio mast, the air is comparable to the electromagnetic radio frequency transmission, the people in the "room" are all the TV receivers, those in the neighboring room may be equivalent to receivers in a neighboring country, and those standing on chairs listening through the window are notionally comparable to pirates who are using hacked receivers or some other forms of tuning that are not officially sanctioned.

What is immediately obvious from this model is that when we first talk about an audience, it seems that we are being fairly deterministic about who we are addressing. Yet, when we penetrate into the detail, it becomes clear that the scope of the term "audience" can have a wide number of permutations. We think we can understand simple sounding terms like "content," "audience," "medium," and "media" when we use these terms, but in practice, many such terms are mercurial, and one person's use of a term may be interpreted differently by other persons who are approaching from a different context.

In my career, and in particular, where I have been writing for trade press or speaking at conferences, I have long lost count of the amount of times I have been talking at cross-purposes with other parties about some of these concepts. Heated debates can arise when people with strong opinions that they have well-cultivated to adhere to get stuck on a different interpretation on the use of particular words.

The worst misappropriation of terms comes with the two words "medium" and "media." We often talk of "the media," and yet the term can refer to the corporation that operates the medium or to the concepts that are propagated through that medium. Let's avoid a drawn out political critique of the distortion of media by medium here (!) as it is important to highlight the broad point that perception is a highly subjective thing. So, when we talk of "audiences," there is a visceral element that must be managed before we attempt to make "objective" comments.

To wrap this section, just one final comment on the analogy: the "wall" for a live event is an important boundary. For the promoter of the live event selling tickets to get into the room, that wall is a well-defined boundary. If the space the boundary defines is too small or too big, the volume of tickets or the price of the tickets will vary, and this may affect the profitability of commercial activities inside the wall. Equally if the wall is not strong enough to create an effective boundary, then piracy will negatively affect profitability again.

Obviously, as we move the model into the broadcast telecoms environment, any concept of a wall is defined by the network and services architecture. Since it can be as much a "logical" boundary, I like to think of the wall to be defined not by security boundaries or encryption methods but by the "perimeter of effectiveness to which a rights management system can be held accountable." Or to put it simply, ask yourself: does the network operator collect money (from subscriber or advertiser) for the end user accessing the content? If a third party does collect that revenue, then the services is "over the top" of the wall.

Because traditional commercial models used real-world walls to control supply, and increase price for services that offer the same value (mercantilism being the finest abstraction of this), the content world has struggled to adapt to the Internet where restricting supply is rarely an option – because the walls are not physically defined. So, to increase price/profitability, there has to be focus much more on the value proposition to grow the volume of market share. Ultimately this is healthy for the future, and start-ups and new entrants can embrace this, but established operators need to adapt, else they will expire within the next few years.

2.3.1.1 Target Audiences to which the Networks Reach

To a network operator providing distribution services for a media source, there is understandably a finite boundary at the edge of their network – particularly when dealing with live linear content. There has to be some synchronicity of participation, whereby an end user is connected to the network and the data flows from the source to the user in a continuous manner, much as I discussed in Section 2.1.1.

Although a user may have its receiver turned on, we can never be sure that the user is listening. Often much is made of how many TV sets receive an advert, but the reality is that most users will have muted their TVs, and perhaps headed to the kitchen to make a snack rather than watch the advert. And for that reason, over and above the push of content, it is important to understand that the audience needs to engage in the adverts, to watch the screen and listen to the advert's audio, and to digest the content before the advert has any chance of interesting the user in the product or service being advertised. The actual audience is smaller than the intended audience.

2.3.1.2   The typical Audiences that Demand Content from Networks

Starting at the other end, and taking a user centric view of the distribution chain, the audience may actively seek the content by tuning into the TV broadcast or selecting the on-demand film to play. These situations are solid success cases for the relationship between the media source, the distribution network, and the engagement of the target audience. However, when the TV is in a family front room, or a public place, the person who has chosen the content may be only one part of the group of people watching the TV. The rest of this audience may be disinterested, although they may become captivated by some of the content, and thus become engaged. So in this instance the *actual* audience will be wider than the intended audience.

2.3.2   Traditional Ratings Companies and Audience Measurement

Clearly there is a challenge to accurately defining and measuring the audience of a particular item of media, distributed over the medium of the network, as it is, at best, inaccurate and misleading and, at worst, impossible. This applies almost universally, be it in a ticketed event in a closed room or on a TV platform or an online distribution network.

In practice, access to a closed room is fairly tightly controlled, and in many circumstances access to an online system is also fairly tightly controlled, and this does limit the error in estimating the audience somewhat. However, we run into problems when we look at the most familiar broadcast networks. We have no connection to the edges of broadcast radio networks, and to all intents and purposes, we have absolutely no way of knowing if an end user of a TV network is "out there" and connected.

For this reason a variety of estimation systems have been evolved, and they rely on statistical sampling systems where a representative group within the expected audience has an extra system put in place that connects back to a measurement platform. From the activities of this representative group, extrapolation can form a basis for the estimation of the "real" audience size.

2.3.2.1   How They Measure

In the UK the main TV audience measurement system (BARB) has approximately 5000 sampling boxes in 5000 households, and each represents somewhere between 5000 and 10000 viewers. They call this group of people a "panel." This panel is meant to be demographically and geographically (and supposedly "perfectly") representative across the entire populous of the area being sampled.

Obviously, in reality, even with the best intentions a sample size of this scale is prone to an incredible skew and errors that really would bring into question the validation of the data were it in any other context.

I did reach out to BARB in the UK to see if they had any comments about some of my cynicism. Despite several attempts to communicate with them, they did not reply.

2.3.2.2 The Discernible Inaccuracies

So where do these problems take us? For example, the current promotional video on the home page of the BARB website describes the panel as having insight beyond that of logging and page impression type analytics so commonly found in website statistical analysis, and further indicates that the panel system gives them a completely accurate picture of how long and who is watching the TV program. They claim that this is something not possible with online statistics. The examples they give indicate that they have the ability to tell if a teenage girl was watching a program "with her friends" and that is something that cannot be done by the sort of online measurement systems that exist today. They also make light of the fact that estimation and extrapolation by three orders of magnitude is not in some way highly inaccurate when compared with the one-for-one data collection that is possible in the so-called Big Data scenarios represented by online media, despite the fact that their panel systems rely on human user input very often, and that data set is then collected in exactly the same way – online – as machine generated data that is inherent within streaming systems.

2.3.2.3 Who They Work for/are Owned By

It is important to also think about who are the owners of BARB? BARB itself claims to be a not-for-profit organization. It is owned by major broadcasters, whose audiences it claims to measure, and also by the advertising agencies who use the data to underpin their advertising sales. While the organization is clearly complex, to arrange a measurement system that all parties can accept, there are undeniable and questionable conflicts of interest here.

2.3.2.4 The Value They Create

Almost an entire sector lives in a world where they consistently extract one column from a set of data, that has one figure that can justify an argument, and then they seek to dismiss or disregard all other data that could be used in context to counter their argument.

The reality is that of the roughly £4.7bn of TV advertising spend in the UK, the vast majority is distributed against these audience statistics, and this goes to fund many independent production companies and the like. The idea is that while the panel model is accepted, the status quo remains. Much the same as the recording companies that were slow to adapt to the Internet and lost nearly all their market share in the distribution of the intellectual property of music, the TV and advertising industry have become incredibly cosy, and fear change. Meanwhile a generation is coming through that will correct this, and it is clear that that intransience, if not better and more honestly managed, will cause a severe correction in the value of the TV advertising industry in the not too distant future. What is more, if that contribution to the production and creative talent is not managed into the forthcoming Internet broadcasting era, then there will be considerable cost in the change and attrition of all the intransient organizations.

I have seen first hand the disruption to the record companies over the past 20 years, and even their occasional re-emergence here in the "digital era." Likewise (often less discussed than the music Industry on which *everyone* has an opinion) radio has evolved, and the Internet radio industry is showing every sign of having to adapt to the huge correction in the value that targeted online advertising has brought. There is no more "spray and pray" value underpinned by some conjecture. Online the successful Internet radio stations know exactly who their market is and sell access to that market to sponsors.

I would liken it to the evolution of the weather forecast services: once we used to forecast with some wet seaweed hung outside the office. Now we have satellites. This is how I contrast traditional panel measurement with "real user measurement" available to Internet distribution. The frustration I have is that there are many who still defend the seaweed method, and this legacy culture makes it challenging getting access to the advertisers' roughly £4.7bn to "launch the satellites" needed to service the next market cycle. Interestingly this has led to some notable successes in the subscriber-driven side of the TV industry, but often those subscriber networks struggle to get rights to content from the legacy content houses. It has to be said that Netflix and Amazon Prime have proved the viability of subscription OTT services and won an independence to produce content directly with the production houses. This is a huge step forward, and one that will accelerate when ad revenue can be concentrated in one place – YouTube being the key market leader in this particular model.

Anyway – I digress for now! OK – let's get back to tech.

2.3.3 Streaming Media and Measurement

In the "connected" world of Internet delivered video, we have a number of advantages over the broadcast world in terms of audience measurement. First, and most obviously, we are connected to the same network – the Internet. Note that we often talk about being connected "to" the audience, but in actuality this may not be the case. While the users are connected to an IP network (their ISP's last mile access network), the content service provider is (with the exception of IPTV) invariably connected to a *different* IP network. There are usually many other networks spanning the delivery chain between the users, their ISP, the core Internet backbones, and the content service provider (CSP)'s publishing origins. Some forms of data such as those transferred using HTTP and TCP may transit these networks reliably and consistently, and these have become very successful in the delivery of ad hoc on-demand data – as we will explore in Chapter 10 when looking at the notionally more scalable multicast routing and the User Datagram Protocol (UDP) delivery methods. However, we often do not tie reliable, accountable delivery inherently to the delivery model. The reliability and accountability is often layered in as an application layer function that examines the network activity and then makes an "out-of-band" return path (with the logging, and sometimes the user control data shares this return path). So everything from metadata, recommendation and selection to bitrate, program dwell time, etc., can be captured, limited only by the programming ingenuity of the end user application design team.

The truth is that it is very difficult to give a meaningful interpretation of such data sets. Perspective is everything when interpreting sampled types of information. Fortunately, the most interesting data are top-line macroeconomic indicators such as overall traffic and overall audience size. A graph showing variance in such key performance indicators over a period of time is universally more informative than detailed granular reference to particular volumes. Trend is more important than specifics.

2.3.3.1 How We can Measure Online Audiences

In many successful implementations – particularly RTMP and RTP (so-called session-based) transports – the user activity is almost universally connection based unicast back to the server, or at least the CDN that originates the stream, and this gives the CDN an instant view of the current activity on the platform. The data is aggregated from the back end of the delivery servers in a quality-controlled environment. While this information can be post-event analyzed to understand many aspects of the user interactions, it is also valuable for real-time statistical analysis – typically used for measuring the "concurrency," or "how many are watching right now," or indeed "is it live?"

In the non–session-based (typically progressive download or adaptive bitrate) technologies, typically each tiny chunk of video that is delivered generates its own record in the data set, and this needs to be aggregated into the wider data sets and processed – albeit in much the same post-processing way as session-based information. Anecdotally this can mean that some programming can generate more data inflow load to a CDN's logging systems than it outputs from its core video traffic delivery service. This also means that the processing of adaptive bitrate data to reveal real-time insights requires log pre-processing before the data can be analyzed – a step that is missing and therefore operationally a little bit simpler – with the session protocols. There are nonetheless many other ways to examine server load over and above reviewing the streaming service logs.

Network operators often use an MRTG (multi-router traffic grapher) or variants to create traffic graphs from data points such as network interface cards or CPU metering.

Again, in these models we can sometimes view numbers of concurrent network sessions, and our network topology may allow us to use this to determine concurrency, in real time without inspecting the application layer data at all.

The truth is that all these techniques can be employed. The successful analyst will cross reference as many such data sets as possible, and then find a frame to that reference and stick to the frame to spot variance over time.

2.3.3.2 The Inherent Problem with Accurate Data in a World used to Guessing

The detailed analytics available to the unicast online delivery systems gives immense possibility to audience understanding. Privacy issues notwithstanding, the amount of anonymous data alone that a network operator can gather simply by delivering a service is staggering, and this has to some extent overwhelmed the audience measurement industry. The system analysts have moved from a quiet world of estimation and extrapolation into a nightmarish brave new world where others may call their estimations into account with far more granular and atomically accountable models.

While the advertising industry relies on BARB figures – to the tune of £4.7bn annually – the fact is that the data BARB publishes is, by its own admission, extrapolated on a 1 to 5000 ratio. This margin of error has historically been hard to challenge – there was no alternative. As audiences go online, these organizations are struggling to, on one hand, publically fault the endless discrepancy between their estimations and the "real" figures that online systems produce and, on the other hand, announce their own integrated systems, and explain why they have more credibility than others but not as much as their estimation …, etc.

Let's get down to the point of this book, and to bring up a little backroom chat. Some years ago I was working with a major UK sports broadcaster. They wanted to try to stream some key golf event on their website, and we were going to carry it.

Broadcasters always work in audiences of hundreds of thousands or millions. The anticipation for the audience on this webcast was hundreds of thousands. Apart from a one hour TV broadcast, the webcast was the only way to follow the event through the day from 2 pm UK time until 9 pm.

We set up the platform for 30,000 concurrent. This made the customer uncomfortable, but we explained that concurrency, because of churn, would represent a larger total audience.

Our own experienced guess was that would still be a high number, and indeed the peak concurrency was about 12,500 – a fairly big event for its day mind you, but no where near their expected hundreds of thousands.

What I found interesting is that this was a free stream, well promoted (on TV as well as online), and this was in 2009, an era when most people had broadband at work or at home. It would seem, however, that the entire fan base of the golf dropped off our stream and over to broadcast TV for the one hour show, and then jumped back again – to the same level. There was no change to the audience despite the TV show announcing the stream. There were, in my mind, about 12,500 people who were actually interested, and when the TV stream came on, they switched to the TV and then came back again, but no one new joined them. And that hinted that the stream had hit its near maximum audience.

Imagine my shock when the ratings agencies reported, the following day, that 1.2 m had watched the TV one hour show – an impossible difference against 12,500 online. Given it was promoted to 1.2 m households apparently, there should have been a significant variation after the TV show.

It was then that I realized how exaggerated and inaccurate the estimation from panels must be.

The problem underlying this outcome is that the audience estimation agencies are the historic bedrock of the TV advertising industry. Many such agencies are *owned* by the broadcasters and advertising agencies, and while they purport to be external/third party/neutral, they are almost invariably private entities, and act like cartels. The audience figures they give out are vastly inflated, and that feeds into the advertising pricing by reflecting an inflated "demand" (or at least "opportunity") for advertisers.

After building this value over many years, this sector is now fighting to reposition itself in a digital world where the accuracy of the data deflates the value as it becomes clear the "demand" for video is fragmented, and that there are no longer "millions" watching most TV advertising campaigns.

However, to try to get the attention from within that diverse and fragmented market by attracting "big budget" advertising to a niche content platform is made harder when the production reports only 12,500 wanted to see it.

Interestingly I would argue that therein lays the greatest opportunity: those 12,500 webcast viewers were a very closely defined audience – much higher in value per viewer than the viewers on a generic broadcast channel. Ostensibly, if you promoted a new set of golf clubs to those 12,500, you would probably see a much better return on your Investment (ROI) than spending a proportionately similar amount in promoting to the 1.2 m estimated to attend the TV broadcast.

2.3.4 Predictions of Others

This seems like a good point to segue into another favorite example of why a change-resistant attitude to disruptive technology, and in particular to the changing landscape of today's media environment, is the story of the collapse of the record industry at the turn of the twenty-first century.

You may recall from earlier in this chapter that I spent a little time very close to mp3.com and a couple of others including Scour and to a lesser extent the start-up Napster. It was an interesting time. The RIAA (Radio Industry Association of America) had recently had to drop its case against audio device manufacturer Diamond for their portable mp3 player – and this was some time before Apple launched the iPod. Then, having seen that case fall, a number of mp3-based initiatives all started to kick off, and that meant so did the regulators. I was asked at one point to provide some written statements to a court case that was looking at if a large DVD-RW producer should pay a small premium on each disc into a royalties collection system, to compensate for piracy that was rife at the time thanks to the newly arrived CD, and later DVD burners. It was quite an interesting time.

What was always apparent to me was the number of people in and around the recording industry who wanted to "make a living off royalties" and just how difficult that became, particularly in a market with almost infinitely unlimited supply and almost completely monopolized distribution models. The hope that they would get the venture finance to record, print to CD, and market was perhaps parallel to what chasing angel finance in dragons den became 10 years after the record industry started to fall apart.

After the DVD-RW advice I also gave some comment to a government-formed group in the UK focused on where music and the Internet could find harmony. I spoke about DRM, and about the arms race that encryption is. I also spoke quite freely about the fact that the "cost of ownership of the printing press" had changed, and that no longer was there a control on the mechanized reproduction of content – and thereby something that could be regulated. The key argument is that until the mid-1930s all musicians ever in the entire history of musicianship had survived on either patronage or minstrelsy. These would today translate to sponsorship or live performance. The royalty model was introduced as an opportunity to capitalize on the ownership of initially Vinyl and latterly CD/DVD presses. The first royalty deals were introduced specifically to tie one musician to one press and, by doing so, share the added value of that control of the supply. These were not trivial plants to run. Mp3 changed that. Now the voice-telecoms market was very interested in using the Internet for voice calls, and it became a challenge to use the patent and licensing system to restrict the use of technology for one group's particular gain. Telcos make trillions of calls a month. Vinyl sales are still measured in tens of thousands. To harmonize both at a price that made sense in terms of restricting competition and regulating the market was impossible, and for this reason mp3 escaped into the public essentially free to use, meaning that from then on they could create and easily share audio themselves, in turn disintermediating the entire CD/DVD and other "fixations" that had, for 80 years or so, both created and monopolized the music distribution industry.

2.3.4.1 Koranteng Got it SO Wrong

So why was the music industry so inert? In my first-hand experience central to this was one report that was produced in 1997, and circulated over 1998, called "Music on the Internet," by Juliana Koranteng[5] (appears to be out of print).

It essentially supported an event by the FT of the same name that was well marketed, extremely expensive, and for a premium of "a few thousand" you could get the report too. To this conference went all the leaders of the music industry who were getting asked a lot, by various parties, what they were going to do with regard to the Internet.

They left with the understanding – and get this, it is very important – that *the Internet will never be capable of delivering the content itself and so the industry should focus on its use as a CD/DVD "e-commerce" sales platform.*

And so that's what they did for the next three years, while MyMp3.com, Scour, and Napster tied up the "test case budgets" and resulted was in effect a disastrously counterproductive marketing campaign for peer to peer and illegal piracy, and a polarized stance against the very medium to which their entire audience had moved.

I recall having a conversation with one of the world's top digital media lawyers at the leading London firm, and around this era he said to me that "if it wasn't published through a reputable label, then it wouldn't be worth listening too ..." – I cited the millions using mp3.com to discover unsigned artists, and begged to differ. Ten years later he very politely acknowledges that he, and his clients, would agree they were very wrong. We are good friends these days.

Also, while on this topic, it is worth noting that I only found out about the FT conference because I was contacting events like this to offer them live webcasting services. I have always thought it ironic that we could have webcast their statement that "the Internet won't carry content" live to the world using the Internet.

2.3.4.2 The Millennial Delusion

Fortunately, I am not one to be intimidated by standing out in a crowd. For that reason I have always been very freely spoken, when asked (I do try not to be a bore in company!), about my views on the emergence of disruptive technologies. At the moment the topic is drones. Some 15 to 20 years ago it was audio. Yet Spotify and Apple Music still stir strong debates about the fairness of organized distribution systems and the questions about "how artists are expected to live from royalties from streaming" make headline news quite often.

---

5 http://www.amazon.co.uk/Music-Internet-FT-management-report/dp/184073017X/
ref=sr_1_2?s=books&ie=UTF8&qid=1448556061&sr=1-2

But meanwhile what seems to slip the attention of many is that only those artists who logjam the distribution networks, largely down to common financial interests shared between the distribution networks and the media companies, are presented as a Hobson's choice: it feels like a choice, but rather the options are so limited that in many ways the consumer is provided only an illusion of an option.

This is reflected in music clearly. Only artists who have big budgets get promoted on college radio and advertising networks, and sink into the public's subconscious as the music is tied to various other memories and experiences (where they first heard the music) and by the time they consciously ask "who is this," they already have a relationship with the music. That process of engaging the audience is inaccessible to those without the same "big budget."

Well piracy aside, the fact is that mp3 allowed the artist to spend their resources solely on self-promotion. Until mp3, artists had to find both the production budget to make the CDs or records and the promotion budget to create the demand. To do both, in a relatively controlled and monopolized market, was inaccessible for all but either die hard touring "indie" bands or those with immense private wealth.

(Not unlike the dot-com industries!)

As the cost of production dropped away, with both mp3 distribution reducing the need to find capital to print a stock of CDs, etc., and as laptop studios reduced the cost of production technologies, artists have had to adjust and look for tours and promotions to hitchhike on to get profile, and what money they did have had to go to promotional strategy only. This created hundreds of small, unidentified bands that worked much more closely to minstrelsy of the era before royalties, than the "rock stars" of the monopolized recording industry that has ultimately had its day now, unable to demand attention for any individual new act without huge TV profiling.

The story is not much different for the news channels either. Technology that enables real-time high-quality video from even the remotest site makes for deeper coverage and more immediate content. With the technical advantage gone, the amount of alternative views available to the average consumer as an option to watching mainstream agenda-driven news is incredible.

As those who "started" their media lives on the main terrestrial over-the-air broadcasting to a radio or TV, we always return to these sources of content for our opinion of "what is the definitive popular perspective."

But the generation bought up on ad-free subscriber video on demand, and on YouTube is a different generation to the MTV generation. At my age I will probably never know what is "cool" in this generation, but I can see all around me the way that the native Internet children are establishing their use of these technologies in a way that as they come through their usage will be very different.

I put it to the TV radio and content production industry regularly that their worlds will change entirely and in the space of two to three years. Much like they did as cassette was replaced by CD, much like DVD was replaced by VOD, and radio is now huge online, the TV experience will move online, and the users will consume all this in ways we simply cannot predict.

There is no monopoly in the same sense. ISPs are the most likely candidate for developing a closer and controlled "walled garden" model, but these days they are more like "good gardeners" who keep the lawn open but try to upsell you fancy flowers to decorate the lawn. I think it most likely that 4 k will take off (if it hasn't already by the date of print of this work) driven by online delivery rather than traditional broadcast delivery. The IP networks are much more versatile and can be made to widen their bitrates almost at will.

It will be interesting when the millennials simply laugh at the idea of a cable or satellite subscription because the stream on their phone is 4 or 8 times higher quality than that on their parents' TV that they can pay for as a bolt-on on top of their basic HD quality streaming mobile Internet service.

2.3.5 The Pending Collapse of the Value of Broadcasting to Advertisers

When the millennials do take the industry through that cycle, there will be an inevitable market correction. The advertisers will see huge, inflated "finger in the air" BARB ratings for streaming that in no way correlate with the streaming data. The streaming audience will be validated in a way that the panel and estimate process simply cannot compare to. The argument that the "millions" on broadcast are more valuable than the "real" hundreds of thousands watching online will weaken as the close engagement with streaming services proves a concrete return on the advertisers' investment, and the spray and pray model for broadcast advertising moves from being a central market driver to being relegated to "vanity publishing" while the real audiences are becoming valuable partners in a working ecosystem.

Those traditional models won't go quietly. Much like the recording industry employed the RIAA to essentially victimize their own audiences, the TV industry will continue to overvalue itself for some years – until it dawns on them that they are the only ones left drinking that Kool-Aid.

Those broadcasters that are embracing online will span that bridge, but any TV network that prioritizes its broadcast business today over the new models of tomorrow has their risk management out of balance.

2.3.6 "Device Effect" and Formats

I mentioned earlier a little about the evolution across formats. I became interested in formats and protocols in the mid-1990s. I penned a (now lost) paper called "Protocol Migration and Management." The thoughts at the time were more notes of my own discovery that a protocol is not only agreed, but it must "travel" from the point of agreement outward to become effective. Be it a political agreement or a technical specification or even a cultural protocol, they all migrate as they become successful.

The classic discussion is VHS vs. Betamax. These two standards used for recording video to magnetic tape emerged at the same time, but JVC's VHS, while inferior, was driven to popularity by the success of its consumer video recorder. In the meanwhile SONY executives were trying to establish Betamax in the production companies, assuming that uptake there would drive the format out to the consumers.

In the end the market played out such that VHS was the runaway success in the consumer market until DVD arrived a decade ago, when it almost disappeared overnight. In the meanwhile (and most of the general public are unaware of this) Sony Betamax was a longer term success in the smaller higher value broadcast space until only the past year or two, since its quality was excellent even for HD video.

We have seen the effect of mp3, and of course, there has been much debate over the last 20 years about what is the best CoDec. Fellow StreamingMedia.com writer Jan Ozer has written extensively about video compression for many years and provides a great reference for the ever-raging debates. The fact is that many of the modern formats either conform to interoperability standards over time or they burn bright from the backing of their proprietary owners' marketing, and then fizzle out quickly as the platform they were custom designed for either fails or is superseded (Real Networks, for example).

For many years the alignment between CPU chipset vendors and GPU graphics processor vendors was somewhat chaotic, and for this reason there was a schism in the manufacturing and device development. Some specific machine builds such as PACE Set-Top Boxes, or Apple Computers could often determine what graphics capabilities would be supported in particular commercial releases, providing developers with clear ways to support video and drive it with middleware. However, in general terms, the market was highly competitive for a long time. That was until the advent of h.264. h.264 targets HD video at acceptable domestic broadband bitrates. It also decodes in software runs on CPUs and on GPUs very well, and this has been widely adopted by Intel. Their laptops for a long time have supported h.264 decoding using GPUs, and now they are releasing server grade GPUs for heavy encoding. This commoditization of the GPU has changed the traditional encoding market significantly over the past decade. Once a hardware encoder capable of delivering high-definition video capture and compression relied on an expensive NVIDIA or MATROX (or similar) card. Now the same performance can be carried out with a GPU that is included in the servers CPU chipset. Where once a card alone would cost many hundreds, if not thousands, and the integration of that card to the motherboard and CPU chipset would add significant cost too, the capabilities are today available as standard on the computer. This has reduced vendor lock-in and opened the market for software driven hardware encoding – ideal for cloud-based transcoding. This trend has been empowering for h.264 and ensures that it will be around for a while.

The successful compression technologies tend to be the ones that are widely adopted by large content publishers, and this usually leads new entrants to play chicken and egg until, if they are lucky, they reach a critical mass in the sector. Since the value relies on partnerships with technology providers and content providers, it is a complex challenge to enter the market with a CoDec.

At the time of writing 4k is a topical subject. Very few would say that 4k offers a great deal of new value to the end user. Indeed, while the picture is only marginally better to the general front room user, 4k costs four times the cost of HD to deliver in terms of bandwidth. Yet 4k also allows more to be done in the production workflow – zooming into pictures without distortion, higher frame rates, and better color dynamics are all useful capabilities offered by 4k workflows when composing (in particular) live sports coverage. So while there is little real benefit to the end user, the fact is that 4k is widely believed to be inexorable.

2.3.7 Video Formats (in Particular, Multicast and UDP) and Network Architecture

Some readers will consider this section the hub of all the discussions. Others will disregard it as esoteric and irrelevant in practice. It's up there with Marmite!

First a tech briefing. The Transmission Control Protocol (TCP) is a particular way to reliably send data across IP networks. If you are sending data that needs to arrive intact, TCP is a very reliable way to send data. It ensures that a dialogue between sender and recipient is carried out that confirms sending, receipt, and checks the delivery as intact.

TCP is a well-known network layer application that sorts out that dialogue.

UDP – the User Datagram Protocol – allows users to define every step of that dialogue themselves. In some circumstances reliability may not be the imperative in the network link. When sending a video picture, a few missed pixels won't have much impact on the viewer. There seems little point in stopping proceedings, rewinding the transmission to the missing pixels and getting going again.

UDP allows the developer to define how this type of discarding may occur, and when too much data has gone missing to discard, and so on.

This is a very simplistic example, but it helps highlight that while the dominant use of IP/Internet is perceived to be accurately copying data from one end of a network link to another, actually the way this is done is not deterministic. In certain circumstances network operators may choose to use non–TCP-based transmission layer protocols.

Critically TCP quite quickly reaches a maximum transmission speed when used over long fat networks (LFNs) such as transatlantic cable or satellite.

In these situations UDP is needed to maximize the transmission throughput over the link.

UDP can also be connectionless, and receivers can listen and receive data without needing to acknowledge each packet. This in turn can allow an operator to optimize distribution of data to many locations. UDP underpins IP multicast, and while we will cover that later in some detail, multicast is without a doubt the best way to scale live or one to many distribution of content.

However, much as in the CoDec wars, albeit with fewer options, TCP and UDP actually emerged as battleground opponents in the late 1990s and early 2000s causing developers to split into two factions.

UDP promised better scaling and finer control for high-bandwidth video delivery. However, TCP, in particular when combined with HTTP services, was very accessible to web developers, and at the time it was web developers who were driving the traffic to video online, and not large scaled up high-bandwidth TV platforms (which had yet to emerge).

Essentially, while inferior from a purists point of view (yes, I would include myself in that group), HTTP/TCP was cheap and easy, and good enough. While Windows Media and Real Networks had worked hard to support both TCP and UDP transmission models, the fact was that Adobe Flash proved a simple way for web designers to add a little video to their webpages, and this quickly attracted audiences. Very soon content delivery networks were seeing a huge demand for this type of short form high-bandwidth video, not least because it worked very well for advertising online, and the relative value of continuing to develop better and better technical solutions for UDP (and some niche TCP-based models) became unjustifiable.

The UDP technologies did, however, find a home with IPTV network operators. In the context of an IPTV network all points on the network are under the operator's management, and this means that the scaling and quality advantages can be maximized, making IPTV a better quality proposition for premium customers.

In the meanwhile for Inter-network delivery HTTP/TCP was simple, and commoditised with all the other web traffic. For CDNs this meant, and means to this day, that they need only support a single type of traffic, making their jobs more profitable.

While the market is still emerging, HTTP, despite its inefficiencies, copes extremely well with the audiences we have today. However, we are still drawing breath when a CDN claims to deliver millions of viewers to a live event. This contrasts with the many broadcast measurement systems that report audiences of tens of millions on broadcast infrastructure.

This gap has to be bridged for the Internet to truly evolve to be considered a broadcast medium for scaled up live/linear streaming.

HTTP/TCP is a brute force way to do that, ultimately requiring that every user has a termination at the edge, and the edge itself has the resource to provide an effective proxy service to minimize the core network requirements. As we scale to the point that one TV broadcast regularly requires "much" of the CDN's resource, the question has to be asked how the model can scale to its best efficiency while using TCP.

Those of us that believe in this scaling issue, believe in IP multicast and other UDP- based dark arts that have been left to one side while there is an HTTP gold rush. However, those capabilities are increasingly going to show real value. Aspera, Motama, Zixi (my own company's "GRIT"), and others are already finding seams of new opportunity in this space, and arguably this is true for the channel-bonding live contribution platforms (CellMuxes) and other similar production broadcast telecoms technologies that are still evolving in the enterprise but will eventually reach into the wider consumer market for sure.

2.3.8 Discovery, Curation, and Social Media

There are a many external influences on the online video distribution market. Some have strong effects on the success of individual models. So far we have discussed the consumer proposition in terms of technical delivery, audience measurement (to underpin commercial models), and the ability to offer good content.

On top of the primary foci of ensuring that good content can be delivered well when it is requested, a successful model will also ensure that consumers are able to watch *what* they want to watch. At the top of these influences is "discovery." Discovery in this context embraces a range of technologies and service modes, ranging from the familiar billboard and "TV" promotion, through to textual search of metadata, image and audio fingerprinting, and ultimately refined into a fine art with "recommendation engines." While recommendation engines are complex and involved, they are in many ways an attempt to "artificially" replicate the intelligence of a human curator or editor, or even "the DJ."

Also important to understand is the effect of the audience on itself: social media is now a central communications capability that at least a quarter of all net users regularly visit, and far more visit on an occasional basis. The ability for social networks to create "herds" or "flash mobs" to various online events or publications is proving to be complex to harness but invaluable in engaging audiences, and the "share" ability that most such networks thrive on ensures that the individual can do a lot to avoid being isolated in a case of "left-out-ITs." Once something "goes viral," the overhead of growing an audience is passed, in a massively distributed way, to the audience itself, making audience growth "frictionless." Thus risk gets reduced to producers, publishers, and promoters of that content alike.

Used well, social media can be a massive asset, but there are also many online streaming companies that have launched naïvely optimistic strategies, reminiscent of the dot-com era, and obsess about volumes of "likes" or "re-tweets" and gauge these as a currency that they infer is empirically "valuable." In fact that "currency" is just as fickle, and the supply in the market (the competition to the model) is also endless. This easy to attain oversupply means (at best) a social media response has a short-term burst of value, and then invariably quickly fades, but more often than not even huge continuous numbers though social "engagement" have proved difficult to directly correlate to value.

2.3.8.1 Personal Recommendation

Without a doubt the most influential of all discoveries is a direct introduction by a trusted third party.

When a friend endorses (or even rejects) some music, and it sets a tone for the moment and creates a memory with you, that music will always have some form of personal value to you.

This rule ultimately stays true for what accounts for "taste." Some is unarguably "genetic" and takes any detailed discussion into a complex biochemical world (beyond scope here!), and yet the vast majority of the influences on an individual's taste are unarguably "environmental."

Be the "friend" a close personal friend, or the DJ with whom you empathize, or the director of a motion picture series you adore talking about his favorite films, if you trust that friend when they "endorse" that media, your taste will become receptive to discovery of that media. It may be that you dislike the content yourself, or you share your friend's endorsement, and that itself will have an effect on your future "trust" of this friend's endorsements.

If you want to explore the concept more fully, Rachael Botsman and Roo Rogers's book *What's Mine Is Yours* talks about "trust currency" at the heart of their "collaborative consumerism" idea. It is certainly an interesting, if idealistic, way to forecast the future of economics, but some of the concepts are definitely well-evolved explorations of "trust" in social networks, and their increasing value in modern consumerism.

Once you have been "turned on" to the content directly, you are a customer at almost no "cost of acquisition" to the publisher of the content. This makes you the most valuable type of customer.

2.3.8.2 Offline and Broadcast Promotion

In contrast, probably the highest cost of acquisition for a publisher to grow an audience is to use existing broadcast radio, TV, and print media to raise awareness of the content. As with any product promotion the cost of using these mediums is not for the feint hearted. Trust for invasive high-street advertising is extremely limited, and perhaps works better used to reinforce rather than introduce the subject. Once the target of the promotion has engaged with – for example – a favorite magazine, the context of the magazine can engender more trust to print adverts for example.

Large broadcasters have their own networks and relatively captive audiences, so much of a channel's promotion is often for its own content. Accessing their audiences is a low-volume/high-demand service that ultimately powers the advertising agencies.

The broadcasters themselves have to promote across media to ensure that nonsubscribers become aware of the programming – and subscriber acquisition is a key measure of the success of TV and radio networks. Through the channel's own marketing and promotion many individual content promoters "hitch a lift" – think of all the shows promoted on billboards as Christmas approaches for examples of this coexistence.

In the limited volume markets of spectrum restricted radio broadcast networks, promotion has, over the past 50 or 60 years, industrialized and structured itself well into a few closely guarded networks of promotion/production and distribution, and their coexistence had, for a long time, protected and regulated the sector.

Since 1994 the emerging Internet has disrupted the exclusivity of many of those networks, threatening their monopolies and cartel nature. However, with so many small emerging models appearing at the same time online, the overwhelming competition in "grabbing eyeballs," which they all had, was generally from each other. YouTube changed the conversation because YouTube combined technology convergence with audience aggregation (it became a "go to" destination for both side of the value chain), but it also bought into sharp view the relative futility of hoping that "being on YouTube" meant fame and fortune.

So simply whatever the promotion model, and even if it was supported by a great technology proposition, the reality is that more needs to be done to reach the audience. A big part of that is to help users find the content themselves.

2.3.8.3 Text Search

Ever since the early days of archie and excite.com, it was clear that computers could search through huge amounts of data quickly. If you knew what the needle looked like, the size of the haystack was not so important.

The key to semantic text search in the context of audio or video media is metadata. If content has good logging at the point of creation, and top level titling, referencing, and indexing, then textual search can be extremely effective. The most complex part of metadata is that it is often not actually "part" of the encoded data that comprises the video and the audio. Consequently, while the metadata can be bundled with the audio and video in, for example, an MPEG transport stream or an MP4 container, there is rarely any consistency in how encoders and transcoders encode and maintain the metadata layer found in one when creating, for example, a Flash video file or even a different transport stream. While the audio and video are central, the metadata has most certainly been considered a bastard-child, where its importance has emerged as the sheer volume of content becomes otherwise unsearchable.

The advertising industry – with a keen appetite for monetization realized very early the value of metadata consistency in creating the "currency" of their campaigns, and understanding the usage of their video. As such, long before a gold standard has emerged, indexing and logging general video in the online world, VAST (Video Ad Serving Template)[6] has become widely adopted – driven, of course, by the commercial interests of the advertisers.

Sadly, the interests of "generic" content providers are never quite aligned. Indeed in most production houses, still to this day, scripts and shot logging are added manually as an early stage of post-production, and yet all the data that is entered is lost as versions of the content are mastered into various digital formats. Unless there is a specific effort made, most metadata beyond a basic sheet of title and perhaps creator is lost, and any chance of being able to search for content within the video using text searching is lost without regenerating the metadata again.

When working on the Parliament Live website in its initial incarnation in 2003 or thereabouts, one of the team, Lee Atkinson at Westminster Digital, whom I was contracted to for the project, merged a number of interesting technologies to make a semantic search option for the videos. This worked because, as part of the tradition in the UK Parliament, an organization called Hansard take formal dictation records of everything that is said in the Houses. The original video feed we were handling was made for the BBC Parliament TV channel, and this meant that they had an automatic subtitle system, which used voice to text conversion to bring up a roughly accurate subtitle on the live video feed.

This subtitling data was stored as part of the original video source, but in a format that Lee could extract to a separate data channel in the Windows Media based workflow, and so he initially carried this on to enable subtitles on the webcasts we were looking after.

However, it dawned on him that he could search the subtitle data and retrieve time codes where there was a match. By combining the partly inaccurate data from the voice to text system with the highly accurate data from the Hansard scripts, it became possible to offer a usably accurate lookup on our video content management system that enabled the public to explore video relating to references to various subjects they wanted to search for. So it was possible to search for "Weapons of Mass Destruction," and every mention in the House of Commons was brought up in a search result set, offering a direct link to the point in the relevant video where the comment was made, and referencing the Diaries and other supporting documents along side.

Although some years later I saw a smoke-and-mirrors version of something similar from the now discredited Autonomy, Lee's system was the finest

---

6 http://www.iab.com/guidelines/digital-video-ad-serving-template-vast-3-0/

working semantic video search I have yet seen, and that was nearly 15 years ago. While Windows Media was particularly easy to set up, that inherent capability that gave Windows Media the edge was lost, and sadly, even if that system were still live, very few people would have a Windows Media Player set up suitably to benefit from that capability.

Still to this day my iTunes collection is chaos. After using a couple of "magic apps" to tidy my metadata, I would conjecture that 30% of my music collection is now named incorrectly. So, even if I do manage to thumb my way through the search window on my Apple TV music search, the chances are that the file I eventually select may not be the one I want to listen to anyway.

So while obviously a central part of both the search and the tracking of the use of digital media assets, there seems to be some way to go before content is commonly deeply searchable based on metadata baked into it.

Naturally a large amount of content is legally published through well-ordered content management systems (CMS) – often a service provided by an online video publisher (OVP). Within the confines of a single CMS there will be a metadata structure. Typically content workflows are designed to ensure that both the asset and the correct metadata for that CMS are carried forward. This makes the CMS searchable, and because the setup is proprietary, it also provides OVPs with lock-in, since migrating the assets and the metadata to a competitor is going to add complexity to the workflow, until and unless a metadata standard is established.

2.3.8.4 Curation

Curation is the job a librarian, an editor, or a DJ does when gathering all the options and working out how best to present them to the end users, readers, or listeners. It implies "personality" in the taste of what is presented and with what priority, and this can be thought of as representing the brand of the service, or the DJ's cool name. The very selection of movies licensed by Netflix or music playlists pushed by Spotify is critical to engaging audience.

More important, curation has a key role to play in live and linear content, and this is why even in the much acclaimed "watch what you want, where you want, and when you want" world, the fact is that often we don't want to get out of the chair after every single track, we want to put on an album and listen for half an hour. In the same way we may put on live TV news and leave it on, or we may have MTV on for the day selecting music. We make a single decision to activate the brand and from there on we "trust" that the brand will deliver content that is "within scope" of my own taste, and the taste I identify with the brand.

For this reason the brand's own curation and taste must be fairly well established to maintain the audience, and encourage users to return. In today's media world the curation of the content library is central to almost every media business with repeating revenue streams from growing audiences.

While this spans both live and on-demand libraries, the brand associated with a live channel is extremely reliant on the curation of that "pushed" media feed. Users will quickly turn it off if it conflicts with their taste or expectation of what the brand should be providing. On-demand users will typically only become disenfranchised with a brand if they cannot quickly discover something suitable for themselves.

In my mind curation is absolutely paramount for the success of a good modern digital media company. While any technology firm can deliver a project once, it takes recognition and good audience alignment from the curation team to ensure that the audience favors you with good reputation, and returns, ideally with friends.

2.3.8.5 Data-Driven Recommendation

As one clicks through various items of digital media on an online platform, and as semantic text searches are gathered against your user profile, it becomes possible to infer recommendations for other items that you may appreciate. So as you search sci-fi movies for *Star Wars*, it is logical to recommend the latest *Star Trek* video. The business and technology of recommendations is a sector and a topic in its own right. Amazon has built their success on their recommendation engine, and its ability to uplift sales dramatically.

In the same way a VOD provider such as Amazon Prime or Netflix works hard to ensure that as I browse my movies they "learn" my interests and push a queue of things that by and large do interest me and become part of the value I get from my Netflix account.

Of course, VOD services can be badly implemented. I find it tedious that when I search for a product to buy, and buy it, I then spend several weeks seeing offers and deals for whatever it was at a lower, better price. This type of overly eager recommendation system has its backlashes; pushing adult movie recommendations among the kids movie search results, for example ....

Data and the inference of behavior, if used carefully, can work at massive scale. With today's Big Data sources around users, it can be possible to push complimentary second-screen content to users who are engaged in a broadcast channel. A significant attempt to address that market was introduced with Anthony Rose (former CTO of BBC iPlayer) as he launched Zeebox along with the concept of "social television." Zeebox was the first of many to attempt to merge social media and broadcast. The idea is that most users today are using a tablet or smartphone while they watch TV, and if that experience and engagement can be combined with the TV experience, then two things potentially happen: first, stronger audience engagement, which has value to the show's sponsors, and second, a back-channel of Big Data emerges, helping the producers better understand their audiences.

Success is varied, and seems to be short-lived even when it works, since many of these projects are attached to events or single TV series.

2.3.8.6 Social Media

While some of the larger "user-generated content" sites such as Vimeo and YouTube do have relatively interesting social elements, not one brand has really excelled in specifically combining social networking with broadcast entertainment. Certainly none that I am aware of have managed to find a strong competitive and defensible differentiation, and until a dominant "search, learn, and recommend" workflow architecture has emerged, most examples of recommendation system are highly proprietary and primarily exist within a single CMS/OVP. While they offer a great deal of value, the data workflow will often lock operators into certain partnerships.

In-house development is often strategically sensible for companies that really see recommendation as a key value for their audience proposition. The main issue is that self-build can come with a large upfront ticket to get set up. Much like "intellectual property," the interface with the audience that a good search and recommend platform can provide is a primary intangible asset to a successful online brand content publisher, and it requires vision, belief, and wide investment across the organization to implement before its value can be realized too.

This capital investment into their digital asset metadata and workflow makes companies resistant to opening up their CMS for external searching, limiting access to commercially engaged "syndication" partners. However, direct "searchability" and instant access to content is key to reaching generally fickle social network users.

Most publishers want to only allow paying /ad-monetized subscribers that search capability. The complexity, for example, of Facebook auto-starting YouTube adverts opened up the entire Facebook market to YouTube's ad network in a push mode. Facebook quickly shut that down, and now only auto-starts videos uploaded directly to Facebook's own servers, for which they have usage information and can work toward their own ad revenue. However, because Facebook has not completed any movie publishing deals (to date!), it is not a destination to, for example, log in and watch the most recent episode of a box set you are following. This latent potential is therefore more to do with the complexity of rights and audience ownership than any technical challenge.

Some of the more successful audio platforms will allow external search, but only allow (for example) 30 second clips of tunes, or in the case of some online video services they may provide previews of videos to play to nonsubscribers (the adult industry is built on this model). The thinking is to create one's own revenue generating audience and, in so doing aggregate eyeballs away from competitors. In turn this conflicts with a demand for interoperable metadata standards (as mentioned above), and thus the "portability" of content to social networks, while potentially desirable to the social network's users, is seen as having no commercial value to rights owners so far.

However, like movie licensing, which we talk about more in the next section, over time it only takes one organization to demonstrate and grab market share to cause a landslide of investment into such opportunity.

2.3.8.7 Release Windows and Piracy

So we must now pause to explore another key issue relating to online content models. Rights are ultimately the kingpins of content delivery models. If you are interested in growing an audience, you must have a continuously growing source of content that they want. While some niche services provide extremely successful video blogs and resources for their core market, to have broad appeal, and to become nightly viewing for residential users (one of the largest markets), you need to have a supply of rights that you can monetize.

For many years the movie industry carefully controlled access to media assets. In my early career I recall helping BT establish a workflow for manually digitizing from tape to digital media for their early video-on-demand platform. The whole process of delivery of the source tapes was fastidiously documented, with an end-to-end chain of paperwork and CCTV logging every handling of the tape as it was delivered to a secure room in the facility, and from there used to master digital encodings for online delivery.

This reverence with which the "masters" were handled (even though they were themselves duplications) was to me almost endearing, and exemplifies a tradition of the traditional content industry. Each "fixation" (as a media asset was called in legal terms for many years) was treated with a unique value. Exposure to duplication immediately reduced its uniqueness and therefore its value.

The fact that once digitized into the BT system the content was then widely available to customers who could fairly freely pirate it, and at good quality, seemed to conflict directly with all the processes that attempted to prevent that up to the introduction to the digital world.

Early systems seemed so porous to piracy that they fell, half-hearted, by the wayside.

Gradually something important changed. Over the late 2000s the movie studios were convinced to experiment with adjusting their "release windows." A release window is a period during which a movie is released to air on a particular medium. The most important release windows are usually the first ones and are known as the "theatrical releases" – and they target cinemas. Often the theatrical window rights can recoup the cost of production of the film, and with many of the cinemas closely affiliated with the movie studios, this relationship is a central part of the movie production industry.

While theatrical releases use steganographic visual indicators to help police "from-screen" filming by theater staff, inevitably the moment a big film makes the screen, pirates are already at work attempting to get a copy into a digital format.

By the time the content has been aired on the second and third tiers of release windows (typically in-flight entertainment, then premium movie on-demand services, followed closely by DVDs), the content has been pirated widely, and at high quality.

Increasingly the release windows have shortened, and thinkers such as Mark Cuban have often spoken out about the need for simultaneous release. To date, no major theatrical release has yet ventured to also release nontheatrically while the film is still in the theater, but increasingly the movies are appearing on many other formats extremely shortly after they are finished with the theater run. There is no doubt that giving users access quickly to legal content has dramatically reduced piracy. However, it is yet to be shown that a theatrical blockbuster, made available simultaneously to an online audience can drive as much revenue as a cinema release, and that is not least down to the fact that every visitor who views at a theater pays whereas only one user pays for a family to watch on a TV-based movie service.

It will take a long time for that model to change – if it *ever* does, and for this reason I foresee there always being a theatrical release window, followed by a digital one. A two-tier model would help too, since it would be easier for online services to procure wider ranges of better quality rights.

For many years it was impossible to negotiate for movie rights in the UK for release on IP networks. Every attempt I made on behalf of clients to contact a studio between 2002 and 2006 was forwarded to Filmbank Ltd who in turn was defending DVD licensing, and saw IP services as cannibalistic, which resulted in queries being black-holed. Filmbank has now finally changed, some 10 years later, but I am still amazed and frustrated by how difficult film studios make it to license moves for venturing commercial platforms. This intransigence is also a contributor to piracy in my mind. As Netflix has shown, if you make it easy for an audience to find something they want to watch they *will* pay.

Rights and release windows do have their place, but once the cost of production and promotion of the movie is recouped, more effort to help channels, syndicators, and licensors of all types propagate and monetize rights will return far better long-tail returns that most producers and rights holders believe, purely on a basis of ludditism!

I will touch on "service velocity" in more depth in Section 2.7, but I want to note that the concept applies to movie rights negotiation as much as it does to movie distribution. Well-executed rights models of the future will *certainly* have to be easier to do than they are today, and the entire rights industry needs to become more adaptable with the way it is clearing rights in order to capture revenue opportunities, and encourage increased partnerships with a myriad of new media and OTT service providers. Yes, this will cannibalize existing models, but if left unchecked and uncontrolled, the erosion will be one way, and inexorable, to the point that the movie sector could risk repeating the errors of the music sector.

The brave reap rewards on the Internet – content owners should definitely be streamlining their syndication – their workflows are immature at best, technology led and confused at worst.

2.4   Encode > Serve > Play

Having touched on rights and Intellectual property from the perspective of content producers, I am going to segue in to some deeper technology discussion now, but starting with the focus on intellectual property and a look at the elemental building principles of content delivery networks.

2.4.1   The Basic Building Blocks

In nearly all streaming paradigms there is a very established and common theme throughout. A simple broadcast or transmission network, be it used for video transmission or other types of signaling, will typically have a simple start and end point, or if you like, a client and a server.

In the distribution model we have to scale this up somewhat so that there is a client/server model established between the original video signal "capture" and the distribution "hub," and then there are typically "many" client/server connections between the hub and the end users.

Thus at its very basic level, as shown in Figure 2.3, a typical content delivery network architecture will comprise three basic building blocks of Encode > Serve > Play.

From a computing perspective this is actually a pairing of client server systems where the "server" stage is both a "client" of the encoder and a server for the player-client. Note that this is why a fuller workflow (as seen in Figure 2.1 for classic live streaming workflow) splits the central Distribute stage into "acquire and distribute").

We will explore this model in some depth, and go into some detail on the internals of the various stages. We will also see how many such models can be orchestrated to run in parallel, and equally how each of the stages in such models can be scaled out independently.

Figure 2.3 Basic building blocks of a content delivery network.

For now though, it is sufficient to simply follow this three-stage picture and quickly apply it to some analogies we may be familiar with:

- TV broadcasting might have an encoder in its outside broadcast truck, a server at its play-out center, and the "players" could be considered to be the TV sets.
- An enterprise video platform might have an encoder connected to a TV camera, a server on a central office platform, perhaps integrated with a knowledge base or perhaps a training platform or something like Microsoft SharePoint, which would then have the capability to serve each video browser as the "player."
- A financial data network may encode real-time data into a form suitable for trading desks at the stock exchange, aggregate that in a high-frequency trading platform ("server"), and then deliver that to many banking terminals "players."
- A content delivery network (in the common sense of the term) that would typically think of the "encoder" as a stage in the process that their customers take control of, leaving them to offer a "server" as an entry point or "origin" on their distribution network, which may in turn comprise a "tree" of servers that form the distribution topology, each of which then provides the "edge" services to which the end users with Set-Top Boxes or mobiles (etc.) can connect ("player").

I included the financial data network because while at first sight the nature of the content makes the system look unrelated to the delivery of TV and video, the fact is that architecturally there is very little difference between these distribution models – the nuances are actually to do with quite fine details.

This is a good thing: most distribution challenges can be broken down to fit this three-stage model. However, this simplicity has also been exploited in ways that were counterproductive for the sector, and an example is covered in the next section.

2.4.2   The Acacia Patent

Some years ago – in the second half of the 1990s – a private company called Acacia sought out and bought rights to some patents that had been granted some years before. So Acacia essentially had a claim on any video or digital media transmission that included a "server" stage between the encoder and player.

A fellow StreamingMedia.com writer, Geoff Daily, followed the story closely at the time, and I caught up with him to understand more.

While the original patent owners had not themselves sought to protect their patent, Acacia was making an aggressive move in this way, and in fact given that the only activity of Acacia was suing for patent violation, its sole purpose was to drain the sector of resource and funding, and return nothing for the privilege (beyond a license to use "its" intellectual property).

In reality Acacia proved to be one of the first really dedicated "patent-trolling" companies. It was predatory, looking to build a base of settlements from "frightened" smaller entities and gradually use this resource to snowball up ever-larger settlements from larger and larger companies.

At first Acacia set its sight on the adult sector. Often adult content is less concerned about many issues that are a focus for more "high-street" content, so the adult content producers compete more wildly and are thus typically very advanced in terms of their technical capabilities. Acacia thought targeting adult would be a good soft target, with many not wanting to go to court, and opting for settlement instead. Evidently, by doing so, they hoped to establish some precedent to then use in chasing larger targets. Unfortunately for Acacia, it totally misjudged the adult sector, which amassed a significant war chest, formed strong alliances to defend themselves, and then mounted a robust defense to any attack from Acacia.

After a year and only limited success, Acacia turned its attention to production studios and broadcast, cable, and TV technology companies. Disney, SONY, and others, surprisingly, settled, and this returned a significant war chest of funds. With this Acacia broadened the attack, and over the following five years they managed to settle with the majority of its targets, with only a few mounting a defense in courts.

While Acacia had amassed a startling $650 m of payments for the patent holders (plus what it took for itself), it ultimately lost court challenges. The Acacia patent was finally invalidated in 2009.[7] Acacia was rich, despite contributing nothing to the sector, and using this fund, it moved its focus to targeting other sectors in the same way.

In many ways this episode delayed the innovation in the streaming on digital media technology sector, and the story is a classic example of the exploitation of "submarine patents." Interestingly Acacia remains active as one of the archetypal "patent trolls."

Sadly, such activities are all too common these days, and ultimately make a mockery of the very purpose of patents. The term "patent" translates from Latin as "laying open," and the original intention of patents was to encourage small inventor teams who had discovered new designs, techniques, and so on, to share them publicly so that large corporations, which could take the invention to market, would do so while returning licensing fees to the Inventors to encourage other inventors to share their ideas.

However, the exact opposite has come to be true. Today's substantial financed organizations, such as Acacia, use the patent process to simply create

---

7 https://www.techdirt.com/articles/20091001/0211456380.shtml

monopolies and prevent competitive market growth, crushing innovation, and discouraging small inventive teams from introducing their new ideas to market, for fear that a submarine patent may emerge to invalidate their innovation. And without recourse to huge legal fees to fight their corner, inventors are effectively locked out of the market.

2.4.3 Akamai vs. Limelight

It would also not be right to discuss patent suits in the streaming sector without looking at Akamai's history. Famously predatory, Akamai has on several occasions tied up the senior management in patent law relating to core, common CDN processes. Akamai is notorious for producing submarine patents and claiming the competition is infringing on those patents, and does so with deep pockets.

Now I am not arguing that all the R&D that companies do to maintain a competitive edge should not be defensible, but the regulator will at some point need to decide if some patents are actually preventing healthy competitive markets from developing, with strategic value for many other sectors as an outcome.

In July 2016, after nearly a decade of legal wrangling, Limelight settled with Akamai (for $51m) for infringing US Patent 6108703.[8] Even on a cursory read, it becomes apparent to any engineer in this sector that despite a relatively early filing date in the history of CDNs (August 2000), every single webpage had been delivered with elements coming from varied locations from the invention of the web nearly a decade later. Indeed, with so much common prior art that could be cited, it is amazing that such a patent stands – although the devil is in the detail, of course.

The core of the debate is focussed on where the execution of the logic that decides which of several distribution locations a particular element is delivered from, with Limelight's claiming that the execution is outside of its control and ultimately essentially different than that of Akamai.

I honestly doubt that Limelight are alone in (intentionally or not) infringing this technical detail, although with such a heavy cost I doubt Akamai will be applying an expensive claim to any more CDNs: their action was clearly intended to tie up Limelights team and resources. To protect its core business, Limelight has had to keep capital reserves to weather any adverse outcome. That cash is out of circulation and could have otherwise been used to develop new services, benefiting the market, and also stimulating Akamai to do the same to maintain its competitive edge.

Akamai's activities over the past few years have been relatively dull, and focused more on these types of competitive moves and acquisition, rather than innovating and showing how to lead in the space. That is not without exception, but I think I make my sentiment clear: too much patent law makes the

---

8 http://www.google.co.uk/patents/US6108703

sector a dull place, achieving the exact opposite of what patents were set up to do. It may offer wonders for the shareholders of the financial organization, but it offers nothing to the consumer, and absorbs funds that could otherwise be used to increase human or intellectual capital. Sadly, this predatory pseudo-monopolistic practice is all too common these days.

2.4.4 Standards, Standards, Standards, ...

As is so often repeated, "the great thing about standards is that there are so many of them"! It is a very true statement. However, that is more the case in the application space than in the network space.

While the complex and varied nature of applications talking over a network is essentially infinite, two ends of a network have to be able to communicate and send binary data, and since we moved to the commoditized IP world, all layers (of the network stack) lead to doing that transfer ultimately using IP these days. I think it is useful to understand some macroeconomic conditions that influenced the emergence of the Internet, and to use this to help underpin what has helped the evolution of the successful protocols we see in use today.

There are an infinite number of ways to set up a private or managed network, and this heterogeneity is a central facet to the success of the network in so many use cases. Successful network protocols are often highly optimized for one particular function and relatively transparent to all other use cases of the network. But when something is highly tuned for communications over its own signaling system, that setup (configuration/protocol) is most likely to not be something that can be "copy and pasted" to other network setups – simply because no two networks are identical.

Function-led proprietary network design was a natural evolution of the specific telegraphy and voice communications business models of telecoms networks over the century or so since they had emerged. Deal making between the International Telecommunications Union members in 1988 saw the International Telecommunications Regulations changed so that the classification of information services was determined as "data," rather than "telecoms." By doing this, the ITU members protected their then-primary and strong voice-telecoms market. At the time this voice-telecoms market was quantified largely in "minutes" – a quotient that was a legacy from the pre–packet-switched and circuit-switched networks era, where the importance in network provisioning was primarily concerned with how long a circuit would be tied up exclusively between two points and one that at the time was what the sales reps knew how to sell.

Even in the much more efficient packet network era, those same sales teams carried on selling minutes as if data didn't exist, since in some ways, back in 1988, it didn't: unrecognized for its potential, the "information baby" was thrown out with the 1998 "deal-water," and general sentiment at the time was that "information services" were just a small sideshow, barely worth putting any investment into. Frankly if opening networks up to transit, a small amount of third party information services, without charging, was the price they had to pay to maintain their own autonomy in pricing their valuable voice minutes, which then it seemed worth, at the time, giving away.

With all these proprietary Telco networks now secure in their core voice businesses, a few small Internet service provider start-ups came to them seeking to buy wholesale quantities of minutes to then offer dial up Internet services to consumers, and indeed many of my generation will recall that the 1990s was taken up with engaged landlines, and huge phone bills for long calls to information services.

Some of these ISPs grew significantly, and as the subscriber revenues gave them more negotiating power, many of them moved to deploy their own termination technology, meaning that the dial up connection was terminated on their own switches, and then aggregated behind a routing infrastructure, which itself was connected into not one but several other backbone networks, ensuring that by having some vendor diversity the ISP could maintain cost pressure on its largest suppliers. Indeed some of these ISPs grew so significantly that they took over their own telecoms infrastructure entirely.

This in turn has meant that traditional switchgear vendors providing technology to the telecoms sector have found new customers in the ISPs. This is where the standards story comes back on track!

Switch vendors such as Bell, Alcatel, Nortel, Nokia, Motorola, and Huawei have long produced technology stacks for the traditional frame relay and ATM telecoms networks. They have a long history of finding a niche (often historically with nationalized/state telecoms companies as customers, in highly regulated (easy to monopolize) markets. Combining patent law, huge capital resources, and complex licensing and regulatory frameworks (which undeniably created cartels), the voice- telecoms operators, and their supplier ecosystem, were supercharged as we entered the 1990s.

Small, relatively misunderstood start-ups like Cisco and Juniper were seen as operating outside of the Telcos' core business. They were thought (by the larger Telcos) to service ISPs and a few large enterprises. Indeed VoIP took until the second half of the 1990s to emerge in any usable sense, so these "Internet protocol" focused vendors were considered to be a nonthreatening minor eccentricity by the rest of the telecoms sector for a long time.

Now IP itself had been around since 1973 (see the earlier chapters on history of the sector), and had superceded as the main network protocol adopted in initially academic and research information services (I first used a Starlink IP node on Sussex University's VAX machines in 1991). However, with economic and regulatory conditions right (or more to the point, the monopolies looking the wrong way), and the widespread and low-cost availability of IP capable technologies, coupled with rapid commoditization of the personal computer, a variety of unstoppable standard ways to do things emerged. As so many competing stakeholders created "versions" of email systems or of webpage servers, the movements such as WWW3C and the IETF became increasingly important for helping customers of vendors ensure that technologies would interoperate – ensuring that there was no vendor lock-in (something that ensures price pressure/control).

However, as those committees and groups evolved (and not just in the network stack but also in the application space – think about CoDecs such as mp3 and h.264 and document formats such as.doc, etc.), there mounted an interesting, unending battle between open and proprietary standards.

There is no right answer. Most technology stacks require an ability to work with third party technologies, and for this reason standards are critical to interoperability. Developing proprietary interfaces between parties extends the lock-in, complicating sales and service velocity and requiring continuous redevelopment each time a client mandates a different third party interface.

Of course, standards are not a panacea. As any implementer will tell you, each implementation of a "standard" will have nuances and variations that will vary with the implementer's skills, and the approach to programming to some extent. Certainly in some cases this can render the standard a failure in its own right. A couple of examples follow.

2.4.5 D-Book Connected TV Standards from the Digital Television Group

In 2013, id3as, my company, was commissioned by Arqiva (UK TV infrastructure providers) to build an encoding and distribution workflow to underpin the UK hybridization of the national digital broadcast television to include OTT services as "red button" features on the services.

The digital television group that oversees the main DTT service called "Freeview" publish the technical model for the service as a standard called the "D-Book."[9] The D-Book is only available to DTG members.

As we came into the project, there was a sense of achievement internally at Arqiva that 16% of the target D-Book compliant Set-Top Boxes and smart TVs were already able to receive the new standard of TV programming and delivery. However, all their attempts to increase this were resulting in a two-way finger-pointing exercise between vendors, with each saying that they were implemented correctly and that any changes needed to be carried out by the other party. This endemic intransigence is all too common. It is typically a result of the fact that primary developers are rarely a resource afforded by integrators farther up the tree (the ones that typically own the project/client), so there is rarely a sense that "going back to the code to make it work" is feasible

---

9 http://dtg.org.uk/publications/dbook.html

or affordable. In turn this means that the badly made core tools are extended by shims/workarounds and hacks at the integration points, rather than fixing the problem at core.

Once id3as got involved, we (owning the encoding platform) took a pragmatic view, looked at the actual packet capture of the sessions between our delivery points and the individual devices, and adjusted the core system to be able to accommodate all the different platforms. We managed this in a matter of two weeks, and took Arqiva from 16% to 96% penetration (the remaining 4% had several unsoldered chips on their circuit boards!). The essence of our approach was to throw the D-Book out of the window and look at what the system actually did in practice, and pragmatically just make it work with no regard to the standard.

The interesting thing is that our resulting platform is arguably one the most universally compliant with D-Book standards, but we simply didn't follow the standard ourselves. So it would be difficult for us to badge the system as standard compliant.

There are obviously many examples like this, and they highlight the complexity faced by operators and developers as they attempt to harmonize standards to produce cost controls, while also competing with each other on features and function.

2.4.6 The CoDec Concerns

No set of standards has caused so much disruption, debate, division, and success (in some cases) as those around COmpression–DECompression protocols – so-called CoDecs or codecs. A CoDec is a client server application that may be synchronous or asynchronous, and it typically has the role of compressing audio or video data for transmission to the remote client, which then decompresses the data and makes the data available for rendering or storage further down the workflow.

The classic CoDec, which everyone from age 4 and up has heard of, is formally known as MPEG Audio Layer III but is much more familiarly as mp3. A huge runaway success – as covered in Section 2.1.2 and other sections in this book – mp3 emerged at a time when network speeds were very low and disc storage was very expensive. So the ability to compress a music file to approximately 1/10th of its uncompressed size was more a consequence of context than technology that foresaw its ultimate success.

The fact that mp3 compression could allow a stream to be rendered as it was transferred from a remote server over a Dial Up network instantly made it invaluable for those interested in using the Internet for multimedia services. And once it had become widely distributed as part of Nullsoft's WinAMP, and subsequently as part of Windows Media Player and Real Media Player – its ubiquity became unequaled.

Much as happened between the VHS and Betamax videocassette standards, the quality only needed to be good enough to function sufficiently, after which point the success was driven by market timing and commercial opportunity rather than purely by technical prowess. So mp3 likewise has many pretenders to its crown – all of which notionally improve on compression ratios, or "quality" – but none has had the timing and opportunity that mp3 had, making it the most successful and most ubiquitous audio technology available in the consumer/online market place. It is important to note that in the professional audio space.aac (advanced audio CoDec) is now dominant, and nearly everything that can play an mp3 will also play an aac. However, most users' libraries are stored in mp3 because they have a confidence that mp3 will always be supported. It is good enough, and so it is widely adopted in the consumer space.

There is a natural draw to the CoDec space for investors and entrepreneurs. The sense that their technology could be inserted into every workflow as a central component draws those who believe they can chase licensing revenue from all over.

Over the past 20 years I must have seen at least half a dozen "revolutionary" new CoDecs introduced to the market. By and large, each brings a small incremental capability, but very few take the sector radical steps forward despite all the hype and claims.

In recent years HEVC (high efficiency video coding) – also known as h.265 by its ITU reference – has been pushed hard. While the main point of these compression technologies has been to attempt to deliver the same quality as their predecessors at increasingly lower bitrates, at the same time as the emergence of HEVC the consumer market has seen widespread sales of 4k and even a limited adoption of 8k screens, and often the focus for HEVC is higher quality at the same bitrate.

HEVC is definitely technically superior to its predecessor h.264. It is, however, faced with some challenges with proliferation. First and most important, there have been some questions about its licensing costs and models. Whenever there is uncertainty in this licensing space the big blue chip "whale" influencers, who would otherwise drive adoption of such a technology, immediately switch to caution-mode – worried about becoming sitting targets for huge licensing fees. This then pushes the responsibility for finding market traction onto less risk-averse SMEs, which may leverage the CoDec to create significant market advantages and help the whales commercially evaluate the opportunity better, albeit delaying the time to market for the CoDec.

The second issue HEVC faces is that it requires considerably higher processing power than h.264, and this means that pure software compression workflows, utilizing CPUs, and so on, all require significant compute resources to work. It takes some time after a standard for a CoDec is made available for silicon manufacturers – be they GPU, DSP, or FPGA – to catch up and mass-produce hardware compression/decompression solutions. During 2016/2017

Intel have been introducing their Skylake chipset range including the HD530 GPU variant, which supports HEVC / h.264 compression and this is exactly the sort of support and impetus that the CoDec will need to become widely adopted.

While CoDec wars have historically caused disruption right across the sector, there is now such wide support for h.264 (and h.264 is clearly good enough for most video workflows) that there is an increased complexity for new entrants involved with trying to churn out incumbent technologies. In trying to make organizations change their entire workflow to support HEVC, the proponent needs to have a commercial driver that is commensurate to the change effort involved.

When trying to decide if updating to a new CoDec is going to be useful, you should be looking for particular capabilities – such as the ability to include multiple languages, accessibility features, or better metadata – and bear in mind that quite often these capabilities can be determined with the transport or container format within which you are distributing the content too.

End-to-end support and the ease with which they can be supported are also key.

There is no hard and fast rule, but I personally defer to the rule of the highest common denominator. Both h.264 and aac are dominantly deployed in production at the time of writing, and look set to remain so for a good few years yet.

2.5   What is a CDN: A Simple Model

2.5.1   Setting the Scene for CDNs

CDN is potentially a huge topic. I'll jump about a bit with some analogy and a brief explanation of the key things in the formative landscape at the time the CDNs emerged.

A CDN is, in logical terms, a very simple thing. It is a way to ensure that many users can consume content.

A traditional audio engineer would think of a CDN's function in much the same way they think of a distribution amplifier. There is a source "input" signal. There are then n channels of output signals replicating the input signal to n downstream receivers. For both upstream and down, there needs to be some processing to achieve this "splitting" of the source to many destinations.

In the analog world of distribution amplifiers, this processing is the essential "amplifier" stage. Without that processing, then as you add more receivers the signal gets progressively divided between them and becomes very weak as the audience grows. In the same way in the digital world of a CDN, the signal needs to be properly replicated to each user, and how this is done affects the quality and cost of the service that the CDN can deliver.

If we head back to the early days of the web, we need to look at the networks as they operated at the time. In the late 1980s (1988 to be exact) the ITU had settled on regulating phone companies' international activities by regulating their trade of "minutes" (explained in a moment). Information services were negotiated out of the regulations. They were deemed, at the time, to be niche services not requiring much capacity on the networks, and so not worth developing a billing system for.

Telco's had evolved to price their main commodity as "call minutes," so their existing billing systems were effective points of contact between the Telco and regulator to ensure regulatory compliance.

Unlike minutes billing, packet billing was complex. A minute refers to how long a private session between two ends of a network link is available. A packet of data moves across "public" third party networks that have no billing relationship with anyone at either end of the route, only with their direct peers and transit providers, and measured in Mbps for a fixed amount of billing and capacity per month, or MB for a flexible amount of capacity and accordingly a variable amount of billing.

For this reason it took until the Internet was well established before packet billing could emerge.

Telcos started to realize that international trunk routing over an IP pipe, where you could commit to a certain consistent level of versatile IP traffic, could be significantly cheaper than paying for "circuits" of 64 kbps to then run two channels of 8 kbps audio over in a fixed ATM or frame-relay model. These circuits were ultimately shared with the operators other clients, but the contention was calculated in minutes that the circuit was reserved solely for the use of that operator.

Given that operators had always charged end users in minutes for their usage, this minutes market was very simple and very strong. However, the appearance of IP was highly disruptive.

Operators essentially resell "routes of minutes." With IP appearing as a cost saving for their interconnections with destination operators, the Telcos worked hard to sell access to that cheaper IP route as a premium calculated with minutes. This in turn gave birth to the least-cost routing market. This market dominated telecoms businesses in the mid-/late 1990s, for minutes and particularly as dial up took off. Often hours (many minutes) online on a dial up connection translated to only a small amount of IP traffic actually passing over the Interconnections from the access provider to the rest of the Internet. Very few users in that era were heavy multimedia users. These dial up ISP businesses sold at many times value, which in turn caused a financial market focus on the information services space. Telcos realized that laying fiber was a good thing, since either way ATM/frame-relay voice focused services were going to sell and so were IP services, and funding was abundant. As they laid fiber, they supported subscriber retailers in creating "always on" dial up services, not least to stabilize the wholesale of both minutes of dial up connections and to shore up commitments to IP traffic.

Once the consumer market had discovered "flat rate Internet," the complexity of packet billing, on a packet by packet source network to destination network, the transit billed basis fell away (or latterly passed to OTT operators), and the possibility to deliver large amount of multimedia over the Internet became affordable for the general public.

The only problem was that while huge funding had gone into fiber, it takes several years to lay transoceanic fiber. Indeed, while this rollout was going on, the international network Interconnects were now filling up, and at the same time the consumer business model no longer scaled revenue with their usage.

Usage was obviously running away with itself.

While consumers could now talk internationally 24/7 for no extra cost, and download or stream audio at good quality, the network operators, in ensuring their network could deliver the service their customers demanded, saw scaling cost at their Interconnects.

Smaller ISPs would buy their access to backbone Internet services on an MB of data transferred each month basis. This meant that increased usage directly increased cost of operations. Equally, those that had significant and consistent enough traffic volumes to be able to commit to fixed Mbps peering with a larger operator had to carefully watch that commitment because these connections were not cheap to establish, and they would still need a data transfer model to "burst onto" at a premium to ensure availability of service under peak loads.

While on a domestic country by country basis, settlement-free peering through (in the case of many locations in Europe) public peering exchanges such as the London Internet Exchange (LINX) softened the impact of direct-scaling costs, there was still a clear challenge to face as demand for the global resource of the Internet scaled up.

A few private peering network operators set up "backbone" IP networks – essentially peering networks with entry points in many cities, so a single connection to them would ensure availability in multiple locations. These were often themselves IP networks using a variety of incumbent Telcos fibers buying in wholesale quantities. However, even though these guys could offer a highly tailored IP network service, and enable a publisher to guarantee that their webserver could be reached from many locations, the issue remained that all traffic had to transit many long network hauls to reach the webserver.

As such all the potential global traffic that might hit (as a working model – not referred to as an actual example) CNN.COM would be reaching the CNN.COM webserver from all locations around the world – and that may be huge during a strong breaking news story, but the rest of the time it might be significantly lower. So should CNN.COM buy expensive burstable MB pipes, or put in place large fixed capacity pipes to ensure that it can meet the peak demand

and yet not simply pay for every byte of data that a consumer reads? Also that topology made the CNN.COM webserver a single point of failure; never a good thing.

With web services becoming more critical to dissemination of news and popular media, it was clear that some scaling architecture needed to be introduced to ensure that service would be delivered.

It was at this exact moment that the CDNs appeared.

2.5.2 CDNs as Money Savers

Many people think of the CDN as solving technical problems such as scaling, lowering latency, and increasing or ensuring availability.

The fact is that the first CDNs emerged in order to save money. It was reasoned that by having a "local" "forward" proxy server, the international/long-distance connectivity requirements could be reduced. Forward proxy servers were hugely popular in enterprise networks during the mid- to late 1990s, and indeed on through most of the following decade. They served two purposes. First they reduced the amount of capacity a branch network needed to be able to provide the users on site with broad access to the data that the central head office wanted to disseminate to the branch offices. In the simplest model the users in the branch office would make a request of the company's webserver, and the proxy server would check to see if the data being searched was already cached locally, and if so, it would serve the user with that content without having to use the IP connection back to the head office. At scale this meant that an office with 100 users might see significant percentages of the calls to the company web service served locally, and this would directly reflect on the size of the expensive leased line IP connection that the branch office required.

The other major purpose of this type of proxy server is to act as a security gateway out of the office, ensuring that company employees are surfing websites they are supposed to, and so on.

There are also reverse proxy servers; these help core network services scale. Ultimately both forward and reverse proxy servers perform the same role: they act as a point of service for downstream end users, and they reduce the traffic "pressure" on the core.

Speedera, and then Akamai, managed to win the responsibility of delivering some large software updates for major software vendors, and positioned themselves to deliver proxy caches in many locations. This meant that they could achieve scales of delivery to end users, and yet offer cost savings to their clients who effectively put these early CDNs into the role of lowering their peering and Interconnection costs.

So a thousand users in the UK accessing CNN.com no longer needed their ISP and CNN.com to ensure that the pipes were large enough to handle their every request over the Atlantic. Instead, the CDN installed a proxy server in the UK, to which all the users connected through the ISP and the ISPs domestic connection to the CDN, and the CDN has a very small transatlantic connection over which just the initial update to the website was copied, once, costing the CDN very little, while effectively giving the end users a transparent and slightly faster (less latency) service.

At first the early CDNs had huge margins of cost to offer to save their clients: CNN itself would pay the CDN to handle delivery rather than increasing its core webserver/reverse proxy cluster size and its connectivity. This represented a significant scaling cost reduction to content publishers.

Second, CND reduced the subscriber ISP's need to keep scaling direct peerings and interconnects with expensive transatlantic routes, instead connecting locally in the UK on a low-cost co-located route to the local CDN proxy server. While CDNs' relationships and deal architecture with ISPs vary hugely to this day, they remained competitive with the alternative cost of the ISP's direct connectivity to publishers' source networks simply through an economy of scale. Further, even where the cost differential would be negligible, the CDNs developed a secondary value proposition as a way to maintain price in the hugely commoditized market it has become today; today, they focus metrics such as low latency for the timely delivery of content, and latterly they deal in more and more "split-hair" differentials such as jitter/time to first byte and myriad other metrics that, to be honest, help sales more than they really help the technical delivery in any practical terms as far as operations or the good enough expectations of the audiences.

2.5.3 Request Routing

One feature is particularly important in a CDN's architecture and that is its approach to request routing. In the early UCL MICE days, multicasts on their MBONE network were announced using a Session Description Protocol (.sdp) file that essentially contained the multicast address and application port on which to listen for the multicast signal.

In a predominantly unicast world, and one that was evolving surrounded by the explosive World Wide Web, discovery of multimedia would typically be reasonably unstructured. Requests for the content might be generated by any number of technical devices and software. This itself presented many issues, central to which was ensuring that the end user would be directed to the CDN's proxy server.

This process is called "request routing." There are two main schisms of request routing: passive and active request routing.

2.5.3.1 Passive Request Routing
These routings typically are not specifically user, or content aware, and they much more concern the pure networking of the contents request. The main

topics relating to CDNs are DNS, ANYCAST, and routing protocols such as OSPF.

A well-managed DNS is a central part of the CDN architecture. In a single DNS reference it is possible to provide a list of server IP addresses that the single DNS can refer to. Should any one of the addresses not be available, the DNS lookup will return a further IP address from the list. This is relatively First In–First Out and cycles – and hence is known as "Round Robin DNS." Round Robin DNS can provide an extremely simple way to ensure that a service is always available. However, there is no way to simply use DNS in this way to route a request to the users "nearest" proxy server.

IP ANYCAST is a networking technique where the same IP address is advertised in multiple locations, and the network processes such as Open Shortest Path First (OSPF) determine which is the closest to route the request to. ANYCAST is an excellent first step in refining the route to a regional geographical location, while purely using resources within the network.

2.5.3.2 Active/Intelligent Request Routing

Once the request is being directed to a specific region using processes such as ANYCAST, an application server will typically determine if the request is valid and which part of the infrastructure is best placed to serve the response. This layer is business process specific, so it has to run on the CDN's own logic, and that logic needs some form of intelligence about the network resources to be able to then direct the request to the final point of contact within the infrastructure.

In 2001 Global-MIX, my own CDN, used php to handle all our request routing. The two request routing clusters were ANYCAST and shared DNS. Either server cluster could service any request, and there was a private line between them, simply ensuring that everything was replicated in both cluster sites. A major CDN today may have dozens or more such locations, and they may or may not replicate all or parts of the required intelligence everywhere, depending on how the network and DNS routing is setup.

In terms of scaling this model, recent developments have ensured greater decentralization. Most modern CDN edges handle requests directly. This means that an edge cluster may be discovered by a combination of DNS and ANYCAST, and then the edge itself either serves the content or issues a 302 redirection to an available source (which is very fast and lightweight for the processor to handle), perhaps using deterministic hash, etc., to keep the whole process very fast.

Akamai has acquired and developed many patents in the request routing area. They are famous for aggressively defending them to tie up competitors' executive management as a way to weaken them, which highlights the central role request routing takes in the CDN sector.

2.5.4 CDN Brokerage

It is such a central capability to a CDN that it has been said a CDN is, at its essence, "just" a request routing platform.

Traditionally request routing required a deep understanding of the underlying available infrastructure, awareness of where content is, and as services scaled up, the Big Data feedback from end user systems has been contributory to the intelligence on which the route is formed.

In the past few years a number of providers have emerged that were initially focused on performing measurements of the performance of delivery networks to, as we like to say in the sector, "keep them honest." Initially these organizations were termed "measurement companies."

With many publishers – particularly those publishing premium content – it has been common to adopt a multi-CDN strategy. In part, this has been to create price pressure, and in part, it has ensured that they can achieve high availability in the event of a single CDN failing.

The measurement companies started in a position where they created static periodic reports on the performance of the CDNs, which were used by procurement to make weighting decisions about which CDN to predominantly use. Over time the gathering of the Big Data, its analysis, and incorporation into a form that can be fed into request routing intelligence, has become linear, and fast; some would even claim "real-time."

Publishers' value is being able to finely decide how content is going to be delivered from their CDN partners on a per-request basis. However, these same publishers also see this sector as so heavily commoditized that they want to procure the service through a single provider. This in turn has meant that those who have been providing trusted measurement, and even inputting that data to the request routing process have been ideally suited to take over the entire CDN contract from the publisher. So, without running anything more than a request router and their original Big Data systems, they are able to take on massive distribution contracts, with their request router acting as a high-frequency broker, fielding millions of transactions an hour, and to all intents and purposes delivering exactly what the publisher expects from a globally distributed compute network, and picking and choosing which of the actual CDNs gets the traffic and thus generates revenue.

This competition in the CDN space is causing tension by increasing price pressure in a sector where margin is hard to come by. With those brokers also having very low capital outlay to get started (much of the Big Data infrastructure is operated in public cloud) and having minimal operating overheads, they can keep their margin low, and yet play God with the traffic volumes more or less at will – just so long as the end users' experience is good enough. And if it is not, they blame the CDN, tweak their load balancing (between the CDNs), and continue.

Those measurement companies that have taken this particular position are becoming known as CDN brokers, and their market is typically measured in GB or Gbps of traffic – competing exactly with the companies that they were originally "keeping honest." Being philosophical though, this is also part of the cruel nature of a relatively unregulated economic environment.

The biggest risk the CDN brokers face is that they may make it economically ineffective for CDNs to continue to operate, and if they put a significant number of the major CDNs out of business, then there will be nowhere for the broker to forward a request to, and if that happens, then the model will change.

What is, however, much more likely is that the Telcos will themselves deliver internal CDNs, so the CDN brokers may continue to service nonpremium OTT content, but in the meanwhile the higher value premium content will, most likely, be served on net from infrastructure that will be created virtually and on the fly within the networks for the task in hand. The traditional Pureplay CDN will, most likely, move back from subscriber delivery and be focused on the backbone delivery to the entry point in the subscriber networks' own CDN application – often one that only exists when and where there is a demand in the operator network.

2.5.5 SaaS Models within the CDN Ecosystems

CDNs were among the first really scaled up Software as a Service (SaaS) models. The capabilities they delivered, albeit difficult to place across the spectrum of definitions of IaaS, SaaS, and PaaS, have always been essentially charged for as a function of usage. Use of an RTMP or a Real Media capability was made available across a vast infrastructure with little or no capital outlay from the CDN's client. In offering this service model to their clients in a relatively low-risk way like this, the CDNs opened up a new way for media companies to price their infrastructure's operational costs. At first, and indeed for a long time, because this cost was seen as incremental to their existing established costs, the adoption rate was quite slow. However, as it was realized that so many other capital and also secondary infrastructure costs were amortized into these models – largely due to the economy of scale that the growing CDN providers had – the penny literally dropped, and once the procurement teams in these larger organizations hooked on, the cultural movement to IP began in earnest.

Today, most CDNs offer a range of core services as SaaS models:

- Web acceleration
- Streaming
- Security

In creating these three typical top-line groups, at times CDNs have made acquisitions of specific former customers and providers into sectors, and cannibalized their own customer base by entering as a competitor to their existing clients.

That said, in the streaming space there are some technology logical building bricks that are common to all CDNs, and again, it may be handy to refer back to Figure 2.1 for the classic live streaming workflow scheme.

2.5.5.1 SaaS and POPs/Edges/Servers

Today, CDN nodes – be they core or edge – will have infrastructure that offers a range of fairly fixed service models. Traditionally these are founded with services that support the major networking protocols in popular use, so in early days the CDNs supported HTTP for file transfer and web/images. Then separately they supported Real Media for RTSP and HTTP, Windows Media for HTTP, and sometimes MMS, and Flash and Wowza, focusing on HTTP and RTMP, although Wowza integrated a number of other third party capabilities such as Icecast and some options for Windows Media.

Over time there has been a global migration to deliver all services through HTTP, and while ingestion of content from live video encoders requires specialized "acquisition" services to exist using protocols such as RTMP, almost universally the general trend on the distribution side has been to opt for HTTP-based delivery service models.

Just so long as you don't want to deliver something that requires a protocol other than HTTP, the market has largely decommissioned/deprecated the session-based streaming protocols, and the traffic, while characteristically different and perhaps accordingly routed in different ways, is usually delivered over the same HTTP server architecture as the static and dynamic web traffic. One of a number of compromises with this includes the fact that HTTP delivery servers at the edge of a network are not typically very good at manipulating media. This has presented challenges for technology strategies such as those that could enable simple Dynamic Ad Integration, and I personally feel that this "simple edge" strategy heads almost entirely in the opposite direction to where the CDN could best leverage its core distributed compute asset. Higher service velocity will require CDNs do evolve their edges more, rather than less, as they have been over the past five years or so. Dynamic Ad Integration is pretty much the tip of the iceberg for the future of edge compute models in the CDN world (since they will be relatively numerous in style and require a return to a degree of complexity in planning at the edge).

With operators rolling out FOGs rapidly, it is quite probable that the depth (in network terms) to which an operator can deliver a highly tailored solution to its clients will outstrip that of any CDN's edge, and again this reinforces some of the complexity that a CDN architect needs to design for.

As far as offering "services" in an SaaS model, if the range of services is too niche, then the CDN may only be able to target specific large enterprise customers in those niches. While the CDN's have in many ways shown the way as far as large distributed network applications are concerned, it may be that their own attempt to make all things HTTP based would leave them with a service architecture that could not provide enough velocity to match the newer, possibly more agile competition from traditionally slow to move operators.

2.5.5.2 Encoder

In video workflows (and audio too) the encoder is a logical building block that combines packetization and compression to convert a source video of one format into a distributable video format of another. It may be that the source is acquired from file or captured from a frame-grabber (which literally takes each frame of video and places it into the computer's memory), and then the stream of video frames is (typically) passed into a compression CoDec, with the resulting output then usually being wrapped in a transport format (for example, MPEG-TS) and finally multiplexed ("muxed") into the delivery format (for example, RTMP or HLS).

Where the input to the encoding process can be facilitated over an IP network, rather than (for example) through a video capture card, meaning the source video is already in some form of suitable transport and delivery format for the encoder to acquire, and where the stream is recompressed then the service is usually termed "transcoding."

Similarly "trans-muxing," "trans-rating," and "re-packaging" all perform parts of this process with nuances that become more and more specific, but that all are subsets of the broad "encoder" model.

Live video encoders are typically connected directly to a non–IP camera source, and encode that source for IP workflows, and as a result are usually physically co-located with customers' production facilities. The transcoders and other "trans" features are, however, features that may be placed inside the networks and performed wherever there is suitable connectivity and resources.

Accordingly CDNs have increasingly baked into their network the capability to take a single-source stream from a customer and deliver the content in many bitrates and formats. This is common in all the major CDNs, and there are also some independent SaaS providers that can provide these services, particularly for on-demand archive library transcoding – viz-à-viz encoding.com, for example.

Over time encoding has become a SaaS model offered as a service by CDNs to their customers, which also tends to "clean up" the contribution feed, making the distribution role easier – the "garbage in–garbage out" reality that CDNs face traditionally impacted CDN's brand. Until virtual encoding and transcoding, etc., evolved, the CDNs were compromised if a client contributed a poor stream and it appeared that the CDN was responsible for it. This has led to a number of CDNs integrating such features – however, at this point in time most still prefer their client to take on the responsibility, and where they do, they offer such encoding in a few network centres and deliver all the variety of the outputs across their backbones.

A better architecture would be to try to deliver a single high bitrate mezzanine out to transcoders at the edges where the many varied options can be created much nearer to the audiences that actually want them.

Again, this is a change in architecture to plan for over the next few years as increased service velocity accelerates a trend toward optimization.

2.5.5.3 Online Video Publishers

During the second half of the decade, from about 2005 onward, the CoDec wars (see Section 2.4.6) were settling down, and with Microsoft essentially paying Real silence money after its antitrust case just as Windows Media and Flash Media were leading the pack as the streaming platforms of choice for most working in the sector. Between the two it was possible to reach the dominant OS users of the day, namely Windows, Mac, and Linux (to a greater or lesser extent). This was in the pre-smartphone days, so the targets were principally laptops and desktop computers. Over time publishers began to adopt a multi-format strategy; no longer were they only on Flash or only on Windows Media Player (or Silverlight as Microsoft tried to level with Adobe). The easiest way to manage this is to run a little bit of code when a user wants to open a stream. Writing that code well so that it works in every scenario is a labor-intensive race. One or two companies stepped up to focus on that user experience and "player" technology. Brightcove is a significant example. Until Brightcove, all the smaller streaming start-ups focused on providing a relatively end-to-end deployment themselves. As Brightcove began to move into large broadcasters, it represented a way to contract out a technology cost that was felt to only increase as more devices were brought to market. Brightcove solved the client-side presentation issues, and made that capability available to all their customers, finding an economy of scale.

The CDNs, normally the big fish in the online video space, saw this, and all spent considerable time exploring ways to offer this online video publishing capability themselves – which caused upset among the OVPs – which were at the time very large wholesale customers of the CDNs, and which became uncomfortable as the CDNs were felt to be creeping up the stack and starting to compete with their own clients. There was a considerable period of saber rattling as the OVPs matured.

However, quite quickly the OVP hype cooled, as the herd of audience adapted to mobile. Publishing to mobile required a new level of skill, and many of the smaller OVPs simply could not resource the diversity of skills that was needed.

Between 2009 and 2013 there was period of consolidation with all the disruption that that brought with it.

Center stage with that consolidation was a company called Kit Digital. Kit Digital had been formed by a takeover and appeared in 2008. Its growth strategy was strongly focused on acquisition, and this initially created a beauty parade of OVPs at many exhibitions and conferences, and then quick turned into a bun fight as the market clearly became significantly overheated. Thus, despite some significant activity around Kit Digital, and a few CDNs and larger incumbents (which were hedging risk into the emerging but immature OVP space), the real grassroots innovation in the responsive delivery of media player/ stream-decoding technology was pretty limited over this period. In fact, because of this focus on ownership of client relationships in the video ecosystem, in the market itself the video technology services space stagnated for a few years in this period.

The key trends in the wider streaming market at this stage were:

- Slow but eventual adoption of h.264 as a global "Esperanto" for streaming platforms (if you like, the "mp3" of video)
- Emergence of HTML5 browsers as simplified < video > embedding
- Cross-platform portability of HTML5 ("responsiveness") matured
- Mobile data plan pricing and network capacity that opened streaming to mobile
- New mobile users' demand for easy-to-access content and willingness to pay for that content.
- Balance for new rights deals tipped, and emergence of Netflix
- Traditional broadcasters' demand for optimized online content delivery platforms

At this point – 2012 – the Kit Digital acquisition spree was running out of steam. This was a shame because they had brought many smaller smart companies and certainly had the good intellectual capital in the company to fully realize their potential. This all happened just at the time that the broadcasters were deciding to go online seriously.

With Kit Digital then declaring bankruptcy, and new management then having to try to rescue what they could, late 2012 and 2013 was an open playing field for those few companies that were established and stable. Yet for a period the demand outstripped the supply, some open source platforms emerged, and some of the larger broadcasters decided to take the publishing capability in-house.

This all happened at the same time that Amazon introduced EC2 and changed the dynamic and, more important, the economics of IT operations forever with what we all now call "public cloud" services (which I will discuss more in the next section below).

And so the OVP market was left with a few commoditizing market giants (in an increasingly niche space) and competing with in-house teams (with fiefdoms to protect). On the other side the emerging CDN brokerages were offering special players (or at least plug-ins for players) between the players and the CDNs, which would ensure price and quality of service load-balancing from the clients' specific locale. This, coupled with Big Data companies wanting to produce deeper insights from Real User Measurement in the media players, leaves the pure OVP market as easy to enter with low-margin diminishing returns, and it is rare that one sees the term OVP used often in any marketing literature in recent times.

The one large entrant into the sector at this time was Ooyala. Its founders had a specific goal – monetization of video content – at heart, and while Kit Digital was attempting a "roll-up" of the sector, Ooyala was focused on helping its clients become sustainable. With Google roots, and significant commercial focus, Ooyala entered the market hard and very seriously, and by 2012 it was filling a vacuum caused by Kit Digital's failure and Brightcove's (frankly) becoming lazy through a lack of real challenge.

Ooyala and Brightcove now try to sidestep the term OVP. Indeed in the last two to three years across the sector, marketing literature has largely replaced the term "OVP" with the term "OTT," and the OVP companies in the space have themselves tried to increasingly reposition and to creep up or down the stack to offer OTT "platforms" with a more end-to-end range of capabilities through the video ecosystem. However, essentially as integrators rather than core innovators, they would struggle to find long-term protectable positions in a dynamic and volatile market, and have to reinvest constantly (from ever-decreasing margins) to stay ahead of their competition. They also generally do not have much of their own infrastructure. So as they creep down to compete with the CDNs, the traditional OVP can only offer third party service level guarantees, and to compete here, they need to move from a very virtual model to a model where they invest in CDN scale infrastructure. It is much easier for a CDN to build its own OVP – or be crushing on price and command any deal that the OVP may bring in.

Pure OVP is a tough market. Those real success stories out there more often than not tell a behind-the-scenes story of good relationships and support in managing workflows to a good client delivery rather than technical prowess.

2.6 Cloud Inside – New Generation

While the OVP space was increasingly focusing on client-side technologies, there was also a significant macro trend emerging in the Internet and telecom space: virtualization was becoming reliable and accessible, and General Purpose Commodity Compute was becoming powerful and yet affordable enough to be considered to replace the wide range of traditional application-specific highly optimized technology that had been used to that point.

With CDNs representing one of the largest, scaled-up, and most distributed service network applications, they were no stranger to this emergence, although right up until 2015 CDNs still thought they could deliver better service levels on appliances than on commodities off the shelf.

And what is interesting is on an individual machine for a specific task that may be true, but when you scale out the total cost of operations, and match that to the total availability of the resource, it is now almost invariably a better long-term strategy to fully virtualize.

The traditional CDNs are "schismed" about the topic, defending their "value proposition" over a public cloud with an endless list of KPI benefits, the fact is that the quality and pricing is good enough that many small publishers have built their own small delivery infrastructure in public clouds. While to a CDN an individual customer that revenues $100 per month is a client not worth investing in, the fact is that when that becomes hundreds of thousands of small clients who support themselves, the question has to be asked when is "good enough" good enough?

Some publishing companies have moved to cloud entirely. The BBC almost entirely delivers its iPlayer platform to the world from Amazon's EC2 service.

Conversely, CDNs and Telcos are increasingly changing their internal operations to leverage virtualization and cloud and to increase their service velocity (see Section 2.9).

So, while CDNs were themselves arguably the first really big SaaS operators, they themselves are conflicted about Infrastructure as a Service, and at the moment most teams in the CDNs offer considerable variations of viewpoints.

This will probably crystalize suddenly at some point in the next year or two, as one manages to leverage a high-profile release in a specific direction. But for now most CDNs say they are virtualizing only where it adds benefit and that they can't reveal anything, but yes, they can do everything you might ask them to, ..., etc.

In the next sections I am going to explain a little about what I think the CDNs should do, since if they don't, then the Telcos on which the CDNs exist are going to creep up the stack and disrupt the pure content delivery space in a way that, until now, the CDNs have traditionally felt dominant in.

2.7 The Three Generations of CDN

Let me recap on the three generations of CDN.

We are familiar with this evolution in the IT and computing services sector.

This evolution has similarly underpinned the same trend (albeit lagging behind by the time to develop the applications on the hardware) in the broadcast services sector, as illustrated in Figure 2.4.

As we can see from the diagrams, both sectors are closely aligned. Indeed the innovation in the broadcast IT services sector today closely tracks the wider IT and computing trend, with both currently highly focused on both virtualization and distribution.

Broadcast distribution networks have historically evolved built on a number of proprietary network protocols, ones that were tied to very

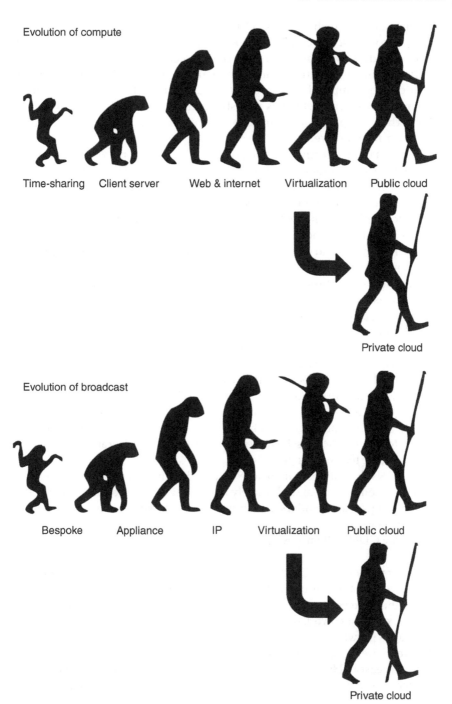

Figure 2.4 Evolution of compute IT with broadcast IT compared.
https://commons.wikimedia.org/wiki/File:Human-evolution-man.png

specific network technologies. Often driving innovation in the telecoms world, "broadcast telecom" was a key frontier in the broadcasters' reach. A strategic decision, opting for a particular technology choice, could fix the position of an entire nation's media for many years. With little interoperability to create competitive markets, this left much of the evolution of the media and broadcast telecoms industry at the mercy of the pace of innovation of their suppliers. They in turn became fat and lazy and this retarded the sector for many years.

IP's key market objective has been to ensure that those provisioning network technologies are no longer tied to a particular vendor. Through encouraging this competitive market we have seen IP disrupt, like no technology before it, and the pace of innovation has rocketed.

As discussed above, in the late 1990s the music industry fell victim to its own "luddite" reaction to the emergence of IP and labored in the misguided belief that the Internet would not affect their business, until it was far too late. Thanks to the time it took to deliver video delivery capable high-bandwidth to the general Internet users, broadcast video has had a little more time on its side to allow it to assess its reaction, to learn from the audio market's struggles, and to find a strong position.

Tradition in the broadcast sector broadened the reasoning behind the resistance to change, and widened the "logic" given for delay in adoption to include issues such as the immaturity of emerging video compression over IP, and the lack of service level agreement that can be formed around IP networks that function, in real-world practice, on "best effort."

These three issues of speed of line, quality of image, and commercial guarantee both set a bar for IP to attain before it would be included as an option and create a forum for those resistant to the incoming and inexorable change to the way broadcast telecoms is provisioned.

The CDNs themselves can do little to directly drive the speed of line that was available to end users, and ultimately are somewhat at the mercy of the ISPs and the compression vendors in addressing both the speed of line and the quality of image issues.

Pureplay CDNs fall into two main architecture schisms:

- Overlay models provision thousands of servers either in or adjacent (topologically) to as many consumer ISPs as possible. The ISP networks that connect all of these devices are beyond the CDNs' management reach, and the core network is a patchwork of multiple public and privately managed routes.
- Managed network models provision a high-quality private managed network between their origins and edge locations, and operate fewer edge locations for this reason. However, their ability to finely optimize the core network to underpin the distribution service level agreements is much greater than an overlay.

As the fiber glut – post 2002 – kicked in, many network services companies found the supply and demand economic changing, and this meant that there was a considerable consolidation in the CDN space between 2002 and 2004. The key remaining players became increasingly myopic about competing with each other.

The sector formed a narrative focusing on where CDN architecture could deliver higher service level guarantees, and in this climate, and in the era before virtualization had taken off, they underpinned this with a "best of breed" strategy – often involving simply buying what was conventionally agreed to be the most expensive, "gold-plated" technology regardless of if it was "overprovisioned" or not. With that commitment made to infrastructure on the basis of offering a belt-and-braces solution, it then became key to recoup that extra expense. This was very much in line to the traditional provisioning process, and enabled the CDNs to "speak the same language" as the traditional broadcasters. Despite the fact that often large sections of the IP video delivery network were not under direct management of the CDN, the focus on the measurement of key performance indicators was carefully trained on where they *could* be measured (namely on the links terminated with the expensive overprovisioned kit). This marketing gave the CDNs a battleground for the commercial teams.

In reality significant chunks of the CDN networks are massively overprovisioned, and the CDNs balance the risk of overprovisioning and cost of operations with the revenue they can charge, and the risk-mitigation capital they need to reserve should they have to pay out on a failure of SLA.

Any "real" SLA in the OTT world is a myth in technical terms: the layer-3 Internet is a "best-effort" network. Period! The best way to ensure delivery/increase availability for an IP connection is to ensure that multiple paths are available. To traditional broadcasters this sounds expensive. Why have several paths of "best-effort" quality when you can pay a premium for a single "very reliable" path?

The fact is that a single "very reliable" path is a single path – an unintended fault on that path could kill a live sports TV event irrecoverably. If you double up that path, you may double your cost but still have no other options if both fail.

In the IP world we approach things differently: if something fails, we have myriad options. Our contribution encoders – which "speak IP" – can connect to any IP network. The IP network itself is highly redundant – almost any part of it can fail, and the failure can be routed around automatically. The commoditization of IP means that backup routes – right down to multiple layer-2 ISP connections at the live event – can be replicated cheaply. Often commercial arrangements can be established that can be paid for only when they are used. This makes it possible to massively over provision those occasional links from outside broadcast contributions. This is no better exemplified than in the evolution of cellular channel bonded 3 g/4 g video encoders and multiplexers (CellMuxes) that have dramatically disrupted the traditional satellite news gathering space, and instead of offering high-capacity guaranteed fixed quality contribution links, such as satellite has provided for many decades, the CellMuxes use "whatever IP network they can" and adapt to deliver the "best effort" – and it turns out that best effort is generally good enough, given that CellMuxes can be bought, commissioned, and deployed for a fraction of the complexity and cost of satellite.

So IP can actually bring high-availability benefits even with "best-effort" operations, but only if it is architected for as "IP" and not as a like-for-like "replacement to circuit switched" (etc.).

Also in the application space the interoperability of IP-based applications was also bringing new capabilities through virtualization, and if architected properly, the virtual application's capability can be offered with much higher availability than if it is tightly tied to a single physical implementation, purely by virtue that the virtual application can be repeatedly launched on new infrastructure and in new locations – allowing high-availability architects to design extremely fault tolerant systems and to replicate them "infinitely" – achieving SLA in a way that can never be delivered on a traditional "fixed" infrastructure.

Let's re-cap:

As operators moved to virtualization, the video delivery networks faced two key challenges:

- They didn't "trust" that the infrastructure would provide the performance they were used to paying a huge amount for in their current expensive (if overprovisioned) kit. They have struggled to realize that by moving to virtualization the infrastructure (as far as the application is concerned) becomes ephemeral. As capability improves, the application is migrated to the new technology. This is culturally alien to a community used to trying to nail down and account for every route and junction.
- Their architecture and thinking was to transpose the existing architectures into a virtualized replication of the same architecture. While this is often a viable option to get started, in practice the "secret sauce" is to leverage the new availability that virtualization brings, to *move capability to infrastructure, just in time and on-demand.* As architects do learn this, it is leading to entirely new architecture possibilities.

And so we have now two generations of the three defined:

- The first generation consists of those that need to tie applications to "tin" (the engineer's vernacular for physical infrastructure). It evolved from (and includes) both traditional broadcast telecoms and IP-based broadcast telecoms with a "traditional fixed infrastructure" architecture.

- The second generation consists of those that have understood that the function of a particular "tin" unit can be replicated on a different "tin" unit. This is "virtualization" as those in the first generation group still largely think it to be. Essentially a "clone" of an entire computer is launched on typically pretty identical "tin" to the one that it was originally created on.

So let us now look at that third generation.

As mentioned above, the common "virtualization" model in practice today is to replicate the first generation workflow but abstract the infrastructure. So, given an available compute and network resource, the virtual machines that construct the workflow's end-to-end application can be run without being (very) deterministic about which computer or where on the network they are being executed. Often "which computer" and "where on the network" are overseen by some form of "orchestration" system, but in broad terms one computer image can be launched "anywhere" and it will function. This means that a failure of the computer resource or network link needn't mean a long-term period of downtime.

Since 2008 a new technology has appeared in the virtualization space – containers.

What a container is (in this context) is an extension to a base operating system that is running on the host computer, which "contains" all the specific additions to the base OS to be able to deliver the computational function required.

What does this mean?

Well one of the key benefits of Gen2 virtualization is that you can host several clients applications on a single machine if the host is powerful enough. However, the requirement for the host to run multiple Gen2 virtual machines is that it must run a host OS – albeit typically fairly minimal – and then each virtual machine much in turn start as if it was running on its own on the underlying resource, with the machines own host OS attempting to "abstract" the new virtual machine's OS from the underlying hardware. Once a second client's virtual machine is added, we now have a requirement from the underlying compute resource to host three OS, to ensure that these OS can share the hardware efficiently, and to ensure that the different machines cannot interfere with each other's process and cause operational or security problems.

With a container model, since the OS is common to all the containers, it becomes possible to install all the client-specific requirements directly onto the host OS, meaning that unlike Gen2 VMs, all applications must be built on the SAME OS architecture. As long as this constraint is not limiting to the overall operations, there are many significant advantages.

First and foremost, a single OS on the machine makes the resource utilization much more efficient.

Second, the containers are completely discrete from each other: there is complete isolation of one client's application from another. Arguably one of the most useful features, this means that when a container is terminated, it leaves the underlying host OS machine completely "clean" from that client's application.

The third really significant benefit is that because there is no "layering" of VM OS on top of host OS, the container is not "abstracted" from the hardware. With direct access, the container can obtain what is termed as "bare metal" speeds from the hardware, and this again increases the resource utilization, both in terms of the compute resources, and – particularly relevant to content delivery architecture – this ensures that maximum throughput can be obtained from network links and internal busses.

Because there is only one OS, and given that often the vast majority of a Gen2 VM image is the OS itself, this also means that in the container paradigm it is possible to launch many more containers on a given physical machine than it is to possible to launch Gen2 VMs. In fact with good architecture, while each container may appear from outside to be an independent computer, it is possible to launch almost as many containers on a single machine as you could launch applications. This ensures that the resource utilization can be made available to more "customers," be they internal customers within a single company or third party customers who are using a publically available infrastructure.

The container boot times take only a few seconds, whereas Gen2 VMs have to effectively boot a whole OS before they launch the application. This makes container architectures extremely dynamic.

Given a particular user may decide to formulate his or her workflows from combining multiple containers, this ensures that software development can become tightly modular if desired, and isolated containers can form networks of resources that can be quickly launched in myriad configurations.

This dynamic capability is leading to a whole new application and workflow architecture.

Here it is worth noting that much the same capability can be obtained in other ways. Purely functional languages – such as the Erlang that my own company codes with dominantly – are natively discrete. Yet the high-level architecture that Erlang (which is 25 years mature) has, if anything, given us clear insight into how other programmers may now access these models of high availability and dynamic orchestration, and this will open up a wealth of new computing paradigms over the next few years.

2.8 Software Definition

Along with the ever-evolving buzzwords in the technical sector, over the past few years the term "software-defined network" (SDN) has become widespread.

Wikipedia defines the term as follows[10]:

> **Software-defined networking (SDN)** is an approach to computer networking that allows network administrators to manage network services through abstraction of lower-level functionality.

At a high level this is a good description. However, if you walk around the many trade shows where exhibitors are using the term in their marketing, and pick up their literature, you will quickly discover that the commonality in meaning is skin-deep when it comes to technical implementation.

Some of the early SDN implementations I saw were essentially widely interfaced network management hubs, consolidating APIs into a single management tool. This allowed coordinated configuration of the existing appliances, very much in a Gen1 model, and with the SDN tool itself being essentially the only software in the system. To me this looks just a consolidated engine for an operations support system (OSS).

Perhaps in reaction to this, or perhaps simply because it was a bigger job to do, it was a little while before I saw SDN moving beyond configuration to include orchestration of "other" software activations within the networks. For me this is much more important than the earlier simple OSS tool. After all most network operations centers (NOCs) were limited in number, so the cost of deploying an aggregated OSS control interface for their network was fairly constrained. Simply moving the traditional, vast array of control interfaces typically controlled in a single NOC into a web browser, or at least a single virtual machine, was only solving a small problem.

A much bigger issue was ensuring the network itself and was being deployed in the most optimal way.

As the approach to deployment of functions such as proxy servers/security gateways – which require compute intelligence to operate – were moved to a Gen2 mode (delivered as virtual machines). This meant that the network operators could deploy services locally to their clients, using the NOC (or SDN controller) to configure the network and adding computers in many places to run the virtual machines. In doing so, they could deploy the proxy server/gateway application machine to a suitable point on the network for that client's traffic, and even scale up to multiple instances of the machine to cope with locales and volumes of use.

While the machines were still highly specific, verging on custom hardware, from the software's perspective the idea was to make all the machines look like a commodity-off- the-shelf (COTS) computer.

Some of the infrastructure management tools of the mid-2000s had evolved, and in particular, OpenStack was emerging as a free and open source favorite

---

10 https://en.wikipedia.org/wiki/Software-defined_networking

of many recognized cloud and network operators. OpenStack (much like VMware, Eucalyptus, or others) enables operators to deploy Infrastructure as a Service. Through a web UI a network of resources can be added, and virtual machines can be deployed to that infrastructure.

Within OpenStack is OpenFlow. OpenFlow is recognized as a protocol standard for SDN. What this means is that (through its controller software OpenDaylight) it can software reprogram layer-3 switches to secure a specific virtual network path around or through the wider Internet/IP network.

This combination, for me, produces a better picture of a software-defined network. While OpenFlow can determine where traffic is going to go, enabling a network operator to sell a software-switched "private network" to their customer, they can additionally deploy function into the network. It may be a proxy/gateway to help the client control access to the "private network," and indeed typically this has been of interest to Telcos because it creates the ability to introduce paywalls and revenue models, but it may also be any compute function that the hardware in the infrastructure can support.

If that infrastructure is COTS, then any function could be deployed by an operator to its client and within the clients own secure QoS-managed "virtual" space within the operator's network.

The combined ability has caught the imagination of operators who have, until now, always had to "roll trucks" to install that kind of capability for any clients. Now they can configure such a deployment from a computer screen. Further they not only can deploy the network configuration but also define the whole networks functional capability, allowing the operators to rapidly deliver highly tailored solutions.

Naturally enough when SDN combined with Infrastructure as a Service, new buzzwords emerged. While the original term is "virtual network function" (VNF), the common phrase became "network functions virtualization" – particularly among the community close to the European Telecommunications Standards Institute (ETSI) that has, since 2012, been working hard to help create standards for their SDN/NFV initiative.[11]

The SDN NFV project has been prominent at many Telco-focused events – I myself chaired one in 2015 in London. It was interesting to see the momentum that ETSI had brought to this area. Coming from the CDN space – where the problem of scaled-up distributed function has been central and inherent for two decades, it was interesting spending time with Telcos. There is a significant cultural gap between the two otherwise closely related groups.

The CDN culture is far more pragmatic. CDNs take a top-down view of the networks, and assume that they must bring to a "simple" network a layer of

---

11 http://www.etsi.org/technologies-clusters/technologies/nfv

intelligence and function that the network on its own lacks. This has traditionally been achieved in a highly proprietary way. In some ways the CDNs have had more in common with clouds and hosting centers than networks. However, because their value proposition – bringing content to users at high quality and with reliability – revolved around distribution of the edge capability, the CDNs have naturally evolved strong network and service automation systems that enabled them to organize in much the same way that the SDN/NFV models were suggesting.

Obviously the CDN's were function/application specific: virtual proxies and private QoS engineered VLANs were not core business to the CDNs. This in turn meant that the CDN's OSS/orchestration systems were highly proprietary, bespoke, and geared toward their specific technology choices.

As the Telcos have seen the CDN sector become significant, they have all sought to deploy CDN within their own infrastructure, and while this only offers a value proposition to those publishers seeking to reach "on-net" customers within that operators network, for large operators such as the former state Public Telephony Operators, these customer bases are large enough that bringing video delivery in-house represents a significant business.

Yet the Telcos continue to move glacially, and – while this is a visceral comment – they look down on the CDNs as if their two decades of experience was at best "not relevant," and in some cases, even more naively they think the CDNs simply do not know about telecoms.

Telcos have bought CDNs. In my opinion, unless that CDN is on-net, this is a daft thing to do for many reasons, and only looks good on Investor Relations PR. In practical terms this brings little in terms of real network optimization in-house. The CDNs have made critical hires from the Telco community to try to bridge this gap. However, those Telco executives have really brought the cultural problem in-house in the CDNs, rather than helping the CDN transform the Telcos and build a larger opportunity for both.

This means that CDNs have largely almost myopically missed the emergence of NFV/SDN until about mid-2015, and in the meanwhile Telcos have tried to differentiate from CDNs by building badly designed CDNs on-net that have often failed to justify the commercial commitments.

To be honest, I think it's all a bit of a mess. And this is not helping large publishers, and their partners (such as AppleTV) get the rights deals laid out to actually bring the possibility of migrating TV in entirety to IP as fast as it could be done if the cultural divides were not causing so many complications.

In summary, the technology works. Those who are managing the transition are surrounded by fiefdoms and wrong preconceptions, and this is preventing proper dialogue between the experienced CDNs and the powerful Telcos.

At some point soon this will watershed. I often joke it will be when the over-50s retire and those who are bought up on the Internet alone take control.

2.8.1 Multicore CPU and Functional Programming

Software-defined orchestration is not limited to network applications. As those who, like my own company, focus on Functional languages know only too well, good software orchestration can be delivered on a globally distributed scale, or on an atomic scale within a single CPU's applications.

As chipsets are produced with more and more cores, the complexity when running many processes at the same time (concurrency) increases. While it is possible to manage this complexity in an object-orientated programming language (OOP), the code to handle every exception and task also grows. This takes time to engineer, and can increase the number of bugs that have to be addressed. In a Functional programming paradigm the composition of the task leads to extremely small tight code, even for massively concurrent process deployment. This in turn reduces the time to engineer and reduces the number of bugs that have to be addressed.

While the paradigms of SDN and VNF orchestration are evolving fast across networks, a similar – potentially continuous – strategy also applies within local clusters and, as core's increase in density, it also increasingly applied within the single computer.

In my own company our adoption of Functional programming (using Erlang) has positioned us some way ahead of many companies that are considerably larger and better known. We are able to orchestrate individual processes within a single compute unit in an almost identical that way we can provision entire global networks. In contrast to OOP languages which have to anticipate potential failure and design/architect for those conditions, Functional programming embraces failure and naturally recovers from such failures by design, seeking to kill and replace the failed workflow instantly. This model ensures that Functional platforms achieve extremely high availability even at scale.

To content delivery network architects, who typically deal with large volumes of concurrent processes ranging from transformation of a video asset within a specific single origin, through to huge volumes of video being delivered via expansive distributed computer networks to ever-increasing audiences, the adoption of Functional programming is a simple fundamental decision that will greatly improve every aspect of their service operations and implementation.

2.8.2 Functional Programming and Containers

There is an additional benefit to the use of Functional programming languages too. Because there is no shared memory state in Functional programming, there is complete isolation between processes. This means that the isolation that containers are used for when deploying multi-tenant applications within shared infrastructure comes baked into the Functional language. While containers continue to be useful for shrink-wrapping large OOP routines (ensuring that when they are removed the underlying infrastructure returns to a clean state) and while Functional programs can, of course, be deployed in containers, it is usual that Functional programs do not need the isolation that containers offer.

A language such as Erlang can orchestrate, achieve isolation, and scale extremely well, with natural resilience and recovery built in. So in a pure Erlang environment we do not need to use containers, and this further simplifies our architectures.

2.9 "Service Velocity" and the Operator

Service velocity is explored in depth in a recent StreamingMedia.com article I wrote and have included in Chapter 5. However, as a conclusion to the context and orientation section I want to stress that all these technical solutions will only find success where they address commercial strategies for users who deploy them. For this reason it is important to note that service velocity is key to understanding *why* one should adopt the techniques I have been advocating above.

Essentially service velocity refers to the speed with which a new service can be provisioned across an operator network in response to either a customer or a business requirement to innovate and bring something new to market.

In the traditional Gen1 appliance-led technology mode, service velocity could be measured to account for the time taken to order and supply the appliances, to train installers how to install them, to test the appliances, and to activate the service. In an extreme example a satellite operator may measure its service velocity in units of years, or possibly even decades. The planning for such rollouts have to be meticulous, since once a rocket is launched, there is little chance to change the satellite's design!

As Gen2 arrived, it was assumed that a Gen1 network of routers and servers based on IP and COTS would still be in place, but from that stage it became possible to commission infrastructure within minutes and deploy services in the time it took to distribute a virtual machine to the commissioned servers within the infrastructure. If "hot-spares" were setup in a redundant mode, then failover for disaster recovery was possible, and this meant that SaaS operators could deploy new services to customers or add new services to their marketing relatively quickly. Typically the business continued to plan and execute much as before, but without needing to wait for physical installation every time a new service was introduced. This meant SaaS operators could measure their service velocity in days or hours. (An interesting legacy of this is that Amazon EC2 still typically measures their IaaS service utilization by the hour.)

Gen3 shrunk the size of the virtual processes that delivered the services once again, and this means that complete networks can be delivered "just in time."

Indeed it is now possible to instantiate a service in response to a request; for example, a user could request a chunk of HTTP-delivered video from a server that doesn't exist at the time the request is made, but that HTTP service can be deployed and respond to the user without the user being aware. This is a heady concept and leads to all sorts of conjecture about the future of computing as a whole; however, more important, it means that service velocity in a Gen3 world can be measured in milliseconds, and makes it possible to always say yes to clients, provide disaster recovery on the fly, and scale or more interesting, moving entire SaaS platforms "on-the-fly" while there may be millions of clients using the service.

It is through this architecture that my company ensured continuity to Nasdaq while delivering hundreds of live financial news broadcasts online through a well-known public cloud infrastructure even when it failed and all the other Gen2 operators suffered a significant outage. We automatically and instantly relocated the service orchestration to an entirely different part of the cloud, and did so between chunks of video. Indeed we only discovered the outage when we saw it reported in the news: we did not receive a support call.

Service velocity obviously changes the competitive landscape – using the right technology for the task in hand means that small agile companies can deliver service levels and times to market that have traditionally been the preserve of very large capital-rich companies. This increases the pace of innovation significantly and will continue to transform not only the content delivery market but many other sectors as well.

3

Workflows

So far I have talked about high-level trends across the sector and expressed my own views and opinions of some of those trends. Then, based on where I have seen them emerging, I have conjectured about where I see the industry sector heading.

Now we are going to turn our attention to the end-to-end production of video, and talk in some detail about aspects of the daisy chains of technologies that can be put together to create what are commonly termed "workflows."

Obviously a good starting point is to agree what the term "workflow" actually means. As with all catchy terms in the IT sector, it sounds very specific, until you realize that different people are using the term to embrace slightly different things.

Let's take the Wikipedia definition as a starting point[1]:

> A **workflow** consists of an orchestrated and repeatable pattern of business activity enabled by the systematic organization of resources into processes that transform materials, provide services, or process information. It can be depicted as a sequence of operations, declared as work of a person or group, an organization of staff, or one or more simple or complex mechanisms.
>
> From a more abstract or higher-level perspective, workflow may be considered a view or representation of real work. The flow being described may refer to a document, service or product that is being transferred from one step to another.
>
> Workflows may be viewed as one fundamental building block to be combined with other parts of an organization's structure such as information technology, teams, projects and hierarchies.

"Business activity" is, for me, a central part of the Wikipedia description. Cynically, marketing brochures of many vendors show how their product can

---

1 https://en.wikipedia.org/wiki/Workflow

Content Delivery Networks: Fundamentals, Design, and Evolution, First Edition. Dom Robinson.
© 2017 by John Wiley & Sons, Inc. Published 2017 by John Wiley & Sons, Inc.

bring a company into competition with all the other customers of that vendor. The sale of "product" solves a problem for the vendor alone – that of needing new customers. However, in my opinion, every "workflow" should not be tied to the current ability of a vendor to provide the same supported product to many clients; it should be tied to solving the specific business problems of each individual customer, particularly in a b2b environment where the customers are themselves seeking differentiation in their own b2c outputs.

In the case of a news agency, that "problem" may be the high-speed delivery of content captured "on-location" in a remote region and to a usable format for a broadcast or online delivery.

In the case of a telemedicine company, it may be that a high-quality video picture needs to be delivered cheaply and securely to just one or two remote locations.

It is unlikely that the physical and link layers of these two customers will be similar, and the financial constraints and objectives will almost certainly be significantly different.

In this chapter I will refer back to these two parallel and yet very different workflows to explore the variance.

In the preceding chapter, in Sections 2.7 and 2.8, I discussed orchestration. In a "software-defined" model, orchestration and repeatability are central concepts. In the latest generation of distributed computing architectures, complex, multi-tenant workflows can be activated at will, and replaced instantly should they fail. This approach is leading to new design considerations, and opening up new business possibilities too. In practice this means that organizations will often arrive on day one at the vendor's office with a loose definition of what they think they need based on taking a previous architecture paradigm into a new context. So today we still see many organizations attempting to virtualize an identical workflow to their traditional workflow so as to validate that there are commercial motivations to "doing the same as they have always done" but "in a new way that is just as good but cheaper." Many have encountered resistance from the corporate/commercial leadership, citing the work as "for technology sake." They also struggle to make the old model work in the less QoS-guaranteed hardware of COTS, and the "best-effort" service level agreements that underpin the IP networks.

The fact is that simply moving a series of black-box capabilities that have been scripted together using the black-box vendors APIs may be possible. In fact, at id3as, our earliest virtualizations were proof of concept works doing exactly this (to ensure we could test end-to-end viability of virtualization and model some of the cloud economics). However, once resource ("cloud computing") becomes cheap and essentially endless, and as that resource can be found in many locations on a network that can be created ad hoc, we can start to design differently.

Traditional architectures in the live video space have usually revolved around getting the source feedback to a central point at as high quality as possible, and that central point has a limited amount of key appliances that can transform the media as required for output, and can then deliver it to a distribution network, again in as high quality as possible. The distribution network then has to commit to replicating that source across its own geographically distributed network and finally deliver it through access networks to end users.

Simply moving this workflow from appliances and "private" networks to COTS and IP networks may bring some benefits. These may include better cost efficiencies: it is common that live networks are used in an ad hoc way, and by virtualizing them, they can be activated across the "cloud" on demand and thus cost nothing when they are not being used. Such approaches may also provide better disaster recovery: a failed COTS appliance is one of thousands in a cloud, and can be replaced instantly – where a failed appliance may require a site visit and physical replacement to be installed. However, the peace of mind provided to the operator by the private networks (on which they have not only evolved but often *anchored* their own key guarantee of delivery business case) is often challenged by a move to IP networks where overprovisioning and best effort are the only guarantees available.

But a first question to ask is whether the network links and topology are still valid in the new compute paradigm.

Traditional broadcast architecture relies on backhaul to a central processing plant and onward contribution to a distribution network. In contrast, the end-to-end design principle[2] of IP networks removes the complex compute functionality from within the network and places it at the edges. This means that in a perfect model the modern broadcast network should be architected in such a way that the source content is encoded and encrypted at source, multicast to all subscribed end users, and if transcoding is required to suit that end users bandwidth/device type, this happens at the edge of the network where the subscriber authenticates on the access network.

Such complete decentralization leaves the modern network simply orchestrating – moving the right functionality/capability to the right resource – and overseeing authentication. The video itself – the high bandwidth data – takes a short route almost directly from the point of creation directly to the end users. There is no "central" broadcast facility. This leads to great scaling, resilience, traffic optimization, and reduced operational complexity.

Yet such a model leaves many traditional broadcast operators uneasy. They have a culture of controlled network core operations. Ask any broadcaster for a tour of their facility and they will proudly show you around their data centers housing huge arrays of appliances. They will also show you to their network operations center (NOC), extolling the virtue of having "amazing" connectivity centralized in that facility, and they will show you their master control room

---

2 https://en.wikipedia.org/wiki/End-to-end_principle

(MCR) where rows of operators oversee the various user interfaces on their different appliances and OSS systems on large screens that give the impression that they are overseeing a moon landing.

Explaining to operators that all the command and control can be available on a web browser, or a smartphone app, and that centralizing all the network links creates a single point of failure, and that the scripts that control their appliances are prone to failing as soon as any of the appliances update their software release is a tough job.

However, what does change hearts and minds is when a large traditional broadcaster has a significant outage despite its huge investment in protecting against such a situation, while a much leaner, more agile modern broadcaster delivers much higher availability on off-the-shelf technology and with much lower fixed overheads. Once the finance director "gets it," the culture has permission to change, and the long-term migration can begin.

Virtualizing workflow for the sake of doing so is unlikely to bring any benefit. Once a business justification for software-defined workflows has been made, then the technology should step up to meet that business' requirements. I often open conferences with the expression *"cloud is not a technical term, it is an economic term."* And it is usually the cost saving made when infrastructure is *not* used that brings the most benefit!

3.1 Live Event Focus

Now I want to focus on some practical aspects of setting up for live video workflows. The narrative will iterate from some very high-level opinions drilling down into more technical specifics. The idea is that by reading this, you will have some of my experiences in your mind as you try to deliver your live event online.

I have, over the years, produced many thousands of live webcasts. These have varied from global news events to music festivals to business briefings and telemedicine. I have used extremely primitive freeware tools, and extremely expensive high-end broadcast systems to achieve different objectives in countless scenarios.

While many guides to webcasting and live streaming are strongly prescriptive they often assume that "all events" are "pretty much the same." Obviously the term "live video event" will typically indicate that there is a specific call to action when the event will happen, and there will be an audience wanting to receive the video "as soon as possible" as the event starts.

Unlike video on demand, the live video event requires synchronicity between all the moving parts to be exact. There is rarely scope for re-running the news event or the sporting finish, etc. Live events also critically require a good understanding of the telecoms underpinning the delivery, something that can be of significantly less relevance to on-demand video delivery. This is in part because of the pressure of the criticality of delivery of a live event, and also in part to the audience behavior: a live audience will typically generate a sudden demand on the infrastructure, and ensuring there is capacity for each viewer takes planning, adaptability and resilience for a successful experience.

All too often, as the industry was nascent in the early 2000s, brave publishers would plan a large live online event, something would fail, the threatened traditional broadcast media would jump on the experiment with cries of "the technology will never be ready," and so on and so forth. In fact it was only through iterations around these failures that we, as a streaming sector, learned how to scale sustainably. And we did this in a period of less than a decade, where the traditional sector has taken some six or seven decades to get as far as they have – and that is far from faultless even now, and has comparatively (to the streaming sector) vast amounts of sunk capital behind it. Today, the ability to scale up to almost any size of live online event is no longer a technical issue. More often than not, if there is any complication, it is to do with rights.

... But that is a different part of the story.

3.1.1 Approaches to Webcasting

I am going to talk through some of the many aspects of producing a live event online. I will take you on a journey from the planning stage, through the deployment – looking in some detail at considerations for repeatability and scaling.

The first thing to highlight is that there is not, and probably should never be, a single way to produce a webcast. While a particular workflow will eventually establish itself as a common reference for any particular operator, publisher or business, there will *always* be nuances in the specific requirements that they will seek.

You have two approaches in addressing this sector as a service provider:

- You can seek only clients that can work around your own technology limitations
- You can prepare for every scenario yourself, and ensure that you have sufficient technology options in your own arsenal to be able to deal with all foreseeable situations.

The first approach requires patience and focus. You will need to position to address that sector, and this may involve specific technical differentiators that are particular to that sectors needs. For example, for telemedicine, you may need to provide specific cameras, and for aerial work, you may need to be able to fly a drone. The range of skills you can bring will help you make that difference, and if you can isolate specific clients with significant continuous streams of work, then you can match your technology to their exact requirements and potentially grow that into a steady business. You will inevitably face a common risk: over time the client will (and I mean *will*) explore bringing the capability they buy from you in-house to increase their own margins. Pragmatically though this is a risk for any service provider in any sector. If you maintain a good relationship and reinvest to always be one step ahead of the client's "can you also do XYZ," then you can remain the thought leader, and with trust, you can become a long-term partner for them. If instead you take the view that you will provide the bare minimum, you will struggle to maintain the business for long. The market has low barriers to entry and is therefore highly competitive.

The second approach requires a broader investment and more intense involvement with the client to align expectations with them. Their concept of what they are contracting you to do may well not be as close to the easy option (your "default" mode) as you would like, and you may inadvertently short-circuit a seemingly trivial requirement that is mission-critical to their operation. For example, wrong metadata insertion into a stream may cause considerable downstream issues. While this broader adaptability to meet a wider variety of projects has some benefit, it is very investment heavy. Almost every event may require a specific production tool. With many such tools costing more than the margin made otherwise on the production, it can become a logistic nightmare trying to preempt the market continuously with the "latest" technology – be it a field kit or developing a new social media plug in.

The answer to which is right for your strategy is going to be unique. Having worked extensively either establishing my own or as a contractor, to many of these webcast service providers the one thing that makes the biggest difference is having some scale at the outset.

This means doing lots of webcasts, and regularly.

The economy of scale means that if you have regular events, you will be able to continuously reinvest and develop your capabilities and reach beyond those initial regular events.

3.1.2   Think Before You Start – Your Client Probably Hasn't!

A question I get asked often is what is the right setup to webcast our events?

Obviously there are myriad answers to this – the previous section will have set you up for this comment! However, assuming your client really knows nothing, then there is a triage I would commonly take them through to work out what answer to give:

- Why are you doing the event? What are the KPIs of its success?
- When is it?
- Is anyone else involved in the production? (Do we have autonomy?)
- Who will be watching it?
- On what devices/where?
- Will it be paid for? (Does it need DRM?)

That said, we have a common set of core functions that will almost certainly require:

- Production of the final composition of image to be broadcast
- Transmission (including compression) of that image to the "hub" of the distribution network
- Understanding of or responsibility for distribution to a target range of devices

The first and most important thing for me is to have a "logical schematic" laid out that becomes the central reference for anyone involved. That will almost invariably start on notepaper during an initial call, and will evolve through a whiteboard session into a simple, but smartly drawn, diagram that will vary as little as possible during the event delivery.

That schematic will show the interfaces between different parts of the production chain, show what different teams within will be expecting from each other. It will show the technology hardware deployed, the network links, and the core service, and applications/functions deployed. Often data flows will be drawn to show where traffic is likely to be routed, and to help stimulate thinking about scaling issues as – for example – second sources are added for resilience or as audiences grow more edges are required to meet demand, etc.

There are more thoughts and details about schematics and diagrams in Chapter 9, Section 9.2.

3.1.3 Budgets

Although always a bit awkward to discuss, do get a feel for "how much budget is there?" While you will usually get a generalization, responses to this typically fall into two zones:

- TV standard – Quality priority over budget. Essentially want to do "targeted" TV.
- Adds value standard – Not really got a budget but will cover human resource costs. Can't we use YouTube Live for free?

Surprisingly, from a webcast operations point of view, and in my own opinion, while the "TV standard" type of events are typically higher profile, and therefore of great value to the webcasters acumen, in terms of profitability the "Adds value" option will usually require much less preparation time, and lower risks, ultimately returning a similar profit per hour of work contributed when you account for every hour of work required in planning for the "TV standard" higher fee events.

3.1.3.1 "TV Standard"
If you want to deliver your live event content online with the same service level agreement that TV broadcasters expect, then a simple strategy would be to

send your contribution feed via satellite to a satellite aggregator (or similar), and produce the event exactly as if it were a TV program, but simply encoding the final output at the production "playout" facility. Often the webcaster in this situation is actually asked to compress a video source provided on a serial digital interface (SDI) with embedded audio. The compression unit contains all the configuration options to encode the video to a compressed form and then to transmit that over a network link to a remote counterpart unit in the target facility. The job is almost identical to that of a traditional satellite news gathering (SNG) link provider. Indeed there is so much crossover operationally that increasingly the SNG link's role is encompassing webcast compression and is being termed digital news gathering (DNG).

DNG engineers these days will usually configure their field encoder to send the stream directly to the CDN's origin server, although sometimes that may first be at a broadcast facility that wishes to modify the stream before forwarding it to the CDN.

While the travel prospects are exciting (!), once the link is established, there is little to do but wait for the event to finish or a problem to need your local hands. It can involve a lot of coffee (!).

3.1.3.2 "Adds Value Standard"

At the other end of the spectrum is the "Adds value" approach. As my drone race example above highlights, at a grassroots level many niche sports have engaged enough followings that a few hundred people will quickly tune into any live media that can be shared socially. Facebook Live, YouTube Live, and before them, Livestream and Ustream, have all provided ways for people to stream without directly meeting the costs of CDN distribution.

These models have opened up webcasting for the masses, and in many instances all you need to become a citizen journalist, live on a broadcast news channel round the world, is to be in the right (or possibly wrong) place at the right time with a smartphone in your hand.

Obviously, if you are going to promote your webcast in advance, it is worth planning the production as well as you can, even if that is going to be only a Facebook Live stream.

To that end, you should be able to control a basic vision mixer, to standard-match and white-balance digital cameras, to have enough basic skill with sound engineering to isolate poorly earthed lines and to switch microphones phantom power on or off where appropriate. Over the years I have had to vision direct, audio engineer, work titles systems, point cameras and lights, and even stage manage. The webcaster is often looked at as the reason the event is being produced, so holding firm, polite, and unpanicked control of those involved throughout the event – even when the fan is turning the ceiling brown – is all part of the role.

So, when you are adding value with a low-budget webcast, do not think all you are doing is plugging it in and pressing start. You are making your client's event very important. That is why there are cameras not only documenting it but actually communicating the event to myriad people who are not present. At the end of the day – like a wedding photographer – you can really make or break a central part of an event. You have to be ready to turn your hand to every aspect of the broadcast with a cool head – be that to calm a nervous speaker who won't stay in shot, or hold a Telco to account that is routing your contribution feed the wrong way between two peerings.

3.1.4 Objectives – Quality vs. Reliability

At the time of writing, HEVC/h.265 is beginning to emerge more fully in production. By far h.264 is still the dominant compression technology for *distribution* models. However, h.265 does produce a higher quality for a given bitrate than h.264, so it has a place in *contribution* technology. That said, bandwidth in most venues is these days nowhere near as scarce as it was 15 years ago when I used to have to channel bond multiple ISDN lines to create a 384k connection out to the CDN from many venues. Today, one can expect conference centers to have 10Mbps to 100Mbps leased line connectivity – but you must *always* check and confirm this beforehand, ensuring that any firewall access is in place.

Why am I discussing this under quality vs. usefulness?

If the site has a 5Mbps connection, you are in a marginal range. Normally it is good practice to deliver two copies of your contribution feed to your CDN – one feed to two diverse locations so that should one fail, the other will give the event continuity. Allowing a little overhead to 2Mbps contribution streams would be using pretty much all of that 5Mbps connection. Should something else happen to unexpectedly try to stream 2Mbps over that same link (as so often happens at facilities where multiple people have access to the IP link), then both contribution feeds may suffer from network congestion.

At that point one there are a few options:

- Increase the budget and upgrade to a 10mbps link.
- Downgrade the contribution feed quality to 1.5Mbps (etc.) to provide more overhead for the unexpected.
- Drop one of the two contribution feeds and hope nothing goes wrong with it, since that would produce a blackout.

Ultimately all webcasts need to undertake this risk/link budget assessment to properly define how reliably the event will be delivered. As budgets become constrained, these outcomes and risk indicators come strongly into play.

Granted, it is not strictly true to say that in a bandwidth-constrained environment that "reliability is inversely proportional to quality," but it is a good rule of thumb to have in mind.

3.1.5 Production Principles

Many webcast jobs may involve simply bringing a video encoder to an existing production, taking an audio/video source from the production team, connecting it to the encoder, connecting the encoder to the Internet, and pressing "start" – followed by coffee and staring at the green light for a few hours, hoping it stays on!

For the majority of smaller webcasts – particularly the "Adds value standard" – cost is a key constraint, yet they will require the webcaster to organize the production too. To deal with this type of client, having a good solid low-budget setup is key. This should be focused on the "bare minimum" setup required. Taking this approach, even when planning to double-up all your key kit elements, is a good idea: cheaper setup means lower cost when setting up a redundant rig in your spares bag.

There are obviously myriad technology options in the market, and while the final choice will be personal, it is probably useful to outline the "rigs" (my term for my webcast setups) that I use in production.

My own main rig is built around my MacBook Air, a Behringer Xenyx 302 USB micro mixer and my Roland VR-3EX.

I include in Figure 3.1 the wiring schematic for a recent webcast I set up to cover a drone race.

You will notice that I carry several other key items in the rig. Since we had four live drone feeds, I elected to take a second vision mixer to create a sub-mix specifically of the racing feeds. In this case I used a Roland VR3 specifically for the purpose, with the Preview output as a single source (four cameras to view) into channel 3 of the VR-3EX, and the main out of the VR3 was sent to channel 2 of the VR-3EX. This meant that at any time we could cut to a "quad" shot of all four race feeds, but by selecting specific channels on the VR3, I would then switch to channel 2 to output that selected channel on the main VR-3EX feed.

The audio feed was being sent to several places, so I used a small Behringer HA400 audio distribution amp to create splits for commentators, for the PA, and for the restricted site license (RSL) FM radio broadcast, which those on site could listen to on small FM radios, etc.

Commentators use radio mics connected directly into the VR-3EX. The VR3 produced no audio in this instance, but I could have those audio feeds connected into the VR-3EX were they required.

Why the Xenyx 302 USB? Well this is ultimately a luxury feature, but it is one I always use, on every webcast. Therefore it is very familiar to me, and my muscle memory, when something goes wrong, is instinctive and can "cut across" the rest of the production directly. This setup allows me to create an audio sub-mix where I can combine the laptop's audio out for playing music, or sound from prerecorded interstitial videos and also sounds from cartridges (I use an app called BossJock running on my iPad mini) and a separate mic mix

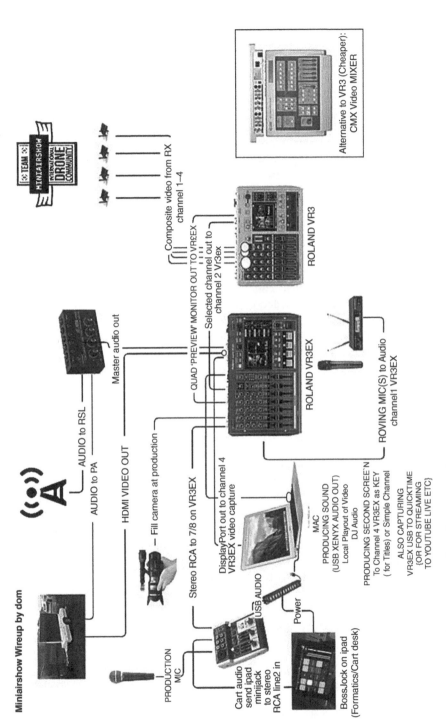

Figure 3.1 My webcast rig set up for a drone race webcast.

for my own booth mic. This means that even if the VR-3EX needed rewiring or adjusting mid-event I can continue with basic sound and commentary from the 302, and even video inserts directly from the laptop to fill in for any production outages. I find that having that extra level of production gives structure to the show, since there are times when I take back control from the VR3-EX producers to run pre-recorded video to air, while the producers set up for subsequent shots, and so on. On its own I also use the iPad and Xenyx to produce simple audio streams mixing music and commentary – I regularly use this setup for TheThursdayNightShow[3] (a hobby Internet radio station I kicked off a few years ago to indulge a personal passion for music!).

So this rig represents a relatively sophisticated shoot. In the preceding example, while orientated around drone racing, the shoot could equally be a five-camera shoot of a conference, or a small sports event, etc. The principles remain the same.

For the drone race, we were producing the output for both a large projection screen, and for YouTube Live. The VR-3EX outputs video to the laptop at 640×480 using a UVC (USB video capture) output. While a little limiting in terms of quality, the drones in this instance all produce 640×480 video, so we worked to that as the base standard. By today's 4k and 8k standards, 640×480 is a small resolution and this may feel somewhat constrained, but our audience was small and purely online. Keeping the quality low like this means a reasonably good image can be produced with a contribution feed of around 1Mbps – great for streaming using 4g as we were on the day. Also this means that the viewers can get a great quality image on smartphones and tablets, and other small screens, while not requiring a high-capacity connection – meaning better worldwide engagement from those in places with limited connectivity. This was perfect for our audience.

At the other end of the spectrum I have used almost the same rig for producing live coverage of Parliament online – the annual meeting in the UK Parliament focusing on Internet governance issues. Again the desired quality target was good enough rather than HD, so this rig again proved its flexibility.

And the best thing about it is I can carry it all in two cases and a backpack – which makes getting onsite easy, and allows me the flexibility to take public transport or taxis without too much strain.

It is also good to note that the market is ever evolving. While id3as – my company – tailor-makes platforms for specific operations, I always explore general-purpose tools. The traditionally limited technologies such as the Flash Media live encoder only facilitate single-channel encoding on a single machine. However, on the laptop I have recently been having a lot of success with some open source software called Open Broadcaster Software.[4] While there are

---

3 http://www.thethursdaynightshow.com
4 https://obsproject.com/

Figure 3.2 Streamstar.com's webcast case-All in One: Great for Sports.

some complexities in ensuring that a laptop can acquire multiple video capture sources, as soon as you move to a small ITX computer you can add any number of different types of capture cards. Essentially this is how we are able to produce live multi-camera mixing with almost all the capabilities seen in Figure 3.1, but using a single computer. This system is under development at the moment, and I will be publishing an article later in the year (which may be available on StreamingMedia's website[5] by the time the book is published) demonstrating this approach. Ultimately that option will be considerably cheaper, although until it is used in production I cannot comment on its suitability for real-world production purposes.

Of course, there are many other tools in the market, ranging from the extensively used software-only Wirecast, to Streamstar's (Figure 3.2) and Livestream's, all in one portable webcast cases that offer compact and excellent functionality, including features such as slow motion and instant replay, and combine titles and graphics all in a single unit.

What suits you will be down to your budget. For high-end production, it is usually best to simply hire kit in – in real terms, buying a specific rig for high-end production will call for considerable capital expenditure, lead to high maintenance costs, and most likely will date quickly – those very high-end features will be superseded before you amortize the capital outlay, so you need to make more and more capital outlays to compete for high-end feature-focused events: it is *normally* the case that in hiring such a kit, and passing the

5 http://www.streamingmedia.com/

cost to each customer based on the specifics they require, you will see a lower operating costs *between* events – although obviously if your client provides regular work, this can change dramatically in favor of owning the technology yourself and including the operating overhead of maintenance, etc., in your service fees.

Every gig, every rig, and every opportunity is different: what suits your situation will be unique.

3.2 Backhaul/Contribution and Acquisition

Let us look in some detail at the most important link in the live webcasting workflow: the link between the event and the core origin of the distribution network. Depending on your own operational role, the terminology for this link varies a little (it's all about perspective), but generally field engineers will talk about "backhaul" (hauling the signal back to the origin) where the network operations teams will talk about the "contribution feed." Those overseeing the event may talk about "signal acquisition from the field" too.

The most important thing to be aware of is that if you have problems on this link, those problems will be replicated throughout the distribution network, affecting all viewers. But, if it works, you probably won't need to think beyond provisioning it at the start of the event; then, if it starts to introduce problems, it will take all your energy, and your stress level will begin to rise.

There are two key bits of practical advice for webcasting live events:

- First, ensure that you have several ways to log the quality of the line setup and run through the day (and make sure that these systems are not at risk of *causing* problems). This accountability is extremely important when you have an outage or need to provide a postmortem. Simple tools like tracert and ping (or GUI-driven versions like Pingplotter) are extremely valuable – they simply repeatedly log the data about the link, and assuming that can be correlated to the causes, any one of these tools can really help when – as does happen – faults need to be accounted for.
- Second, and most important, keep calm. Seriously – when the link begins to fail, there may be tens of thousands of people watching. Everyone will turn to you, be they onsite or remote. You will be the only person who can in any way "tell" what is going on. There will be many people clamoring to know what is going on, when the link is going to be fixed, and this can be extremely stressful – particularly if you are trying to read packet traces or diagnose deep network problems. You will have to politely assert that you will provide periodic updates every 30 minutes but for now you need to be left alone. Then put your headphones on, call someone offsite to help (they are not caught up in the stress onsite and this can be very focusing), and try to

ignore all the commotion. It may even be worth establishing that this is your working protocol before the event so that other members of the production team can ring-fence you and ensure that you can concentrate on trying to fix the issue.

Particularly in the early days of webcasting, when we were bonding multiple ISDN lines in order to get a high bandwidth feedback to the distribution origin, or using prototype satellite IP connections, it was frequent to have issues. Sometimes the issues were simply due to the transient nature of the Internet, sometimes it was third party operations making changes midstream within the IP route, and sometimes it was a mixture of many variables changing uncontrollably. The conditions were almost impossible to recreate, and naturally enough they appeared during the live event and not during the testing.

Over the past decade most of these issues were smoothed away. As we will see in the sections below, which look at various different types of contribution feed in some more detail, many are now commoditized, the Internet service providers are experienced in supporting live streams, and with video now being central to every IP providers operations, most networks are well provisioned to handle live streaming – particularly on a single contribution link.

That said, there is nothing so complex as trying to debug a fault while a live event is counting on you. For this reason I also have one key piece of advice to help you fault-find quickly: *work inward from both ends!*

When debugging a live stream problem try to work from both the video origin and the end users player toward the middle until you have a continuous picture of what is going on. More traditional debug methodology of working from one end through to the other tends to inevitably start at the wrong end, meaning you have to check nearly the whole link before you find the fault. If you start at each end at the same time, and check a little from one end, then the other, then return, and so on, you are far more likely to isolate the fault quickly. This may seem scattergun to those around you – particularly the production team, but they forget that as a webcaster you are often managing more offsite kit than onsite kit, and while, in the hour of panic, this may seem to onlookers like you are not doing much more than sitting at a terminal window, you actually may be debugging across an infrastructure far larger than they are managing.

Webcasting well is a much more broad skill than simply turning up with a box and pressing go. Managing those around you assertively and clearly is a key skill. The Internet and IP networks in general are volatile, and in a sector where broadcasters and those used to working with broadcasters expect the network service to be private, secure, and extremely high level, acclimatizing them to the variability and adaptability they need in the IP space can be tooth-sucking and tedious, but nonetheless essential, and if done well, it can be extremely rewarding.

3.2.1 Broadcast

How did some of the first high-quality live webcasts set up their contribution feeds? Essentially in the early events, cost was less of a limitation, and the webcast was treated exactly like a TV outside broadcast. The signal was produced and uplinked on a facility line (private telecoms connection) or a satellite link (typically from a satellite truck). At the TV studio facility the signal was received from the facility line or a satellite link, and in a baseband video form such as serial digital interface (SDI), which connected to an encoder that compressed the video into a streaming format. In turn that compressed video was transmitted over a high-capacity IP connection to the content delivery network origin.

For TV companies that were offering to simulcast programming, this worked very well: ultimately the online simulcast was a small extra feature that could be added at the studio. In the meanwhile all the telecoms or satellite technologies were already tightly integrated into their normal workflows and also by their service level agreements with their customers.

There was high confidence that the contribution from the event was robust, and the facility was well connected, so there was reasonably high confidence that the contribution from the studio to the CDN was robust too.

For high-end broadcasts – particularly those that were also being broadcast on traditional TV – this model makes a lot of sense. The webcaster would therefore not attend the live event but typically oversee the encoder in the TV studio facility. The extra cost of "going live online" was a small incremental cost on the scale of the overall TV production. For content such as major sports events, this method is still commonly found in TV workflows today.

3.2.2 Wire

For venues that host many events, such as sports stadiums, it has been common to provision a permanent "facility line" – this is a loose term for high-capacity private connections between the venue and the facility capable of supporting (for example) a 270Mbps uncompressed video feed.

Once installed, a facility line may cost only $200 to $300 (indicative) to activate the circuit for the duration of a typical event webcast. In comparison, installation of a private link may run to many $10,000s, which for one off/ad hoc webcasts is typically out of scope.

Satellite links for TV outside broadcast are also a reasonable commitment financially. Although the figures vary wildly, a typical satellite truck (with operator, satellite capacity, and a remote operator to oversee reception at the TV studio facility) could cost $2000 to $3000 per day or more.

For this reason the potential to use relatively cheap and abundant IP connections into many locations has been a key underlying driver in the adoption of IP webcasting. For those who have more constrained budgets, and do not require TV quality production whose cost is prohibitive, the lower link cost of using available IP/Internet connections has been a game changer.

Yet, that said, no matter what the budget, once a webcast goes live and is promoted to the event's audience, regardless of the budget, the brand equity that the clients are placing behind the webcast are proportionately the same. For that reason expectation management has been extremely key to helping them trust IP as a contribution method.

My first webcasts used PSTN telephone lines, which were typically limited to 56kbps but had a number of advantages over today's Internet connections. Most important, when we connected a dial up modem to an ISP on a 56kbps telephone circuit, that circuit was ours alone, for the duration of that session. This meant that our dial up contribution feed had a fixed service level. It typically meant that if we had problems sending an audio feed over a dial up connection, those problems were not between just us and the ISP, but between the ISP and its peers or the CDN we were contributing to. In today's broadband world these ISP interconnections and the peering with CDNs, and so on, are so massively overprovisioned (to deal with the vast amount of video data that is in use) that it is extremely unlikely any issue will arise with the contribution feed.

Over time we began to use ISDN lines. There were several advantages to ISDN: most important, the dial up process (that familiar "phrrrrrra ptwang ptwang" handshake made by dial up modems) took around 8 to 10 seconds to complete, and only once complete could the applications (the encoder and packetizing software) handshake with the CDN again. These 8 seconds could seem like a lifetime in the middle of a sports event. In contrast, ISDN lines connect almost automatically. The result is that a dropped call may result in just a second or two of audio.

ISDN is still in widespread use in the radio and Internet radio sector, providing high-quality private links between studios, and so on.

As early broadband emerged offering 256kbps and 512kbps, the demand for live video came with it. But these broadband lines were based on ADSL technology, and this was unsuitable for contribution for a number of reasons:

- The lines were asymmetrical – so, while you could download 512kbps, you may only be able to upload 128kbps.
- The lines were contended – which is to say, that while you could download a max throughput of 512kbps, this was only in short bursts, since you were sharing that 512kbps with anything up to 80 other people. For downloading your email over 20 seconds, the line would provide a burst of 512kbps. But if you tried to stream a 450kbps video for any length of time, the chances are that your neighbor would check his email, and for a period it would be impossible to throughput sufficient video data to keep your stream running smoothly.

So, while the audience were connecting with 512kbps, in order to provide a usable video, we had to bond together several ISDN lines. To do this, we required having bonding technology at both ends of the ISDN links. So we had to host technology in a data center and in effect build our own small ISP service. By bonding 6 ISDN lines, we could achieve a throughput of 384kbps, and by allowing around 10% for signaling, and so on, we would then encode our contribution feed at around 320kbps. The hosted, remote end of the ISDN bonding system was itself connected to a 1Mbps Internet connection, and this then forwarded the contribution into the CDN.

Interestingly, at these contribution speeds, even contributions to CDN origins in the US from the UK would typically get through. There is a complexity in the "long fat Internet" connections that use TCP, and that is caused by a combination of TCP Window size and latency – increased latency increased the probability of packet loss, and in turn when TCP noted a lost packet, the entire subsequent "window" of data would be discarded as it arrived, while a request was made to resend the entire window, restarting from the lost packet, and onward. Back at the source this would cause problems with buffering and very often, if the buffer was not big enough to hold a few windows' worth of the stream, the stream would stutter and fail as that particular part of the stream was simply dumped.

This problem stumped a number of webcasters for many years. Despite providing high-capacity links onsite, it seemed impossible to throughput high-quality webcasts all the way to the CDN origins in the US. However, as CDNs provided more localized entry points/origins nearer to the ISPs to which the webcasters were connecting, the CDNs could take on the complexity of internally window sizing the long-haul links to their other locations. This quietly but importantly ensured that it became possible to contribute reliably at speeds exceeding 400kbps, and by 2005 most clients jumped to demanding multiple bitrate streams of 1.4mbps, 700kbps, and 384kbps. So the days of bonded ISDN were superseded as the availability of a variety of new fixed line services, like SDSL (symmetrical DSL) and leased lines, were becoming all the more common.

Now, over a decade later, with high-capacity FTTH connectivity coupled with better contention ratios, most IP lines are capable of providing decent bandwidths for contribution feed, and I have produced many webcasts using just a domestic grade broadband line, although typically keep a good 20% overhead. Moreover these days adaptive bitrate has superseded multiple bitrate.

Where you can find a wire, you will reduce a significant number of variables that most of the other (radio) based links below are exposed to. That said, it is important to understand the characteristics of the line, and to have a point of contact to help if the line is not performing as expected. Your webcast will depend on it, and if it is not entirely under your own control, it is key to know who you can bring into account if needed.

3.2.3 Wireless

While I have separated out satellite and 3g/4g from the wireless section, I am going to include both WiFi and microwave here.

WiFi is ultimately not a good technology to use when webcasting anything other than low-bandwidth video or audio-only content. WiFi is prone to great variability in signal strength. A typical setup is to test with WiFi in an empty venue. Then, although everything seemed fine, when 200 delegates arrive at the conference, two things happen. First, they all connect to the WiFi themselves, causing both a contention issue and a radio spectrum issue – literally competing with your webcast for the radio capacity. The second drawback is that human beings are largely water, and water is highly absorbent of radio signals – so by the time the venue is full, your WiFi signal is weak and unreliable. That is not to say that WiFi *can't* be used – and in many cases it may be the only way to get breaking news out – so it is important to practice and test webcasting over WiFi as you learn the general webcast skills. But, if there is another option, then almost invariably that option is better for contribution feeds. Moreover it is important to keep in mind that the WiFi router itself is likely connected to a wired line out of the building – so it is important to have a full understanding of that line and its capacity to support your feed.

While also a radio technology, microwave tends to refer to directional point to point links. A typical microwave link is similar in many ways to a WiFi link in that one end will be connected to a wired line. However, the directional capability means that microwave links can be established over long distances, which can be 50 m to 2 km, and if well set up, they can be very reliable. Microwaves are typically uncontended, so in some ways they are thought of as extending the fixed line to a remote location.

The logistics of finding a fixed line, and establishing a remote microwave link, may be complex, so this should be set up well in advance of an event. There are additionally some problems that are particular to microwave links: one of my favorite stories is what we experienced covering some political commentary in a street in London. Every now and then the signal would fail, and we would scramble around trying to work out why the link had dropped. Everything technically seemed fine, apart from the fact that we would, approximately every 10 minutes, have a 2 minute outage.

It was only when we stood outside our production vehicle for a full cycle that we realized that the number 22 bus was stopping directly between our microwave terminal and the remote location, simply blocking the line of sight between the two points! We fixed the issue by raising the link up to a first floor balcony and dropping the cables down to the production truck, but it was quite embarrassing having to explain to the client that a bus had caused the outages.

3.2.4 Satellite

I have a deep fondness for satellite technologies. Perhaps it stems from a fascination with radio astronomy as a teenager, and there is certainly a real sense of achievement when one first points a satellite dish at an orbiting satellite and successfully establishes a two-way connection over a distance of around 60,000 km!

When I started webcasting in 1996, the only satellite links in use were TV broadcast links, using C-band or L-band to transmit high-quality TV signals. Bandwidth was expensive and only available from the satellite operators in commitments for multi-year periods. Ad hoc contribution was carried out by value added resellers, who paid for the annual commitment and then sold access to their reserved capacity in conjunction with uplink and downlink production services. Because the entry level into this game was relatively high, those incumbent operators were less interested in making the links affordable for budget webcasting than driving their core business at a premium.

In 1998 Steve Flood of DC Sat-Net asked me to get involved in some testing he was carrying out with Astra, using new IP-enabled links to deliver backhaul. Over the following years we carried out many webcasts using Astra's and later Eutelsat's IP services. There was a struggle with the 400kbps throughput problem until around 2003, when UDP accelerators were introduced and our ability to contribute at 2Mbps from "anywhere" opened up the possibility to webcast events, affordably from locations that were previously unreachable with usable contribution feed Internet connections.

Over the same period a number of manufacturers produced increasingly portable "flyaway" very small aperture terminal (VSAT) dishes. Although at first we used to take 1.2 meter dishes in a van, complete with a heavy concrete-based tripod (satellite dish alignment for two-way communication is highly sensitive to movement – for example, by high wind). We would also need to take complex RF meters and configure the modem for our specific location. All in all the kit required was far from compact. If we forgot the meter, setting up the link by eye was incredibly difficult – verging on complete guesswork. A little embarrassingly I forgot my meter once when traveling to a setup in the hills of Spain. It took me 12 days to locate and lock on the satellite by guesswork and eye: it was absolutely the most gruelling link I have ever set up! I do not recommend doing that for a critical live event!

Over time these setups became smaller and lighter, the dishes could be deconstructed and clipped back together, and so on, and the mounts became more robust at the same time. Today, you can get a portable flyaway VSAT setup that can fit into a small suitcase and be aligned with a mobile phone in a matter of minutes.

Here in Europe, Eutelsat broke the market for webcasting via satellite open in 2010 with its Ka-band based NewsSpotter service. The NewsSpotter service can be booked by the hour in speeds such as 20Mbps with a premium for reduced contention and a higher tier for private connectivity. Prices for such a link, by the hour, are typically in the range of $100/hour, making it one of the cheapest ways to get a high-capacity link to a remote location for ad hoc use.

With a little practice to acclimatize to the dish-alignment routing, and with a little planning in advance (which should always be priced into the job), satellite is an excellent contribution technology. Even the introduced latency of (typically) around 800ms is rarely an issue when media players on the end clients' devices are typically buffering 10 to 30 seconds of content.

While on the subject, it is worth mentioning a very popular service in the early days of IP outside broadcast: the Inmarsat BGAN systems. These small portable units were focused on newsgathering teams that just needed a quick to setup link. They typically worked in similar chunks of bandwidth to ISDN lines, clustering 128kbps connections via a small square antenna on a portable modem that was altogether about the size of a small briefcase. They use L-band satellite, which offers lower throughput speeds (it's simply a lower frequency carrier) that are less susceptible to rain fade and easier to align to the satellites, making them easier to use in the field.

The 128kbps was enough for a good audio line but a terrible video picture. Common for war correspondence (because satellite meant that a link directly out of the country was possible), much of the late 2000's TV front line reporting was produced at quarter screen resolution (QCIF) using perhaps 492kbps of bandwidth to send 350kbps of video and 64kbps of audio (with a little overhead for packet loss, etc.). Often affected by atmospherics, these links were successful for quite some time but today are largely replaced by Ka-band high-throughput services. Bandwidth is paid for on a data-transferred model at around $8/minute.

3.2.5 3g/4G CellMux

As with all technologies, just as NewsSpotter was arriving in the webcaster's artillery, a disruptive new dynamic entered the market. With the arrival of the smartphone, the cellular networks "got" video-like religion. Cellular vendors realized that so long as they could keep up with the demand in their networks that video was data hungry, and since sale of data transfer packages has since become a core revenue source, video was to be a key revenue driver for them: they managed to "distribute" the CDN costs to their subscribers, which was a key differentiator from their terrestrial counterparts.

Since the mobile networks were becoming less concerned about the bandwidth demands, several companies began to take some theory from channel bonding ISDN connections over to various mobile connection models. In Linux there is a set of protocols called the Link Aggregation Control Protocol (LACP) – this is available to any engineer and can be used to share bandwidth across multiple layer-2 network connections. Variations on this theme have been deployed by a number of companies, including Live-U (which are arguably the dominant player), TVU Networks, Mobile Viewpoint, Dejero, AVIWest, and several others.

All these technologies combine link aggregation with a counterpart application at the remote end of the link that can work as a client server with the source device, and add layers of encoding and control, forward error correction, and stream buffering. This means that a single video source can be captured, encoded to the best bitrate, and reliably sent over maybe as many as 12 cellular signal paths (GPRS, 3G or 4G, etc.). Since this needs no aligning, and the receiving end of the signal can decode the video to SDI or other such production-friendly formats, adoption in the broadcast industry has been swift. It has also been subtle. Where previously we would see a shot of the leaders of a marathon as they pass a static broadcast satellite uplink (with a bike and camera person using a short-range microwave link to bring the source to the uplink), that shot has typically been limited to the range of the microwave link and the time it takes for the bike to traverse that range. Now the bike is untethered, and can sit at the front of the pack producing a live feed almost constantly.

War journalists are able to find a range of signal paths in all but the most extremely devastated areas (where they can even add a BGAN as a path with some of the devices).

I contracted the term Cellular video Multiplexer to "CellMux" in a long running series of reviews I carried out for Streamingmedia.com some years ago. Some vendors still refer to their kit as a CellMux. I distinguish, a little pedantically, link aggregation and channel-bonding link aggregation from true CellMuxes. The first simply routes requests across the link – for many web users in a building (where the data transfer is bursty but the data is relatively small); link aggregation can ensure that the users take any one (of several) routes to the Internet at any time. However, a video stream will still have to use one or the other routes, and if both are limited to 1Mbps, then 1mbps (or more likely 800kbps) will be the maximum stream rate they can transfer. Channel-bonding link aggregators require a de-multiplexer at the other end, and with this in place, the multiple paths are made transparent to the application. So parts of the stream can pass over one link, and parts over the other, and in our model we can approach 2Mbps as a total stream bitrate. Indeed a true CellMux has feedback over the link from the channel bonding that ensures that the encoding rate can be dropped if the link becomes congested, and enables the stream to adapt to variations in overall capacity – something that is a constant issue in a mobile production.

While each has its own approach to the channel bonding/encoding and handling the variations in the signals, etc., ultimately the differentiators between vendors are more often than not down to ancillary features such as talkback/tally lights or form factor.

It is worth mentioning that increasingly audiences are tolerant to compressed pictures so long as the story the video is conveying is engaging, so we are seeing more and more live video from smartphones making major video productions. With a smartphone in billions of pockets, it is usual that "citizen journalists" are the first responders for news video, and as crews arrive onsite with more and more link options, the quality of video pictures increases until eventually the traditional satellite uplinks arrive and the quality reaches "broadcast" KPIs.

3.2.6   Reliable UDP and HTTP/ UDP Solutions

The derivatives of LACP are not confined to cellular field encoding solutions. Over the years there has been a considerable amount of work focusing on maximizing the "goodput" (useful throughput) of IP networks.

I mentioned above about satellite networks solving the 400kbps problem with UDP acceleration. TCP has a number of limitations when transferring long sessions of data that must be delivered reliably. Principally, when a packet is lost, the transmission has to stop, any data discarded that has already been sent subsequent to the error, subsequent data de-queued from buffers (etc.), and the sender requested to resend the lost packet. If the buffer in the decoding media player empties while this happens, or if it happens frequently and the buffer gradually empties over a series of errors, then the stream will stop until there is enough data to restart.

TCP itself is really a particular implementation of a control protocol that sits on a UDP connection. Of course, it is possible to implement your own control protocol, and simply use IP's native UDP to send the data, relying on your own system to acknowledge packets, recover lost ones, and control the flow rate of the data, etc.

There has been a rash of such protocols introduced to the market in the past few years, and common names include Zixxi, Aspera, and Motama, to name but a few. Mostly what they do is aggressively fill available Internet connections, treating the links as if they were private (where TCP is designed to be considerate to other users). Once they have maximized the throughput, they have their own forward error correction (FEC) implementations and recovery routines to cater for lost packets. Quite often in video a lost packet can be ignored, costing perhaps a macroblock of data, or a lost frame of video. The eye barely notices. This means that the recovery routines can be a little more pragmatic than reliable – this is not financial data here, so a few discarded packets is inconsequential – particularly if the cost of recovery would stop the stream or at least make it stutter.

These UDP techniques are effective, albeit in purist terms they are not "good net citizens." TCP has a great design advantage – the one that has made it the success it is – and that is all to do with its ability to back off its bit rate to share the network link with other traffic. Where the link is private – such as on a LAN or a privately owned/managed WAN – then switching to an alternative transmission control model is something the network owner can choose to do.

Within the confines of a content delivery network with a managed underlying IP network, many operators both tune their windows correctly – to ensure that what TCP traffic does exists can flow in an optimized way – and make use of alternative transmission control models.

One of the most interesting of these Google's SPDY initiative, which has become part of HTTP/2.[6] Google support SPDY across all their CDN edges for all their major properties. Leveraging Chrome, and more recently all major browsers, the speed of interaction on Google site – despite their scale – has always been exemplary of good CDN architecture. SPDY helps the underlying TCP (OR SSL/TLS) by establishing just one "tunnel" connection to the server, and this provides a number of benefits to the client-server pair in terms of optimizations.

Perhaps because of the practical experience of running such scale, Google have subsequently introduced what may become the next evolution in this space: quick UDP Internet connections (QUIC). QUIC both multiplexes the various sessions a browser may open to the server in a traditional model into a single session, while also providing, at a transport layer, the ability to optimize the transmission control of UDP data. Because sessions are no longer waiting for TCP to set up, this makes small bursty sessions possible, and because there is no "permanent tunnel" path, this also means that the QUIC datagrams can take any route, even varying mid-file transfer – and this brings resilience and scalability.

At id3as we have our own similar model too, called GRIT. This model is extensively used by our clients' contribution workflows to enable them to instantly benefit from channel bonding of various connections, resilience, and reliability, together with optimized throughput of those connections.

3.2.7 Throughput vs. Goodput

Most people are familiar with the term "throughput." Even relatively nontechnical Internet users have a good mental image of what is going on when they think about the "flow" of data to their computer screen, and get the concept of measuring the volume of flow at a specific point. It is likely that their picture is almost exactly like an image of water flow through plumbing pipes, and to be fair, this is a very good metaphor for throughput in general terms, and holds very close to what is going on in traditional circuit-switched phone networks such as traditional telecoms voice networks.

However, if we dig a little deeper, we have to get a little pickier. Unlike the water flow analogy, data flows are not a continuous stream when they are

---

6 https://www.chromium.org/spdy/spdy-whitepaper

transferred from source to destination. A refinement to the picture would be to think of bottles of water, each with a source and destination address label stuck to them, and each sliding through the network of pipes on their journey. At any pipe junction (IP multicast and broadcast notwithstanding) a bottle can only slide through one exit, but there is no guarantee that the subsequent bottles will follow the same path, only that they will all try to get to the right target destination.

If we manage to pack the pipe full, with no spaces, then we have to account for the fact that the bottle plastic itself is taking up some of the space in the pipe. Indeed, if we are going to be truly fussy, the address label is taking up some of the capacity of the pipe too.

So even if the "throughput" of bottles is 100% of the pipe's capacity, the first thing we note is that the amount of water actually being transferred is slightly less than 100% (because the pipe is also carrying all the labels and bottle plastic). Thus the amount of throughput of the pipe is not quite the same as the amount of useful water that is being transferred, and that measure is known as goodput. ISPs and other IP service providers fail to talk about goodput because it is hard for them to measure how much of the overall traffic they are transferring is actually useful to the end users, and also because the throughput number, while only a theoretical maximum, simply sounds bigger in their marketing literature. Thus an Internet connection marketed as 10Mbps will typically achieve a goodput of around 60% of this value, but if you are an ISP, you would rather sell a theoretical 10Mbps service than an approximate, but realistic approximately 6Mbps service.

I mention this because many publishers, webcasters, and others involved in stream engineering simply fail to grasp this, promise their customers a service that they genuinely think they can commission, given the advertised "throughput" of services, and then simply cannot, in practice, deliver.

3.3 Cloud Saas

As streaming emerged in the broadcast industry, there was a natural tendancy to replicate the daisy-chain model of lining up different appliances to "treat" content as it was format or standard converted, encrypted, stored, or distributed. Since there were logical parallels to the traditional models, facilities and teams that were responsible for part or all of these traditional workflows simply added a new appliance to deal with the new format for streaming.

The demand for the standards in the streaming space was, however, much less under the control of the broadcasters, and rather than dictating TV standards, they struggled to adapt to the myriad formats required by the ever-increasing range of streaming devices – be they PC, tablet, smartphone, or smart TV, and any number of different models of each.

Since TV broadcast technologies such as MPEG2 and SDI were so ubiquitous, they had not had to scale, both technically and operationally, in the ways that streaming now demanded. As they attempted to do so, they soon learned that where previously one encoder or one SDI router met all their delivery requirements, now they had to operate dozen of systems to cater for many different bitrates, encoding profiles, and unicast demand loads.

As cloud took hold in the architects' understanding, it was decided that scaling services in a cloud model, particularly where a production may only require the capability for a day, a week, or few months, was much more straightforward when hiring computers from a cloud service provider.

As IP-transported video qualities were equalizing (if not exceeding) many TV qualities, the fact that video could be processed "anywhere" started to provide options. So long as the delivery protocol ensured that the stream was delivered well, in the cloud any number of treatments could be deployed and to almost any scale.

3.3.1 In Workflow "Treatment" (Transcode/Transmux, etc.)

In 2007 and 2008 at my CDN we launched a service we called "transmuxing" – it is now more commonly called re-packetizing by those who are offering similar services. The idea of a transmuxing system was that a webcaster could send a stream to our servers in a single format, and we would, without re-encoding the video, replicate it on a variety of other transports. This service meant that the operator could provide us with a transport stream and we could replicate the embedded and already encoded video to other media players. Because we didn't demand the CPU to re-encode the video, we didn't have to dedicate a whole machine to each customer. In fact we had two large machines that delivered the transmuxing of all our clients' services.

We also offered trans-rating (where a single format stream was re-encoded to multiple bitrates), and of course, we offered some of the first live transcoding services too.

Subsequently other providers emerged with similar services, and now there are hundreds of online video and audio processing bureaus available that can receive a source video (live or archive) and transcode and packetize it into myriad output formats. With pricing generally being use based, this model was accessible equally to small independents and large enterprises, and it has changed the affordability of video processing technology, and therefore the market place dramatically.

Today, at id3as everything, apart from original video capture from analog, is processed in a virtualized model. We may be a few years ahead in some ways, but for sure, the rest of the market is moving to the same way of thinking.

We have moved to an era where we can move our capability to the best place to solve the problem being addressed – when needed rather than always having to network-route the problem to the capability. This architectural theory becomes even more efficient as the capabilities become smaller and easier to move (see Section 3.2.7 below to understand how this positively affects service velocity).

This ability to treat content in the workflow is also spawning new models for production. The system we designed for NASDAQ allows the field engineers to concentrate on the contribution of live video; while web-based operators elsewhere in the world can see the live stream, they can additionally pause and scrub backward/forward along the time line to mark in and out sections such as coffee breaks and "top-and-tail" the live archive, trimming off unwanted video before and after the event. Once this edit has been made, they can issue a command to all the related cloud services focusing on that task, and all the archives for all the different formats are instantly processed. Once the resulting edited archives are cut in this way, they can be reconstructed without re-encoding them, and this means they are available within a few seconds of the operator issuing the edit decision list.

Most interesting, and highlighting the power of moving the workflow to the cloud, the entire workflow infrastructure relating to that event is literally destroyed the moment the archives are delivered to the distribution and origin "NAS." This removes any further costs for maintaining the infrastructure.

The scale of operation is effectively now limited only by their sales activity and field operations, and not their infrastructure.

For me, the NASDAQ model is a near-perfect example of how critical live and on-demand live video workflows should be architected.

To illustrate, I grabbed one of our system's introspection views, as seen in Figure 3.3.

As the image shows, a series of contribution streams are acquired, subjected to various synchronization processes, and then the video workflow and audio workflows are distributed into a tree of processes including transcoding/re-packetizing and reformatting and security, etc. The core id3as.media "bricks" (as we call them) may run all on the same machine, or they may be deployed by the system on a wider range of resources to ensure a balance between cost and provisioning.

While I do not know the details of their architecture well enough to discuss them here, the engines behind Google and Facebook's live video features must be similarly architected, with resource provisioning on-demand and just-in-time services as requested by a user. They are operating at vast and incomprehensible scales, and this is undoubtedly down to management of a virtualized core.

Other providers service niches. Worth mentioning are Encoding.com, which have led the way for archive transcoding in the cloud as a service from the core of their business. Amazon too now has the ability to batch transcode files as a service, and many other CDNs and online operators also offer these services.

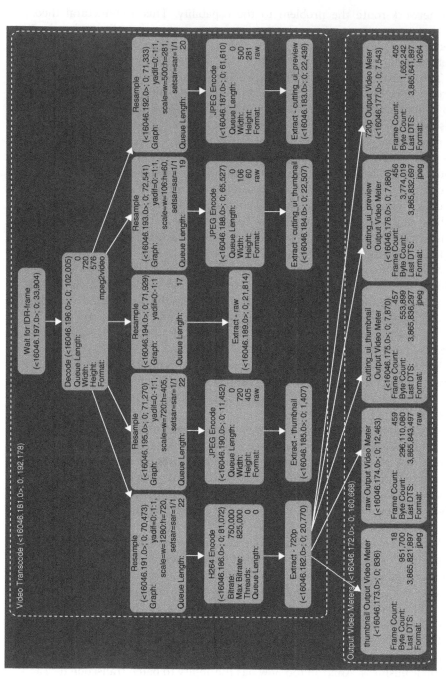

Figure 3.3 Virtual workflow example - Various source videos being acquired, synchronized, and treated for delivery.

Some use cloud, and are typically the easiest to use for a layperson. Other have more rigid video-focused infrastructures and monetize this in a different way, which suits some larger enterprises, but ultimately they will move to a fully virtualized model too, if for no other reason than to keep up with the inexorable diversification of format types and devices being targeted by those formats. With a cloud/virtual model a new feature can be rolled out continuously while it is being developed, or it can be deployed across a global infrastructure in minutes.

3.3.2 DVR Workflows

Digital video recording (DVR) workflows and their cousin personal video recorders (PVR) are services that allow the user to jump out of a live broadcast and instantly start jumping to new positions in the archive of that broadcast. This may result in pausing live TV, and rewinding to see parts again. It may result in bookmarking the stream for a later return, and by presenting this marked point in a stream as if it was part of a personal video library – then pressing the "record" button need only bookmark that video and the location in the stream that the user pressed "record" to produce the same effect as pressing "record" on a local video recorder. So long as the user's application can keep track of the position in the stream that is required, the overall effect is the same, and typically it is simply a matter of managing time-code data that is already present in the broadcast.

In fact so "trivial" is this that the technology required to archive a live/linear stream and instantly make that archive seamlessly accessible to the audience of the live stream has been in existence for nearly a decade. However, the main complexity in delivering the service to audiences has been in the content licensing.

For our workflow at Arqiva, where id3as delivers the hybrid TV functionality for many of the YouView and Freeview public broadcasting services, we have had technology ready to install that can instantly allow a viewer to bookmark a file to watch later, or to program "recordings" against an EPG. Yet, due to licensing restrictions, broadcasters in the UK have so far been limited to the delivery of "start-over" services, where a viewer who joins a program halfway through can opt to switch from the broadcast feed to an online service where the same program is started from the beginning and plays to the end. Even the ability to pause and forward wind/rewind is restricted.

There are presently two extremes of the technical models. The first is slightly more complicated to deploy but is simpler to understand: it is called "private copy."

Essentially when a viewer elects to archive a program for later viewing in a private copy model, the technical systems create a copy of that archive and allocate it to storage within the particular user's workflow. Typically private copy systems work well in a highly distributed Set-Top Box model, where the private copy is actually stored on the viewer's own hardware. Indeed in the earliest online models – thinking back to the BBC and its early experiments with the peer-to-peer platform Kontiki in the early 2000s – once a viewer had selected to archive a program for later viewing, the Kontiki client would download that copy and the viewer would simply play it locally when wanting to access it.

To some extent this helped the rights owners with their royalty models, and licensing models emerged to cover private copy models relatively quickly. However, from a technical point of view, they were incredibly inefficient: as the general network speeds increased over the second part of the decade, so that high-quality video could be streamed ad hoc from servers to clients, it became clear that there was no need to store the entire program in multiple locations. Indeed a single copy of the program could be accessed by the entire audience, with only transitory caching of parts of the program in the CDN networks required to ensure scalability. This model became known as "shared copy" as the two diverged.

In simple terms, private copy appealed because there was deemed to be a discernible volume of copies of the content and – when coupled with DRM-limited access and forwarding of the content. This gave rise to a credible model for royalties to rights owners who were used to dealing with "fixations" (the legal term for content that is somehow "engraved" in the body of a unit of media such as a DVD or tape). For organizations that wanted to maintain friction in the distribution, to ensure that only capital-rich distribution networks could participate by maintaining a high barrier to entry, private copy was brought in early. This was a regulatory strategy intended to be of advantage to the few distribution networks that could invest in a massive storage unit for each home or establish large intermediary online storage farms.

Sadly, for those hoping for advantage from such attempts, the Internet consumer doesn't pay much heed to the "friction" needs of the rights/distribution providers, and where pirate sites would crack the DRM and publish the content un-traceably and illegally, but in instantly available streaming formats, the consumers simply voted with their feet. This in turn meant that it became very difficult to chase those models commercially.

For this reason many on-demand services – and DVR and PVR are essentially a specific version of an on-demand model – have launched very slowly. There are, in some territories, legal obstacles to providing catch-up services, protected by lobbies of trade associations that represent the incumbent rights owners and underlying service providers. Shared copy is a far more elegant model, scales far better, and is much lower cost to deliver. However, because there is only a single replication of the file, organizations that are used to monetizing "copies" have struggled to develop agreeable licensing models with publishers. The world of mechanical copyright was separate to the world of broadcast rights, and as the two blurred, the resistance to develop new models, and fear that it would cannibalize the existing models has meant that a simple service to deliver has been slow to reach market.

Despite all this it is inevitable that shared copy will inexorably become the ubiquitous model. This is not least because all Set-Top Boxes that are being developed at the moment are attempting to reduce the storage requirement as much as possible to remain competitive at the point the unit is sold. A TIVO box will cost many tens of dollars – in part because it contains a hard drive that itself is a reasonably expensive component. In contrast a Roku or Amazon, Fire Stick today costs about $30 to $40. Given that the same user service can be delivered on either, there is no doubt that over time all content will be streamed from a remote service to the user. In turn this means that those service operators will seek to optimize their storage costs, and share copy is a natural optimization in that process.

One thing is certain: if the content rights permit it, or if the content is yours in the first place, then shared copy is architecturally the best way forward.

3.3.3 Catch-up Workflows

Catch-up, as mentioned in the previous section, is a relatively simple workflow to engineer, although there is a wide scope to the interpretation as to what a "catch-up service" is! Essentially the customer proposition is to enable them to review a library of content through some form of electronic program guide (EPG), and allow them to see programs on-demand that have already been broadcast.

Catch-up differs from DVR in as much as the user doesn't need to proactively request the content is made on demand: the content is available to any user with access to the EPG. For example, if you join a TV series at episode 3, you could elect to find episodes 1 and 2 in the catch-up library and watch the entire series from the start.

Some rights may mean that content is only available for a short period. For example, news headlines can be "replaced" every few hours, since the requirement to watch "last week's news" will probably be very infrequent. However, this is not a technical decision, it is a business decision between the broadcaster and the rights holder.

One aspect worth commenting on is the instant availability of live-to-air events. Given the diversity of devices on the market, and the corresponding formats of content encoding that are required to service that array of devices, some good planning can accelerate the availability of the archives to the audience.

I would quickly like to provide a couple of contrasting stories to help clarify how that planning can make a difference.

3.3.3.1 Prime Minister's Questions

In the early 2000s I helped establish the online streaming of Prime Minister's Questions – a specific weekly session in the UK Parliament where the Prime Minister takes questions from other members. This stream was watched live by around 15,000 to 25,000 viewers, and then – particularly if the content was interesting – could be viewed in a catch-up mode by as many as 150,000 more parties (typically news agencies). It was an exciting stream – one of the largest regular live webcasts of its time. The turnaround time of the archive was quite critical.

When the workflow was initially established, the stream was archived from live to an AVI uncompressed file. After the event it was manually copied to an edit suite (a process that itself can take many minutes to around an hour). In that edit suite it was "cut" tightly to the start and finish, an animated parliamentary logo "intro" was affixed at each end ("top-and-tailed," in engineer jargon), and then the final file was rendered out to multiple formats such as Windows Media and Real Media, and in several bitrates. All the formats were uploaded to the distribution server. The whole process could take several hours.

I was not happy with this workflow, so I changed it and removed the AVI archival and the edit suite process. Instead, I used a different tool to simply cut the various recordings of the Windows Media files and Real Media files and stitched pre-encoded logos to the front and back. Because this also removed the requirement to re-encode the video, this entire process took a few minutes, and within just a few minutes of the end of the event, the archives were uploading to the distribution servers.

3.3.3.2 NASDAQ Market Disclosures

Similarly, when id3as was approached to optimize the NASDAQ market disclosure workflow (Thomson Reuters prior to acquisition by NASDAQ), we initially saw a very similar workflow to the early Prime Minister's Questions model. Partly because these workflows had evolved organically from the initial delivery of a live stream and had followed a more traditional broadcast architecture – where large video files would be moved around to be "treated" (processed) by rare and expensive hardware – their workflow also suffered considerable delays between the end of an event and the availability of the catch-up offering.

Our approach was to centralize the delivery of the high bandwidth into a cloud model and to *move the capability to video*. The software capability – particularly with our highly virtualized model – was comparatively small, and because it was not tied to a physical unit, it was much faster to bring many encoders to the virtual end point of the source video in the cloud, perform all the transcoding into the 38+ formats that NASDAQ deliver, to provide a web-based UI (see below) to top-and-tail the archive – which itself simply provided an edit decision list (EDL)

Figure 3.4 NASDAQ web-based EDL editor and "cutting interface".

to mark up *all* the various archives, and to cut and top-and-tail the various archives instantly. The final archives are then initially made available on an internal point of origin within the cloud, from where the content delivery network can "pull" and deliver them. The NASDAQ turnaround for completed archives is now a few seconds from the end of the event. This transformed the speed at which their catch-up service could be offered, and has been a benchmark for the financial disclosure market ever since (Figure 3.4).

3.3.4 VOD Workflows

Having explored the two specific examples of DVR and catch-up services, I have little more to add to explain the simplest use case of all online video: VOD. However, some comments and thoughts that are not so far covered may be of value.

The vast work effort in a VOD model is typically focused on the searchability and discoverability of content. Good metadata is essential for text-based searches and recommendations. Applying this is easiest done at source, but given that the elementary streams where such metadata can be stored vary greatly from one file format to another, maintaining continuity as archives are transcoded can be incredibly complex. Notably schemes such as SCTE35 are emerging as a strategy to try to unify some of this metadata where it is used for workflow signaling.

There are search systems that can fingerprint/hash multimedia content. For example, if you upload content that has already been fingerprinted into a platform such as YouTube, you will find that it is quickly spotted by automated processes, and these can effectively take down the content, or at least alert you that you are in breach of someone else's claim to the content's copyright.

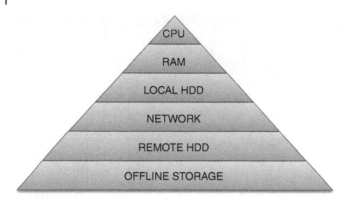

Figure 3.5 Storage model.

Digging deeper into the technology models for delivery, I like to think of a pyramid (Figure 3.5) whose base is remote storage, and whose pinnacle is the CPU and the local machine's memory.

As we work up the storage model, access time decreases, and yet typically cost increases. In a thin-client streaming device we can flatten the model to exclude OFFLINE and LOCAL HDD, and the content is copied directly from the remote HDD to the RAM, and then rendered by the CPU (or possibly by the GPU that would sit alongside the CPU in the model).

Obviously the cheapest storage model is typically OFFLINE – so storage on a DVD, for example, the one created, costs very little to maintain – there is no electricity involved, nor any need to maintain a system to host the DVD, unless it is mounted in a robotic retrieval system. While I was helping BT Rich Media in the early 2000s, they had a large DVD storage system with a robotic arm that could, within a few seconds, locate, pull, and bring online any one of thousands of DVDs. This was fairly practical, until the volumes of on-demand content grew vast, simply because a single film may be encoded into many formats. What typically happens today is that there is a "mezzanine" high-quality archive stored on REMOTE HDD, and as it is pulled through the network, "in workflow treatments" (see Section 3.3.1) can create ephemeral transcodings of the file suited to the particular client. While this bucks the end-to- end model of classic network architecture, it proves to be efficient as a balance between cost and speed. If the network caches the content for a period, and if several users all want a popular file and all request the same transcoding, it can be retrieved from the network cache rather than repeatedly pulled from the REMOTE HDD "origin." Then the cache can be purged once the file is no longer popular.

Good cache management can reduce the workload, so CDNs are masters of tuning and optimizing this balance.

While much of the recent decade has seen a move to place SSDs into the HDD layer, which is naturally faster, what we increasingly see is a top-level trend to massively enlarge the RAM layer. Platforms such as the Open Compute Platform are working hard to enlarge the role of RAM in ephemeral storage of increasingly large data assets.

There is a great book called *Multimedia Servers*[7] by Sitaram and Dan that digs into this space in considerable depth.

Up to this point, I hope I have given you a high-level range of thoughts and anecdotes that will help you think widely about your workflow architectures and plan them properly. Small differences to design can make massive differences to your operations, so take your time when developing even simple systems, particularly if you are anticipating scale.

---

7 https://www.amazon.com/Multimedia-Servers-Applications-Environments-Information/dp/1558604308

4

Publishing

"Publishing" is a broad term. In the print world we think of a publisher as someone who commissions writers and takes a risk on the print run. When we try to translate that model to traditional broadcast, we find a split between production company and broadcaster. Together, the production company (which takes the risk on the creation of the master content) and the broadcaster (which takes the risk in creating the content distribution infrastructure) could be argued to work together to "publish" the content, but nuances between the models are so abundant that I think – should I have made the same statement before a combined group of publishers, producers, and broadcasters – I would be beating a hasty retreat by now!

To further complicate things, adding "online publisher" to the discussion opens up more parallels and more nuances once again, since barely any capital investment is required to create a "print run" or a cloud-based "distribution platform." Indeed most online publishing models ensure that their costs are simply a function within their operating expense, de-risking the business significantly.

Obviously that lowered risk in turn makes the online publishing space a reasonably competitive space, so over time hairs will be split over increasingly irrelevant (in any practical terms) but differentiating technical capabilities.

So what we have found over the 20 years of the emergence of online publishing is intense commoditization on the infrastructure technologies and service models, which has diversified to reach an ever-increasing range of capabilities on end user devices – and this has largely been driven not by the technology partners but by the consumers at the end of the chain. Despite this diversification of devices, in my opinion, the rate of diversification of the underlying software models is *actually* trending toward a unified and highly commoditized range of mature technologies and service models.

To clarify: I think that while we see more and more devices, and ways to display videos, this means that we have become acclimatized to developing workflows that can produce specific encodings of a video for many types of

Content Delivery Networks: Fundamentals, Design, and Evolution, First Edition. Dom Robinson.
© 2017 by John Wiley & Sons, Inc. Published 2017 by John Wiley & Sons, Inc.

target smartphones. Moreover we have at a slightly deeper level seen that HTTP has become dominant in the distribution chain, where there once was fierce competition among HTTP, RTP, RTMP, UDP, and many other transports, and while h.264 is dominant today, HEVC and possibly VP9 will emerge tomorrow, and that emergence is from a very limited and easily identified group. Indeed, 20 years ago, there were literally dozens of CoDec prototypes available and commonly in use. Today, change in that space is slow, fairly deliberating, and does not present a high-risk strategic range of options.

So while the technologists provide the publishers with myriad configuration options within the workflows, actually the underlying workflow is usually, in its own right, almost entirely static once it is established.

4.1 Publishers, OVPs, CDNs, and MCNs

Online video publishers (OVPs) disrupted the space somewhat in the latter part of the first decade of this century.

As online video emerged, it was very much the role of the CDN to provide the "publisher" with a simple way to present the content in layer 4. In many of the early CDNs this meant that they provided a URL pointing to the content within the CDN infrastructure, and this URL was passed, through webpage interaction, to a local media player that was either spawned from the webpage as a standalone "pop-up" player such as Real Media or Windows Media Player, or as those technologies advanced, these media players were embedded within the webpage itself and the media played "in-line" with the surrounding text. With so many variations on how this could be achieved, the CDNs drew a line in the sand at the URL, and while they might have provided advice, and even examples as to how that could be done in specific circumstances (combinations of players, browsers, operating systems, etc.), the CDNs operated with the expectation that their clients were responsible for that final stage of presentation.

As more browsers, variations of operating systems and media players diversified, let alone new devices appearing on the market such as smartphones and smart TVs, the complexity in this montage only increased.

The OVPs, seeing this as an opportunity, emerged to offer their services to the publishers, taking on the bridge between the CDN and the publisher's content management systems. A single integration with an OVP passed the responsibility to maintain compliance with all the diversifying models from the publisher to the OVP, and the OVP more often than not resold the underlying CDN services.

Solving the problems of presentation layer integration for any one scenario usually meant that that solution would work for all the OVPs clients, and the OVP abstracted the underlying technical issues for the publisher. While the

OVPs typically were simple systems integrators – offering little innovation or new capability to the CDN or publisher – they commercially and operationally made the delivery of media easier.

At first the CDNs saw the OVPs as value-added resellers – and often the OVP would see a commercial upside for bringing large traffic volumes to the CDNs. This meant that early on there were tight and loyal relationships between OVPs and CDNs. Over time, however, the OVPs realized that by integrating with multiple CDNs, they could offer new value to their publisher clients: they could drive CDN prices down while maintaining a commanding relationship with the publishers, increasing their own margins. Additionally, because they were often the front line point of contact with the publishers, even if the CDN was the cause of delivery issues, they benefited from higher service levels where they used multiple CDN providers.

Also some of the CDNs began to see the OVPs command of the relationship with the publishers as a threat, and they began to invest in developing their own OVP models. This "stack creep" disrupted the sector as the CDNs effectively started to compete with their own resellers. Some OVPs tried to punish the CDNs by reducing traffic to those that competed. Equally the CDNs undermined OVP pricing by loss-leading their in-house OVP capabilities to the publishers, bundling the capability with the traffic delivery fees.

Overall, this caused something of a war between the CDNs and OVPs, and while it made the process of choosing the supplier model convoluted, the benefit to the publisher was commoditized service fees for both traffic and OVP capability.

Once Amazon Web Services (and other public clouds) began to demonstrate that their direct delivery capability was good enough, a number of OVPs moved not only their OVP capability to the cloud but also started to deliver traffic from the cloud direct to the publishers audiences.

Noting that this meant that the whole infrastructure was directly available to their own in-house editors, and as video moved to center stage in driving audiences (and therefore value), some of the larger publishers – notably the BBC as a great example – began to move their content management systems (CMS), tightly integrated with their own online video publishing, and leveraging cloud delivery capability, to these public clouds.

In the past five years or so this is a trend that has been followed by many other very large publishers (those who could afford to hire a few developers to deal with the various cross-platform presentation layer integration issues).

Both OVPs and CDNs found this commoditization, and the loss of the very large clients challenging. CDNs, in particular, began to avoid very small clients, where the cost of acquiring a small client was difficult to recover. They began to define a lower minimum limit to the value of the business, and would only target and take on clients that guaranteed fairly substantial annual revenue.

Smaller niche publishers, which could not risk these minimum commitments, also found the public cloud attractive commercially. Public cloud infrastructure costs scale right down if the demand on the infrastructure is very small, and yet allow the publisher to scale up to meet spikes of demand if needed. Until now they had relied on CDNs to help meet this demand, but with the CDNs now wanting a fixed minimum cost, public cloud was the only sensible strategy. While an individual small publisher would not alone have been worth much to a CDN or OVP, many such small publishers, as a whole, meant that the public clouds took a vast amount of the revenue away from the CDNs and OVPs.

Interestingly many of the public clouds back off underlying traffic to CDNs in a white label model – and while overall the traffic volume may be substantial and of value to the CDNs, it has created even further commoditization of price in that sector. Additionally, because this meant that the small publishers took care of the OVP/presentation layer in-house, the OVPs have really struggled to offer value to the smaller publishers.

And, of course, a few publishers avoided all this by adopting the behemoth of YouTube as a combined OVP and CDN, which is ostensibly free. A number of fairly high finance start-ups have tried to capitalize on this by taking on the responsibility of developing multi-channel networks (MCNs), focusing on taking operational responsibility for creating content and liaising advertising partnerships for the larger YouTube-based publishers, usually in return for a percentage of the ad revenue that the channel earned.

In practice, the MCN model has only proved to work where the top-line brand associated with the channel is a well-known household name.

One or two of the MCN models caught the attention of the markets, and there were a few rapid IPOs based on fairly conjectural financial projections that promptly collapsed. Additionally the sector was widely criticized for its tactics, since it often consisted of some very poor business models that were underpinned by "predatory" contracts and, worse, a real inability to technically or commercially deliver. This led to a significant backlash, and most of the MCNs have since failed or been commercially taken apart. They are, in my opinion, the "dodgy secondhand car salesmen" of the sector, promising to be able to deliver the same models as the few success cases that pre-dated them but that were successes in part because of the top-line brand and in part because of lucky timing.

Even YouTube has tried to distance itself from most of the MCNs, and by 2014 most of those offering MCN services were reduced to significant naval-gazing in empty offices or simply out of business.

Sadly, this type of business has made it harder for well-founded online publishing models to attract interest from investors, and in many ways they have stifled innovation for the past couple of years across the sector.

But, being pragmatic, I have seen this many times before with a variety of streaming schisms over the past 20 years, and these cycles come around.

4.2 Small Objects, Large Objects, or Continuous Streams

In deciding on a publishing strategy, there are a number of considerations that must be taken into account, and the most impacting is what I am going to term the "form factor" of the content itself.

In crude terms there are three form factors: short, long, and continuous. By this I mean that the videos (or indeed audio feeds) are short form, such as adverts or bulletins; or they are long form, such as movies or entire program episodes; or they are live/linear feeds (note live may include "strings" of back-to-back/scheduled programs that run continuously such as you may see on a TV channel or radio station).

We will set aside the production workflow differences in the creation of these different forms of content. To all intents and purposes, in their publication and underlying online distribution, the three modes require three different approaches.

Before we can decide which is best, we must also make a judgment call about the anticipated audience size that the content will be consumed by.

Anecdotally, when I first started streaming in the mid-1990s, each and every publisher was used to audience figures for "exciting live events" provided by audience measurement companies vis-à-vis TV and national broadcasting networks. While I discussed this in depth in Section 2.3 (and I am very cynical about the numbers that these organizations tout), this was an incredibly difficult expectation to manage as a webcaster. Indeed, when a stream was put online, there were often some ridiculous claims that the "servers crashed" because of the massive demand. Because the Internet was seen to be a global network, and because statistics that were being touted about website "hits" were so incredibly and inaccurately inflated at the time, it was often claimed that even the smallest webcast was inundated by massive audiences – reinforcing the expectation that the audience measurement figures were touting.

In practice (admittedly most likely with some exceptions), this was a complete misrepresentation of what was really going on.

Under the hood, the webcast industry was still very much in its infancy, and provisioning infrastructure was, in general, poorly planned. The typical mistake was that the webserver that was presenting the stream to the audience was probably not scalable to meet the relatively sudden influx of requests for the webpage that provided the stream URL to the audience. For a webserver that typically served "a few" copies of the webpage every minute, the sudden demand of "a few tens" or perhaps "a few hundred" copies in that same timescale this event-driven influx was beyond its capacity. This meant that the server did not provide the audience with the link to the video/audio feed in time, and that before the content itself was even reached, the distribution model failed.

CDNs at the time also used web redirection in their request routing layer, and in the same way as the webserver that was hosting the webpage with the stream, the underlying web-redirection servers simply failed to meet the sudden load, leaving audiences with a "404" error – reporting back to the prospective audience that the page could not be found.

So before the audience even got to the streaming of any content, the workflow to deliver the access to the content had failed. I recall statements in the press the following morning, after such events, where the PR guys, to save face, would report that the event had '"crashed the Internet." Sure, "crashed the Internet ..." got to love that!

Over time the request routing issues did get sorted out, and webcasts did begin to scale up as audiences began to trust the experience and plan to join on time, counting on the delivery actually taking place.

In the meanwhile – around the mid-2004 to 2008 period – smaller clips, such as adverts and short videos took a slightly different approach. Since small clips could be cached efficiently by web-proxy servers, they typically loaded quickly, even when progressively downloaded rather than being streamed. Advertisers liked this: the impact of a video clip playing almost as soon as a webpage loaded "grabbed more eyeballs" and converted more of those interactions to click-through. This was a major break for the online video sector, since it turned streaming into a revenue generator. CPM (the unit that advertisers count cost of 1000 adverts delivered online) for video proved considerably higher than the CPM because video clips were more attention-grabbing than static images. While this appealed to publishers, it also came with a cost for delivery. Video is many times larger to deliver, and the underlying CDNs therefore took a large margin of the profit that the publishers made. By simply integrating this within the existing web content workflows (rather than using a premium streaming model for delivery), there was a small saving, and at first this saving was quite attractive.

However, as the market commoditized, and data delivery prices fell, the difference between RTMP streaming (in particular) and simple HTTP delivery moved from price to performance: RTMP started quicker, and because it was effectively a separate session between the browser and the RTMP server, which ran in parallel to the HTTP delivery, the advert neither had to wait for the page to fully load nor had to hold up the loading of the page around it. So, in the "freemium" content delivery space, RTMP became dominant in the second half of the decade. It was also attractive because RTMP was delivered to the cross-platform Flash Media plug-in that was at one time almost pervasive in all OS and all browsers, ensuring that the advert (or other video) could be universally seen with minimum support overhead. YouTube was the benchmark at the time and was an extensive user of Adobe's products, although it stuck to progressive download rather than RTMP for a long time, presumably because at its scale YouTube was easier/cheaper to just scale HTTP delivery rather than scale *both* RTMP and HTTP delivery.

Once we move to the Netflix era, as (finally) rights models emerged that enabled online movie services to establish themselves, then the long-form movie format really starts to evolve. Since premium models underpinned these video services, there was much more importance placed on the delivery throughout the viewer experience.

This contrasted the premium model somewhat. In the freemium model the only important bit of the video was the pre-roll advert, and all too often the advert would start quickly, and play for 20 to 30 seconds very smoothly, only to be followed by a low bitrate, pixelated, and stuttering video. Users were rewarded for watching the advert with the cheapest delivery of content possible.

That could not carry forward in the long-form premium video space. Fortunately, exactly as these rights negotiations were happening adaptive bitrate (ABR) technologies were maturing, and with Apple driving HLS off the back of the arrival of the iPhone and iPad, and HLS "chunking" (although there were other similar models with lesser scale such as Microsoft's Smooth and several smaller players), ABR became ubiquitously available. HLS nonetheless required significant buffering, and this meant that it was neither good for low-latency projects, such as betting, nor particularly good for advertising. To get a "fast start," the advert had to be delivered at a lower bitrate.

For on-demand movie content that was not an issue: once a consumer had decided to pay for a movie, a 20 to 30 second buffering time to then watch 2 hours of excellent quality, continuous video made the wait absolutely acceptable. Given that modern ABR technology is universally (at the time of writing) HTTP delivered, this suited the CDNs well, and pricing was competitive too.

There were one or two issues with the very largest publishers – Netflix being the classic case here – which wanted to move their operations from third party CDNs in-house, so Netflix developed its own CDN cache system called Open Connect, and has been rapidly partnering with last mile network operators, cutting them in on the commercials so that they are not explicitly "over the top" any longer, in return for hosting Netflix CDN caches within those last mile networks. This ensures that the very highest bitrate possible is delivered, which in turn helps Netflix build their premium value in partnership with the sub-scribers ISPs and ultimately to enable them to gradually increase their subscriptions.

We are only now starting to see a combination of fast start and continuous live ABR streaming scale, and here in the UK, TVPlayer has only just announced that it is to launch a "bouquet" of legal, linear/live streams. In the US, HBO Now has been operating for about a year, and similarly Sky NOW is getting off the ground. While live streaming at scale has been possible for some time, the "scale" has always been – for large premium channels at least – always augmented major broadcast distribution channels. The scale that they are hoping to achieve is to be a real alternative to the traditional broadcast models, and over time I have no doubt that this type of scale will come about – for two reasons: first, because multiple operators will carry the rights, and this decentralization of the distribution architecture will inevitably help with the scaling; and second, because the value to the rights owners of being able to reach the dominantly connected audiences on multiple networks will outweigh the value of maintaining a single broadcast network infrastructure. So it is my prediction that over the next three to five years live linear is going to move center stage, and once it does, traditional broadcast networks will slide into terminal decline.

One last comment is to note the rise of dynamic adaptive streaming over HTTP –commonly termed DASH. DASH is a CoDec agnostic format for transporting content over TCP. With HLS more recently moving to support a wider range of CoDecs and container formats, the value of DASH is in some ways impacted. Yet, because it has evolved from MPEG (Motion Pictures Experts Group), DASH is widely adopted by vendors who want to promote themselves as independent from any particular technology. This has kept DASH under the microscope for some time as a potential cross-platform model to ensure device compatibility.

Yet, while adoption has been going well, in the past weeks (as I write), DASH has announced a patent pool and associated fees with use of DASH technology. Now this is not unexpected, but as is always the case when patent pools announce a fee structure sometime after vendors have already widely adopted the technology, there is certainly going to be some push-back from the industry on the pricing model introduced. Unlike h.264, whose patent pool strongly focused on the content creators and those who used the CoDec to compress the original video content for onward delivery, the DASH strategy is more focused on the publishers who present the content to the end user, and the fees are not insignificant, particularly if the publisher has large reach. Given that other technology may be more restrictive in reach, but patent royalty free, the market reaction I anticipate is a push-back toward HLS, which is already very visible, and I anticipate this will delay DASH. It may even be signaling a significant stalling of its adoption. As the book is being published, we are already able to see these trends emerging: DASH is simply not getting the adoption it had hoped for.

4.2.1 Compression

Much is talked about CoDecs. Even in this book I have visited the topic several times. There is a legacy within the sector, where the CoDec choice defined if you could reach an audience at all, to strongly prioritize CoDec choices as central to a content delivery strategy.

Today, in my opinion, there are two video and two audio CoDecs that are important if you want to reach an audience. These are h.264 with HEVC as the emerging successor, and aac for audio (with video) and mp3 for pure music delivery.

I am pretty sure that will have put the cat among the pigeons, but I have become fairly thick skinned to the repercussions of stating my opinion. Most of the so-called proprietary video CoDecs on the market today are little more than variations or optimizations of h.264. Even Google's VP9 is not getting the traction that Google would like, as is evidenced by their recent addition of h.264 to WebRTC support in Chrome. The fact is that h.264 has been extremely successful in much the same way that mp3 was 15 years ago. The universality of support is critical to ensuring that an audience can consume the content. Regardless of any optimizations and special benefits that other pretenders to the crown offer, the fact is that nothing compares in priority to the ability to reach the person (or device) wanting the content. And h.264 and mp3 have that ubiquity.

AAC has had a strong ride on the back of its early incorporation in the HLS standard. Although it is not as widely supported as mp3 as a whole (in part because of legacy devices), it has near-ubiquitous support in the devices that premium content consumers use, so I would think of AAC as the next generation for forward-looking deployments.

In the same way I would think of HECV as that evolution in video CoDecs.

As with the comparison between AAC and mp3, HEVC brings better quality at lower bitrates than h.264. As 4k and 8k video emerge (which both support, albeit with some variance and limitations), that bitrate difference will increasingly impact where optimization is important. It does require support in devices, and for this reason HEVC is already in common deployment in production and contribution, but less so in consumer facing workflows. It is, however, coming fast thanks – in part – to ARM and Intel taking great strides to include it in their recent chipsets.

This tighter compression makes HEVC a good consideration for mezzanine storage too. Where large video libraries are stored or cached behind "transcode on-the-fly" architectures (which may transcode the HEVC to h.264 between the storage and the consumer for compatibility), the HEVC library will require less storage capacity than the same library in h.264. This makes its continued uptake inevitable.

So, for the foreseeable future, h.264 is a solid platform and HEVC is a good option to explore; likewise, for audio channels in video, AAC is perfect – ubiquitous where the h.264 and HEVC are – but for very long-term, backward-compatible audio compression, mp3 is still unbeatable, even if bit for bit AAC compression provides better compression ratios.

I am not going to go on further here about CoDecs, since there are a number of points earlier in the book that dig deeper, but I will say one thing about some of the pretenders to these crowns: always ask yourself if they give you the same reach as the major CoDecs. If they don't, then you must do some serious digging into your economics, including the cost of rolling out the end user device support, before you adopt new compression technology. Always work with a ubiquitous CoDec that is "good enough" in preference to one that offers the world to a tiny audience.

4.2.2 The "Quality Question" ...

As you might have noticed, I am in the habit of using the term "good enough" with some regularity. In a sector that is dominated by conversations of quality, this may seem a somewhat pragmatic, if not heretical, attitude. The fact is that in the early days of streaming it was so exciting to manage to stream anything at all, of almost any quality, that my own experience as the sector emerged was through the eyes of learning to deliver the capability to stream. Image and audio quality were very much aspects that took many years to mature and take center stage. This makes me somewhat pragmatic.

While we do have high-resolution systems for testing our encoding platforms at id3as, I have become so used to watching video over dual-ISDN connections running at 128Kbps that I would never, myself, claim to have the "golden eyes" that those who profess to analyze video quality do. Even to this day I can sit and quite happily bask in the beauty of a full-screen scaled-up video that is normally 240x180 resolution and looks more like a cheap Christmas tree decoration than the video of a 2002 concert. I am not one to spend money on Hi-Fi, and while I realize that many people traditionally go to great lengths to ensure that their production workflows all exceed the quality of my home entertainment system. So as to ensure the "highest quality" by the time it reaches my front room, I help them out by keeping my home entertainment system pretty much as low cost as it can be, and generally quite out of date too. Why? Well it ensures that I have the best backward compatibility so my archives are still accessible, and it generally means that I am in the "long tail" mass market for services whose operators have debugged them and simply work. I tend to "push the boundaries" on my work computers for the latest and cutting-edge technologies, but when it comes to just watching something with my family, I take an almost opposite approach. This also keeps me mindful of where the mass consumer market is. Those who work in the industry and indulge themselves in 8kUHD screens five years before the mass market even understands what UHD means are right to do so, don't get me wrong. However, they are also at risk of disconnecting from the mass market, and unconsciously leaving their own customers with a sense of being second rate: Something that one should never allow to happen.

There are many great books written about "quality." Nontechnical discussions aside, Persig's famous book, *Zen in the Art of Motorcycle Maintenance*, tells the story of a man's eventual breakdown in the search for its meaning.

This story is a potent warning for my colleagues in the sector. Since the 2002 opening up of massive availability of Intercontinental Telecoms routes, the CDNs, in particular, had to alter their approach to market. When transoceanic IP was a scarcity, the supply–demand economics allowed CDNs to charge a huge premium on their IP. This was because the CDNs' proxy capability offered significant savings over multiple direct delivery over each pipe. Premiums such as $1.50 per GB of data transferred were common, even up to 2005 (as contracts expired), but since then the CDNs have fought tooth and nail to maintain price. In fact it was only down to the consolidation caused by careful dropping of the prices (to today's more stable $0.02 per GB "floor") that stemmed the competition and allowed the CDN revenue models to stabilize.

To add value, the CDNs changed the narrative of the delivery story from price to "quality," and – as we have discussed multiple times elsewhere – they have produced a number of key performance indicators that form the typical core of CDN negotiations with publishers these days.

I will explore latency in the following section, but given that very few applications are *really* latency sensitive and given that most media services have to buffer a few seconds before they start playing (orders of magnitude than the KPIs of milliseconds that CDNs differentiate with), we should also introduce the concept of "quality of experience (QoE). QoE is a broader measure of KPIs that takes a more holistic approach to the entire engagement of a customer with a service. While in a lab a particular bitrate may stream to a player, this is a relatively isolated way to view quality. In practice, when delivering commercial services, we must include a variety of factors such as ease of discovery and access, starting up within expectation and consistently, and probably one of the most important (at least according to major broadcasters such as Sky who spoke on this very subject at Content Delivery World in London last week) is "re-buffering."

These factors all add up to how well the client engages with your services. If a service is unavailable, then the user has a million other options, and they are unlikely to return to try the service again. That is unless they are in the middle of a box set, or if you have a monopoly on the content, in which case unavailability is likely to result in a very strong and direct impact on the customer's view of your brand as a whole.

So, while in these circumstances it cannot be stressed how important the CDN is in underpinning the client's perception of the CDN's customer, the CDN may often take its availability for granted and instead invest in differentiating with microscopically faster loading times or supporting higher bitrates. Any publisher who prioritizes encoding quality over availability must either be focused on a niche such as telemedicine or have an eye on the wrong KPI. While ISPs that offer poor connectivity – consistently providing speeds lower than advertised – may see a churn of customers, few publishers loose customers because they offer 1080p rather than 4 k streaming, or because the stream took 6.02 seconds to start rather than 6.01 seconds.

4.2.3 Latency

I recall the delight I had in setting up my first live video stream on a LAN many years ago. With the first frame of video I remember a clear image of the top of my head. The immediate thing I noticed was that when I looked up at the camera I could still see the top of my head. I then waved at the camera. It was some seconds later – with a few moments convinced it was not working in between – that I finally saw my face look up and then my hand waving back.

I have covered the technical background of latency in several places earlier in the text, particularly in Section 2.1.1. I was aware of latency even as I performed my first live video webcasting tests, having for some years prior become used to the effect on audio webcasting. Still, there was a sense of surprise. Not least was because I had until then mainly seen my own image either rendered directly to the screen from the local capture card (a process that neither requires compression nor involves much propagation delay), and further I was used to only otherwise seeing my face in a mirror. So there was, if nothing else, I had to make a mental adjustment to this new, highly compressed and latent video of my hand waving back some moments after the event had occurred.

Now normally seeing yourself on camera provides a very instant feedback on video latency. However, until the event of webcasting it was unusual for the general public to see themselves live on a transmission network of any kind, other than perhaps on the CCTV cameras in a shopping center. Traditional broadcast networks – which, of course, also suffer latency – were expensive, and live broadcasts were involved and complex things to set up. They were far out of reach of the individual, and interested layperson. Webcasting has indeed changed that, but until it happened, it was rare to see yourself waving back from a TV screen. For this reason most people were largely unaware of network latency as an effect.

Obviously webcasting, with its increased need to mitigate errors in the network, accentuates latency over the relatively controlled network latencies found in private broadcasting networks. As the general public has been increasingly able to watch live sporting and other events on both laptops and traditional broadcast networks at the same time, it has garnered more awareness.

Because people watching a TV signal often have no other frame of reference, they always expect that the moment they see something on live TV is the same as the moment it is actually happening. Yes, the sting (extolling the possibility of wire fraud in gambling) had been in the public conscious but only vaguely. In fact betting systems always shut the gate early enough so that even those watching on broadcast links cannot place bets anywhere near the time the race results have obtained.

This segues nicely into the fact that as in betting applications, in a few finance applications the broadcast latency is a key performance indicator of interest to live streaming publishers because it can have a real financial impact on the business for which the streaming is being delivered.

In sports streaming, the issue of latency is considerably less impacting. Yes, it is possible that your neighbors, watching on a traditional broadcast, may cheer a goal a few seconds before you see it on your tablet or smartphone, but you are probably aware of that before you click start on the stream. Indeed in pragmatic reality it is not going to make you rush back to a broadcast network subscription. You are more likely to close your Windows, or wander a little farther away from your neighbors' Windows, or do the social thing and go round to their house with a few beers to watch the game ...!

Obviously that does not mean that the online publisher should not demand low latency from their service providers if it is available. To this end there is currently much interest in WebRTC, which, by its full name (web real-time conferencing) is designed for low-latency video communications. As a mass market proposition WebRTC is not today designed to scale for large audiences: it was designed for individuals and small groups to video chat. At id3as (and I am sure at many others), we are working on technology solutions that can leverage WebRTC in the workflow to minimize latency where possible.

So my current suggestion is to explore WebRTC where possible – particularly as the lowest latency streaming technology – RTMP – is rapidly being deprecated from the market as HTML5 video tags and browsers' own video players replace RTMP-capable Flash players. RTMP may last some more years in the contribution feed market, since Flash per-se is not required to generate RTMP, and it is worth noting that Facebook and YouTube both use RTMP for contributions to their live services. Presumably this is because plug-ins and encoding apps for RTMP are pretty reliable and simple to implement, and RTMP does typically provide latency of around 2 seconds.

However, these publishers then transmux and transcode the content into a variety of ABR formats to reach the myriad devices that the audiences are connected to. Overtime that ingest will likely migrate to WebRTC, since the encoding capability can be delivered without a plug-in or external app, and this will increase the ease with which this user generated content can be contributed.

4.2.4 Application, Site, Web, and Games Acceleration

Obviously beyond the specifics of video and audio streaming most publishers are also presenting a vast array of text and images, and often more complex web applications too. Throughout this book I have concentrated on multimedia, largely because that is where my expertise lays but also because the sheer volume of network load that these forms of data generate need to be dealt with a very broad set of skills combining almost every aspect of computer science and telecoms.

For the types of data that result in text, webpages, EPG information, images, and web applications, the challenges are weighted differently. These comprise vast volumes of very small bits of data. Usually that data has a higher value per byte, since you can get quite a few frames of issues and lose quite large chunks of video without losing your audience, but if you lose even a word in a news article, you can completely alter meaning.

This changes the design architecture somewhat. Fortunately, several of the more modern CDNs can help significantly with techniques such as "in-lining" whereby components referenced on a page can be brought into the cached copies of the page wholesale. A good example of this is with a JavaScript (.js) library: often pages use JavaScript libraries by referring to them in the header. These headers can be stored on separate servers to the web content, but a good CDN will load the js in-line into the HTML and then cache the whole code as a single file. In turn this means that only one file is cached and the user's browser simply pulls that single file from the cache, rather than each component from each origin server. So the proximity of the cache reduces latency, and the single session required between the browser and the cache saves an overhead of initiating multiple sessions.

Another common trick is to compress images on the fly, and then update the webpage with less compressed images over time. This helps the user load the page quickly, while over a short time improving the quality of the data presented.

With streaming games, and soon with VR, we will see more and more innovative techniques being introduced to enhance the user's experience.

4.3   Desktop and Device Delivery Applications

4.3.1   Standalone Media Players and Applications

RealPlayer is widely acknowledged as the first really successful Media Player that incorporated ability to stream or progressively download content, launching in April 1995.[1] The UCL MICE tools, among other academic projects, pre-dated RealPlayer by nearly a decade, but RealPlayer was commercially distributed and designed for more ease of use. Yet it was not well integrated with browsers at that stage, relying on the user to sequentially pass metadata from the browser to the player to begin streaming.

I myself consider WinPlay3, appearing in 1995, as the first widely available media player application that offered a well-integrated streaming experience for the web user. This is because it included the m3u file type (close to my heart – see Section 1.3 above), meaning that so long as your computer's MIME

---

1 https://en.wikipedia.org/wiki/RealPlayer#History

types were set up right (as should have happened at installation), you can click a link on a webpage, launch WinPlay3, and thus start a progressive download stream of the target mp3 (listed in the m3u file) playing in a few seconds (depending on your Internet speed). WinAMP emerged in 1997, and was considerably more successful, made so by its second version including a range of user-friendly tools such as a spectrum analyzer.

Shortly after this, Microsoft released the Active Movie Player: but much like RealPlayer it had a rather faltering start. Although in 1997 it became the foundation of the much more successful DirectShow capabilities, in 1999 Windows Media Player 6.4 split from the standard Windows Release cycles. In my opinion, this was one of the best media players of its time, being simple, practical (it was rolled into the OS for many years), and reliable.

As Object Link Embedding established itself as an open portable way to embed Windows Media Player and, over time, the RealPlayer into the webpages, maturing with Active-X, it was these technologies that largely brought video playback to be a normal, and expected part of the web user's general experience. However, because the media player application was external to the browser, just because the browser could provide access to the metadata describing the stream, it was no guarantee that the player would be able to also penetrate the local firewall and access the stream.

Destiny Media Technologies introduced their Clipstream streaming Java-based mp3 player around 1998, and this technology was notable in that it allowed a single mp3 stream to be delivered cross platform, and directly into the browser (provided that Java was installed).

Clipstream opened up the thinking that cross platform was a good idea. Indeed it was also the first technology to focus on browser streaming integration through just the HTTP streaming ports, whereas Windows Media and Real Media had a number of challenges to overcome before their embedding was smooth and reliable.

While Windows Media Player was bundled with the OS, and Real Player was "freemium," Clipstream based their business on a model of "player activations" that – while it may well be more acceptable in today's mature market – meant that their technology was (comparatively) marginalized. Its tight port control meant that security conscious enterprises took interest in Clipstream for inward marketing, but Clipstream was not really well positioned to take advertising forward to consumer markets. The nascent advertising market was not warm to the idea of paying for a player instantiation for each advert in addition to the CDN delivery costs.

Fast starting for VoD assets emerged in early 2000. Windows Media server, in particular, introduced a number of ways to their configuration workflow to simply insert adverts as pre-roll and mid-roll. In the case of live streaming – particularly multicast – this helped the user experience. Because the multicast usually took a few seconds to join up and buffer, the pre-roll time was an excellent opportunity to give the viewer something to watch instead of a "buffering" message.

By the mid-2000s Adobe had really got going with its acquisition of Macromedia's Adobe realized that video capabilities could be easily added to their Flash executable. Because Flash was so widely installed for rich-media website development (not least because it was excellent at cross-platform support) and because it was invoked within the browser, it could share the same HTTP session as the browser for accessing the content – meaning it was typically simpler for firewalls and offered a widespread, fast-starting, low-latency, and cross-platform video delivery option.

Advertisers loved that, and relatively quickly Flash became the de facto model for launching video streams – particularly in the freemium web-user targeted IP video space. Microsoft ran to try to catch-up, by launching their own "rich Internet application" – Silverlight – bringing cross-platform access to Windows Media streaming. But until Microsoft stole a bit of a march on Flash by introducing Adaptive Bitrate "Smooth" Streaming in around 2008, there was a period between 2003 and 2008 when Flash became strongly dominant in the video delivery and CDN space.

QuickTime is the other key technology in the major vendor space. Introduced as far back as 1991 by Apple, becoming publically available in 1992, the early QuickTime was actually outsourced for development by Apple, and Apple subsequently took the developers to court (although settled) for stealing several hundred lines of QuickTime code when they developed the source at the heart of what became Windows Media Player. This incestuous relationship between QuickTime and Windows Media was probably a complex issue for the companies involved, but ultimately it is also probably one of the key contributing factors to today's cross-platform support for media.

However, it wasn't until version 4.0 in 1999 that QuickTime added streaming support. This made it four years behind Real and Windows Media (whose Active Movie player release in 1995 had supported streaming). This loss of position took some time to recover. Ultimately Mac platforms were targeted by Flash-based publishers, until Apple made a strong separation from Flash to introduce HLS, which was very similar to Microsoft's smooth but was the only way to stream to the disruptive iPhone and subsequent iPad. Leveraging their device dominance, the QuickTime components, and smooth handling of the stream between the i-devices' browsers Apple set the stage for the rapid switch to HTTP-based, native browser targeting that has risen since the smartphone era transformed the video streaming landscape.

Before we jump into the browsers though, we should mention mplayer and VLC. VLC is one of the largest collaborative open source media player projects. The project started in 2001, so it was relatively late to the stage, but it brought together a number of traditional media player features for the consumer, with a range of encoding capabilities for the producer. Until then only

QuickTime had really included any degree of authoring tools, and these were fairly simple. VLC added the ability to compress, packetize, and serve a variety of streaming formats, and though never really a production-ready tool, as a desktop toolkit for a webcaster or streaming engineer it was the one tool that gave a producer a depth of control and insight into the streaming process that meant quick tests, models, and device interop debugging could be conducted through a GUI.

I still always have VLC installed, and while I would never consider using it for a production client, if I receive a file that is difficult to play back, or if I want to test the very latest beta CoDec or try out streaming quickly on a LAN, VLC is a quick and dirty "Swiss army knife" for all of these types of workbench tests.

VLC has been ported to many OS and provides a relatively consistent experience. However, in 1999/2000 there was still extremely limited support for video streaming to the rapidly emerging Linux operation system.

Into the Linux space came mplayer. The mplayer was a command-line media player, with a counterpart mencoder that provided compression and muxing/packetizing for basic streaming. Schisms in the coding team formed mplayer2 as a fork, although mplayer2 had a GUI and did not ship with mencoder.

The mplayer and mplayer2 are still commonly found in appliance-based streaming systems, such as those used for digital signage. They are relatively simple, and being GPL-based coders, they can access the source, which is much more restricted than VLCs, and relatively quickly set up simple Linux appliances that can render video to a display. In my IP Set-Top Box start-up (Set Top Solutions Ltd, 2004–2006) we used mplayer at the heart of the system. It is certainly possible to make it production ready, although it tends to be relatively fussy to add a fluid UI.

4.3.2 Video Tags in HTML5

In 2007 the Opera Browser group proposed to introduce < video > tags to the HTML5 spec, and to make video a "first-class citizen" on the web. Initially CoDec issues hampered uptake of the standard, and while they supported a few "free" CoDecs, browsers essentially worked around the daunting h.264 licensing risk by instantiating third party media objects better, in a uniform cross-browser model, where previously instantiating Windows Media, RealPlayer, QuickTime, Flash, or Silverlight had varied from browser to browser and OS to OS. This pushed the h.264 codec responsibility to the media object, handing over at what the browsers call a "user agent."

Native media libraries may decode other royalty-free CoDecs without needing to use an underlying media framework or application. However, whichever way the local system achieves the playback, the publishers simply inserts "<video > <some metadata about the source > </video > ."

AS HTML5 video has exploded, Flash has been gradually deprecated – even by Adobe. Increasingly all the capability that the Flash player added has become available from the native browser, and in some cases the browsers are also proactively making Flash "click to play" to accelerate the deprecation and migration to HTML5 only video and audio delivery strategies.

4.3.3 WebRTC – Beyond HTML5

While crystal ball gazing is obviously only guesswork, it is fairly clear that WebRTC is emerging as the next evolution of online video delivery. WebRTC, as mentioned in in Sections 4.1.3, brings lower latency, coupled with a useful peer-to-peer model for scaling. While this needs further engineering to make it truly scalable for valuable premium content, and while it is still evolving in terms of being available cross-browser and cross-platform, WebRTC is already getting significant traction. Indeed it will be a strong player even in an HTML5 video-dominated market for some time to come.

4.4   Request Routing (The Dark Art of the CDN)

I covered the technical basics of request routing in Chapter 2, Section 2.5.3. However, there are some considerations that are relevant to the publisher that are worth adding.

Once you publish a URL to an item of content, that URL (where you are using a CDN) is a key data item that ties your users to the content, and their ability to find the content in your CDN. If those links expire (which may be desired in some models), the content becomes unavailable.

Controlling this link is paramount to the survival of your business. If the request router cannot connect users to their content, then no matter how good the CDN is, the content cannot be accessed.

Publisher strategies may include having your own top-level request router, which in turn provides access to the URLs to the request Rrouters of various CDNs, in effect giving you multi-vendor redundancy in the event of an entire vendor going out of service. This is key for high-availability premium services.

It may be that you decide to use a CDN brokerage (also mentioned in Section 2.5.4 above), which in effect measures your various CDN options and chooses the best balance between QoS and cost for you. Again, the brokerage – which is essentially an intelligent request router – could potentially fail, so you may want to have redundancy of multiple CDN brokerages. Obviously that could endlessly cascade, and sometimes the complexity itself can cause more issues than it solves.

In practical terms the only way to get this right is to evolve it in a real-world environment. But bear in mind at all times that if the user's request cannot be routed, then no matter how good the CDN, the user won't get any service!

4.5 Logging Analytics and the Devil in the Detail

I want to wrap this section by making some further publisher-centric comments about reporting and interpreting the data those CDNs and publishing services may provide. Also I want to help you become familiar with some of the interpretations and mis-interpretations that can arise from the data presented.

As the various early media server platforms evolved, and with particular regard to Abode, Real, Windows, and Wowza, there was, even at an early stage, a very significant data management problem that arose from the activity and user logs.

For a start, they all produced different structures of logs, containing different columns of data. Early log analysis tools needed to be "trained" as to how to parse the logs files, and store the parsed data in a usable format. Historically, not least because they were cheap to get started with, these data sets were then stored in ever-increasing relational databases. Given that even a modest CDN can be dealing with tens of millions of log entries each month, the scaling limitations of centralized aggregation into a relational database were an absolute pain to manage in practical terms.

In my own CDN (Global-MIX) the log and analytics machine was by far our most powerful machine, and it had a massive storage array that kept us all awake at night: not because of noise (!) but because, if it failed, it would take out our ability to bill our clients.

As database strategies improved by the middle of the decade, we were starting to see the concept of map-reduction evolve and come to market in an affordable way. The development of ideas such as "map-reduce" meant that we could store logs on the origin and edge servers, and only interrogate them in subsets of data, as the analytics were required. By distributing the problem, and taking the query to the data, rather than aggregating the data before we could query it, so-called Big Data analysis became far more scalable.

Along with this, a "competition" appeared between CDNs to try to present more and more meaningful KPIs from the data. Whereas once we only cared "how many hits a video has had," today we care about entry point and exit point, bitrate received, number of re-bufferings, intervals between re-bufferings, popularity by region, etc.

However, we have seen, particularly with the OVPs, which by nature are very skilled in the upper layers and particularly in web UI/GUI interfacing, a strong trend to create more meaningful data sets relating specifically to commercial models and outcomes, and their accounting. By creating, or trading with "currencies," such as Cost Per Mille – commonly known as CPM,[2] the statistics derived from the media service delivery can be automatically accounted directly to advertisers from the logging and analytics process. Ultimately that data is very much where the business is done.

Unlike the CDNs, which have to sell on some minutiae and QoS of KPIs, the OVPs have to sell on high-level QoE. This is a much broader technical skill space focused on the overall user experience, but one where detail is not focused on the statistics and telecoms QoS, so long as the video at the heart of the customer propositon is delivered "within expectations."

So the OVPs have done some very good deals brokering ad agencies and online video publishers. But invariably a part of the offering is an option for the OVP to manage the underlying CDN relationships, where the OVP aggregates traffic and can command a little of the pricing, and win some recurring revenue from the transaction. Ultimately OVPs often prove to publishers to be better able in monetizing the content delivery ecosystem where the CDNs, with much the same base data, have become more embroiled in defending ever more atomic discrepancies between their service and their direct competitor.

Much the same data is available to both, but the schism stems from different use, and produces different results.

As you can see from my quick sketch of the industry, different stakeholders require different reports from their content delivery. Without the visibility they specifically need, they cannot understand how the technology is solving the problem they need it to.

So any database and logging analytics system needs to be able to offer its owner a full range of flexibility meeting all the stakeholders needs and expectations.

A broad-minded CDN would be able to present itself as a fine telecoms resource to a broadcast telecoms customer, but to a publisher they need to present themselves as part of the rights-monetization system. Few CDNs get this right beyond a tight focus on a particular niche sector.

As a CDN developer you need to design your monitoring, logging, and historic data aggregation strategy as the backbone of your business, and not as an afterthought. Also, to give you the most agility as those business-specific requirements come in from your various customers, querying that data should be as fast and as lightweight as possible. You need to inexpensively make informed decisions, be the decision responses fully automated or channelled for human oversight.

---

2 https://en.wikipedia.org/wiki/Cost_per_mille

5

Service Velocity

(An earlier version of this chapter was published in www.StreamingMedia.com in 2016[1])

Interestingly the term "service velocity" appears as far back as 2007 in the context of networks and telecoms, with citations of the term referenced from some academic papers (which I have been unable to find) within the cable industry's patents of early 2008.

The term's rapid emergence from that point can be seen on Google Trends.[2]

However, it is only within the past few years that I have been aware of the term with relevance to service deployment for streaming media. There is a reason for this, and I will explain both the cause and the effect below. Indeed service velocity is yet another string for the bow of my broader arguments about how we should anticipate significant macro change in the industry over the next two to five years. It also, from first-hand experience, underpins where my own company is finding a strong growth of interest and activities at the moment.

Let me first explain the service velocity concept by quoting a great brief from 2012 where Carl Weinschenk, senior editor of BTReport, gave a good definition[3]:

> Service velocity, as the name aptly implies, is the set of skills and infrastructure that enables service providers to offer the spectrum of sales, deployment, repair, upgrading and other requisite capabilities in a speedy manner.
>
> The idea is fairly straightforward: Operators who anticipate where business will come from will be able to offer it more quickly.
>
> The traditional approach seems reasonable: When a prospect materializes – either by contacting the operator or after being contacted by the MSO's sales staff – an assessment is done to determine if and how the business can be reached and if it makes sense for the operator to do so.

---

1 http://www.streamingmediaglobal.com/Articles/ReadArticle.aspx?ArticleID=110848
2 https://www.google.com/trends/explore#q=Service%20Velocity
3 http://www.btreport.net/articles/2012/10/getting-up-to-speed-with-service-velocity.html

Content Delivery Networks: Fundamentals, Design, and Evolution, First Edition. Dom Robinson.
© 2017 by John Wiley & Sons, Inc. Published 2017 by John Wiley & Sons, Inc.

The problem with this approach grows as operators aim at bigger and more sophisticated potential customers. Since those prospects are bigger, they likely are being courted by other providers as well. If so, they most likely can provide services more quickly – i.e., with higher service velocity – than carriers that are starting from scratch and who also have to spend some time determining if they even want the business.

Now back in 2012 we were in the midst of the discovery of Gen2 virtualization. By this I mean that those network service operators that had traditionally thought only of building their networks from dedicated hardware building blocks (Gen1) were starting to accept that many elements of service could be abstracted from a common commodity off the shelf (COTS) underlying hardware environment – essentially x86 computers. The deployment of hosted servers was no longer a combined hardware and software responsibility, and hardware Infrastructure as a Service (IaaS) providers were inviting operators to deploy their software services within managed hosted networks of computer resources. This meant that in the event of a hardware failure, rather than having no continuity, the service operator could replicate a copy of the software from the failed machine (or another source) to a new machine, and all functionality would quickly be restored. In the meanwhile the hardware operators could send out an engineer to replace the physical unit, and commission it back into the pool of resources that the service operator could draw from as required.

Gen1 physical appliances, where the underlying compute resource was tailored to the application running on that box, were decoupled, and the resulting model has been called "cloud" ever since.

What is key to note is that while various operational aspects of deploying services (obviously resilience and scaling) benefited from this type of virtualization, in many ways the function of the network, and the time to implement functions also became shortened somewhat. There was no longer a need to "roll trucks" to install specialist appliances in remote locations on the network: the idea was that a "vanilla" cloud hardware resource was already available, and an application could be launched as quickly as the image of that computer could be uploaded to the hardware and booted up.

While for a large network operator jumping in and changing all your dedicated routers for COTS servers running routing software has been somewhat scary, for small businesses wanting to create distributed networks of database servers or storage services, and so on, there were several advantages. First and foremost, they could reduce their trips to data centers – the overhead for a small business of traveling across a city or a continent to maintain hardware was effectively amortized into the cost of services fees charged by the cloud operator. Second, the upward scale available to even a one-person business is vast, and is obviously a function of the operating costs of a scaling (and hopefully profitable) business, and that brings great opportunity to small businesses.

Third, an even more important reason that cloud has been successful is that while peaks of demand can be met, huge sunk capital no longer has to be invested in technology that is *only* used for peaks. In nearly all businesses the daily ebb and flow of traffic through e-commerce platforms, and the like, means that the majority of fixed infrastructure remains unused for most of the time. The larger the scale of the enterprise, the larger is the efficiency that moving infrastructure costs to "use based" can bring.

Within the Gen2 environment typically the complete application function of a traditional appliance was "imaged" and optimized a little to run on the higher power the abundantly available compute resources deployed in the cloud's data centers. Where traditionally a video encoder farm had to produce all the different source formats of the video needed to generate a desired target device, now a single top-level mezzanine source could generate and submit it to the cloud infrastructure, activate as many servers (running the encoder image) as needed for all the formats, and quickly deliver the service, with the advantage that you only need to turn on all the servers a few minutes before they are needed, let them boot, confirm they are ready, and away you go.

Once the encoding task is complete, you could turn off all the cloud servers, and in a pay-as-you-go IaaS Cloud (such as AWS or Azure), you would also be turning off your costs, until the next time they are needed. (Note your traditional Gen1 infrastructure, even if turned off, would still be costing you warehousing or office space, security, manpower, to turn it back on when needed, and so on.)

The Gen2 model, where images of the old appliances are run on ephemeral resources, is a great "Duplo-Lego" introduction to virtualization. Most engineers and architects now understand that trend. Indeed we have seen many engineers, who until four or five years ago had very little regard for distributed computing and virtualization, embrace the cloud wholeheartedly as they learn to scale their applications. What is remarkable here is that scale brings the ability for even a very small company to compete for opportunities with large heavily invested network operators.

Quickly to return to Weinschenk's definition of service velocity:

> Since those prospects are bigger, they likely are being courted by other providers as well. If so, they most likely can provide services more quickly – i.e., with higher service velocity – than carriers that are starting from scratch and who also have to spend some time determining if they even want the business.

The Gen2 model has given application developers a service velocity that Gen1 simply cannot provide. Small enterprises usually have much shorter decision-making cycles and agility in their leadership. Larger incumbent operators traditionally had a monopolistic advantage when deciding to offer a service like TV or voice online, and they would set their service velocity to almost completely de-risk even vast capital investment. They could dictate the pace of technological change. Now smaller, more agile start-ups can scale to deliver large subscriber services worldwide and in a few moments. We have moved from an operator-driven technology landscape to a consumer-driven one. Only those enterprises that can keep up with the constantly changing consumer demands can sustain their business. Agility has replaced monopoly.

Such vast change in service velocity, coupled with deregulation in the telecoms sector over the past 20 years, has created a vast thriving market for OTT online providers whose operations depend on money coming from the underlying Telco subscribers.

Back in the 1990s, and even the mid-2000s, Telcos were still very much expecting to provide the shopping portals, the walled garden models of content, and other managed services. These managed on-net services were nearly always so easy to switch away from (just a press of a remote control to reach equivalent OTT providers offering a better/cheaper/optimized service) that managed services had to leverage the advantage of the operator's ownership of the access network for the subscriber (offering higher resolution images or better variety/easier discovery, etc.) else the subscriber could simply shop OTT.

With net neutrality there too is cause for concern. Although the general idea is that the market must be competitive, only one ISP services any particular end user. That access circuit has additional physical installation costs, and the ISP, and the ISP alone has an opportunity to offer "advanced managed network services" over that connection. This can be a headache both for the Telco that invested in infrastructure expecting to upsell with managed services to provide their own shareholders an ROI, and for the regulators who would like the Telcos to continue to invest in developing access networks more widely but are threatened by the risk of opening very unequal markets where only those with large capital funds can deploy managed services within the operator network footprints.

What does this all have to do with service velocity?

Let's recap:

- We have Gen1 – The traditional network with intelligent appliances at the edges and a dumb pipe in the middle.
- We have Gen2 – The virtualized appliance where the application is no longer fixed permanently at the edges of the network. It can now be moved to the resource most suitable for the optimized delivery of the service, and the use of hardware resources is strictly tied to real demand for the delivery of service.

So what might Gen3 be?

While there are many applications that can run on networks, ranging from gaming to banking to TV, there are (currently) only subsets that can run within networks. Almost exclusively these are network protocols of one type of another.

Let's drill into some of the more familiar network applications, and then broaden into some applications that cross the line between the network and the pure application space.

First are a couple of obvious ones: the Domain Naming Service (DNS) used all the time by everyone – it's what turns www.streamingmedia.com into a number that the routers can coordinate to route a request.

Second is the obvious one: Internet Protocol – the very essence of how data gets from one place to another in a mixed mesh networks of networks.

There are a couple of others too – MPLS is a way that IP can be deployed on various forms of fixed line networks. MPLS can be used by operators to designate priorities for traffic, so ensuring that low latency banking data can be shipped faster than a background software update, etc. MPEG-TS is one that is closer to the StreamingMedia audience, and this is just one of many layers of coordinated media and network protocols that are implemented at either end of a data transmission to ensure that a video signal can be transmitted and received.

In the Gen1 and Gen2 world we have often taken blocks of these protocols (such as IP/HTTP/HLS), and using our application-specific appliances, or virtual appliances, we have processed a group of these to acquire a video signal, and then passed these along a "conveyor belt" of appliances to reprocess them until they are ready ultimately for the end user to consume.

That conveyor belt has become much more agile in the Gen2 world – we can daisy-chain a limitless number of virtual appliances together to translate almost any combination of protocol sources to any combination of output protocols – leading to a world of virtual encoding and transmuxing, etc.

But in pure computational terms, these compute-units/appliances are inefficient. If I want to "stack" three tiny network application protocols, and for some reason it needs three separate Gen2 appliances, then I may need to boot three large operating systems on three compute resources to complete my task.

Gen3 computing architectures look beyond that model. They assume not only COTS hardware but also a common OS, live and running on the host computer. Instead of needing to provision new hardware, and network addresses, and distribute the OS image, boot that, clear security, launch the network application needed for that task, a Gen3 model would expect to run the network application on the already available COTS resource, and to launch that application almost instantaneously, not least because it is significantly smaller than the "full Gen2" image previously used.

Historically we have seen what used to be data warehouses gradually convert to providing cloud hosting. Traditionally these data centers were large customers of network operators – or in some cases great markets for sale to common customers.

The network itself, however, has always had Gen1 architecture. Core exchanges and routing infrastructures terminated very specific network types, and this meant that the networks underpinning all these hosted services were very inflexible.

While the network interface cards themselves always require specific interfacing, the routing core that these interfaces connect to has, over the years, begun to look increasingly like a traditional COTS computer core. And this is largely a testament to the progress of commodity chipsets. So a £1m Cisco router of five years ago probably has significantly less processing power than a contemporary Dell desktop. Accordingly those looking to increase the service velocity in the currently Gen1 network operator space are directly focused at the moment about how the actual network itself can be virtualized.

Given that this means managing a distributed cloud of resources, and Gen2 is already being eclipsed by the more agile applications developers that thirst for Gen3 architecture (because it is cheaper, more dynamic and more scalable again than Gen2), these network operators are almost all exploring Gen3 virtualization models. They want maximum availability and maximum service velocity – for where they see an opportunity to offer a managed service, and to create and expand into that market, leveraging their ownership of the network and before the regulator prevents them from doing so, in order to protect the OTT market that competes in the same space but has no ability to manage the network.

What may emerge, and I believe this to be quite certain, is that operators will initially take advantage of this massively increased service velocity to "show the way" and to ensure the capability is well defined, and then they will open up the ability to offer managed network services on-net to third parties, in a continuation of the IaaS model seen currently only available on COTS in data warehouses.

CDNs, IoT platforms, Retail, and FinTech will all see advantages they can leverage within the managed services environment, and to be able to run applications deep over operator networks will create a new generation of network services – indeed the term "microservices" is appearing in this context more and more – many of which we cannot imagine today, but all will become available almost as soon as they are invented, at scale and with quality of service and reliability that will surpass our expectations today.

So expect the very ground the streaming media sector is built on to start moving significantly over the next few years. Traditional alliances may change dramatically, some for the better and some for the worse. Operators may rapidly deploy their own CDN models, or they may even open up to invite third parties experienced with managed network microservices to come and evolve with them ....

Whatever the outcome, as they fully virtualize, this inexorable evolution will radically change the service velocity that the powerful network operators bring to market, and this will have deep and far-reaching effects.

6

Charging for IP-Delivered Content

6.1   Lessons from the Music Industry

Around year 2000 we saw the music industry go through an identity crisis as it realized it could no longer control where its rights were exploited.

My view is that the legal notion of "fixation" – the embodiment of a copyright material in a discrete form that could be sold in a unitary and accountable way – was the only model that had a legal rights framework at the time.

Broadcast and Telecoms data traffic laws relating to video and audio distribution were immature, as discussed in Chapter 7, and audiences were not significant.

Cable, satellite, and digital terrestrial were all distinct autonomous systems that were only just starting to roll out IP. All were closed, conditional access-based distribution networks. They were largely spectrum-restricted in capacity so concurrency was a limiting factor to offering user-specific services. The video on-demand systems that were available were often NVOD (where you wait for a showing a starting within a few minutes) in order to minimize the network utilization by broadcasting those VOD shows to small audiences.

And WAP (Wireless Application Protocol) was a thing on mobile networks …

So around the turn of the millennium it looked like CD and DVD were a great fixation model, and everything felt fairly monopolized and regulated in their favor. The music licensing bodies felt that they didn't have much to worry about.

Then the RIAA took Napster through the mill, counterproductively (for the RIAA members) serving to train an entire mass market in how to file-share using peer-to-peer technology.

The rest is history.

It took the music industry some time to reassert its organizational structure around this new paradigm. And it took Steve Jobs to shrink-wrap it for them, and make it work by leveraging his experience in the movie industry at Pixar to

Content Delivery Networks: Fundamentals, Design, and Evolution, First Edition. Dom Robinson.
© 2017 by John Wiley & Sons, Inc. Published 2017 by John Wiley & Sons, Inc.

negotiate the rights for iTunes at a tempting financial return, coupled with a massive "free" distribution and promotion engine that iTunes brings.

Jobs's iTunes was by no means the first online e-music service – far from it. He was, however, the one who made the music license holders realize that they didn't have much to lose in supplying to a demand that Apple could create, and commit to financially too.

iTunes proved a theory that was widely central to many narratives around the online rights topics at the time: namely "if you make the content easy to find, you can charge for that, even if the content is available for free elsewhere after some more painstaking 'discovery' process."

As the first year returns came in from iTunes, the dying music licensing industry began to economize on its CD and DVD production and refocus on understanding the art of the possible with regard to using the online ecosystem as a proper source of revenue.

iTunes represented the e-commerce of music on demand. Premium online content services came of age.

DRM has always been a "should we, shouldn't we" issue, and the debate intensified around iTunes take-off years in particular.

The biggest complication DRM faces is in moving the culture of music consumers from one of ownership of a record to an understanding that you have a temporary license to use content that is specifically "fixed" in that plastic/storage "unit."

Consumers still feel they have a right to ownership of the content, and struggle to understand that they have a right to it as it is sold but not to replicate it. In fact "copyright is retained," ©, and the rights owners do have law on their side, historically at least.

If you use DRM to protect a file, and then unlock it for a paid-up user, you need to define when it will be closed again. If it is part of a large on-demand library, you end up with a simple model that unlocks all files for the period of time permitted. That naturally creates a basic subscriber service.

If you try to sell individual audio files wrapped in DRM, then every application that may want to de-encrypt that file must be able to authenticate properly, which also means that the DRM licensing system needs to be set in stone, rarely upgraded, and always available. If over time that service cannot be maintained, then at a certain point a whole music collection that was bought, and considered "owned" would become unusable. The risk vector for a music publisher in maintaining such long-term ("in-perpetuity?") legacy licensing systems – available to keep customers who paid them once for the product some time ago – was far more costly than the risk of piracy of long-tail content.

iTunes eventually could drop its DRM (which it did) because its value proved to be more of a payment and distribution system to quickly get the mp3 requested rather than search for it illegally.

The same was not true in the video services industry. DVD was still nascent in 2000. So the expectation of "video of what you want when you want it" was still emerging. As it did, the expectation was better set, with the arrival of video on demand, which always got the viewer only a "showing" or a "rental." The model of "download films to own" also evolved with an expectation that the content was still trapped in the ecosystem, so "ownership" was better delineated between the rights owner and the consumer than had been the case in the music industry.

The video services industry, which was held back from market by the simple fact that broadband networks required longer to roll out than narrowband ones, had the opportunity to watch and learn from the challenges that the music industry faced.

6.2 Success Cases

Compression issues aside, audio delivery and video delivery are broadly technically equivalent models – with the key variance being the bandwidth required by the content. The rollout of broadband availability without a doubt produced a significant drag in the emergence of video services worldwide, while the music services space had emerged some years before.

Obviously there were many smaller models years before these prime names emerged. However, the services listed in Table 6.1 have all been significant in their negotiation of rights. But until these rights vehicles appeared, they had largely been illegally rebroadcast or had limited investment and penetration.

These "big plays" were also markers of a point of critical mass being reached for rights deals in online content distribution.

The drag occurred due to big video licensors being a lot more demanding of video. While the music industry took a considerable hit, the video services industry was able to be more defensive in the music industry's wake.

Video services learned quickly where the music sector has "got it right."

Table 6.1 Drag between music and video services emergence in major rights enabled platforms.

	Music services	Video services
Subscription on demand	2001	2007
	Rhapsody (Listen.com)	Netflix
Pay-per-use on demand	2003	2006
	iTunes Music	iTunes Movies
Subscription linear/live	2008	2014
	Apple Radio	HBO Now

While the technology has been able to deliver the models for around 12 to15 years, it has taken all that time for the major broadcasters to "get serious" about online delivery, and realize that it is an inexorable future. Now the technology piece is pretty much sorted out; the last hurdle is largely a combination of rights negotiations and cultural change.

Let's briefly take a look at two more of the largest success cases.

6.2.1 YouTube

An interesting fact about YouTube is that it only launched in 2005. This was nine years after I personally started engaging with streaming technologies. For much of that first decade it was very difficult to explain to the layperson what it was I did for a living. Within 18 months, particularly after Google acquired it, YouTube was ubiquitously understood, with *Time Magazine* crowning "You" (in reference to YouTube's "zeitgeist" moment) as "Man of the Year."[1] It was the inflexion point in my career at which point my area of work – streaming – became part of the layperson's vernacular.

Today, YouTube spans both the fremium and the premium markets. They have vast delivery capability, and have fine-tuned that with a decade of scale beyond that of nearly all service operators. They have had unrivaled insight into user habits and demands. And to be fair, they have simply got it right. If your video decoder can't play YouTube videos, it is set to fail.

Just to give an indication of success, in 2015 YouTube was estimated[2] to have received around $9bn in ad revenue. With Google taking about half of that as part of a cost of service, it was a significant out payment to its huge publisher base. What Google has never disclosed has been the costs of running YouTube. Now while many expect that in isolation the pure bandwidth of distribution alone would eat up a considerable amount of their revenue – perhaps even making it run at a loss against its direct earnings – what needs to be factored in is that the demand for bandwidth that YouTube creates makes Google a massive buying power in the telecoms market. In turn this leverages very low telecoms distribution costs, and while YouTube revenues $9bn, and consumes the lion's share of the company's online bandwidth requirement, the rest of Google's $400bn business runs on the cheap bandwidth that YouTube enables them to demand. So, while one business may break even or even run at a loss, it enables Google's many other ventures to maintain an extremely low content distribution cost, making them all more competitive.

---

1 https://en.wikipedia.org/wiki/You_(Time_Person_of_the_Year)
2 http://www.musicbusinessworldwide.com/youtube-will-earn-9bn-in-revenue-this-year-towering-over-spotify/

So, while it is indirect, it is clear to me that YouTube is very much a key part of driving the overall value proposition that the wider Google ecosystem offers, and much of this IS premium.

Still, returning to YouTube's own video services, it is worth mentioning the more recent YouTube RED service. This allows subscriber to pay a fixed $9.99 per month to have ad-free YouTube services. Estimates vary, but the indication is that this $9.99 is around double what an average user generates for YouTube as a "free" ad-supported viewer over the same time. Uptake and results are not openly available, but while YouTube is king of the user-generated content, it is still only at the market-testing stage of where it can offer premium content and it is erratic at buying third party rights for the purpose.

My guess is that the one or two very large live events it has experimented with were technically complex enough – where they may have delivered a few millions of live streams – that the possibility of offering many large live events at the same time is still being ironed out by experimentation with their YouTube Live service, where audiences for that relatively low-key content is not likely to cause a CDN failure. There is a world of difference between delivering one live event to a few million viewers, and offering prime-time TV services to hundreds of millions from a single infrastructure.

I would imagine, over time, they will find a positioning that works for them, and they certainly have the technology and resource to enable that. However at this point in time they are taking their time and learning from the market as it emerges.

6.2.2 Netflix

Netflix has got to be one of the finest examples of streaming successes in the online video world. While their technology model is exemplary, and a reference for nearly all engineers in the space, it was not their technology that won them their position. There were many organizations that could see the "quality movie on-demand" service online going viral. However, rights holders were an inaccessible cartel, and they made it incredibly difficult to even engage with their rights teams. Certainly, as an independent, I had immense difficulties licensing moves for a hospital pay-per-view model I setup in 2004 to 2005. The studios would refer us to a local rights agent, who in turn would say "we only deal with DVD licensing talk to the studio" that would cycles us back to the rights agent.

We had to circumvent them and talk to an in-flight entertainment company to get into a discussion and eventually do a deal on a very limited number (12) of movies.

In contrast, in this era Netflix had already built a vast DVD rental business. This was a more traditional (fixation-based) model. It gave Netflix access and leverage to talk to the rights teams and negotiate an online model. It was much like Steve Jobs had leveraged his contacts in major studios from his Pixar career to "do the deal" behind iTunes launch.

So once Netflix brought the screamingly obvious opportunity to market, everyone jumped at the chance. Quality was good, usability was strong, and price was more effective to pay than spending the time spent downloading illegal file shares.

Over time their portfolio of content has increased, although they are still largely resigned to having to wait a considerable time after the "theatrical" run before the rights holders license them the movies. The fear is that immediate online release will impact premium movie on demand services like Sky Movies or iTunes movies, so they are still a little way down the list in terms of release-window availability. However, to combat this, they have started to produce some excellent content of their own, and some of it has been hugely popular, benefiting from Netflix's ability to direct market to their ever-larger subscriber base.

6.2.3 On the Horizon

Table 6.1 mentions several success cases, and I break them down into three service classes: subscription on demand, pay-per-view on demand, and subscription live.

I chose these because most service models are based on the three-stage model shown in Table 6.1, and they commonly result in either linear or nonlinear pass through of the data, ultimately giving rise to live or on-demand models. Ultimately "time-shift" or PVR/DVR models are typically acquiring from a live or linear source, and then making the content available as an on-demand source but adhere to the model.

With such a simple fundamental core set of processes so common to all models, we can see that given commoditization and the deregulated, global Internet market, that rights holders will gradually license content to "unicorns" in the online video sector.

In each of my simplified sector models there will eventually emerge a strong "go-to" player for the consumer to dominantly opt for when selecting their content. It may be that they want to listen to a specific item of music as an on-demand stream. This is highly likely to be iTunes. Or they may wish to watch a specific video on an academic topic – for this they will most likely turn to YouTube.

For a just-released premium movie there is still to be a dominant service provider/player, and some of the traditional broadcasters have managed to keep their audiences interested by extending their subscriber models to allow DRM licensing for short periods of access to those movies. Sky movies here in the UK come to mind. Indeed iTunes actually supports the true on-demand "buy access" for recent releases, but not quite as many as I would typically hope for when I search it. So, though they are well positioned, I personally would not say they are the "dominant" brand I think of when I want "true" on-demand access to recent movie releases.

Amazon's LoveFilm is also well positioned but at the moment is also not yet – in my mind – at "killer-app" level in terms of providing consistent licensing of just released movies. I think there is still room for a leading "brand" provider to emerge here. I also think that the rights owners deciding to do the deals, more than any particular technology evolution, will enable such an entity to emerge.

While Table 6.1 shows lead times between music and video services emerging, the "unicorns" of success are rarely the first to market. Netflix is undeniably the king of subscription–VOD services, and Spotify is the leading subscriber–AOD service provider at the time of writing. This space is quite mature.

We can see that traditional cable and satellite service providers are currently making their debut. Sky GO and HBO Now are both essentially offering millennials, as they move into paying for their own access to content upon leaving home, a way to access the same sort of bouquet of live and on-demand services that their parents had delivered to a fixed location by satellite and cable. This heavy reliance on live/linear programming and a wide range of choices of live linear streaming is all technically possible at the levels that an individual network expects to serve online today. However, the prospect of a gradual "flush" through the subscriber base as millennials become parents and gradually the entire subscriber base expects *all* the live linear delivery to be delivered over IP absolutely requires some changes to our network infrastructures. Broadcast audiences (measurement gripes of my own aside) still reach tens of millions. While the streaming audiences today are typically around 10% of that size, given indicators such as BBC iPlayer's audience statistics, and so on, we can be certain that to move those tens of millions online will take a more scalable set of architectures than we have now. BT Vision is a good example of how an IP service can implement multicast to reach this scale, but (as I will cover in Chapter 10) this is today only really possible at scale on-net for a given access providers network.

So for Sky or HBO to strategize "turning off their broadcast networks," they need to plan for a considerable network strategy beyond simply "use Akamai" to really reach broadcast scale over IP.

That said, it might well be possible in the next year or two, and with that will arrive legal OTT cable services via the Internet. There may even be a group that can secure rights for global service delivery, and they could well become the Global–Cable–TV "unicorn."

We have seen Pandora and Listen.com and Last.FM produce "radio," but actually these services produce playlists of on-demand files. I can see a space for a Tune-In type live radio aggregator to emerge, if for no other reason than to parallel the Global–Cable–TV unicorn model. With many of the radio groups in most major territories gradually rolling up into just a small handful of radio network operators and publishing companies, I can see one of these groups making the right move, becoming 60–70% of the global market and launching a single radio service, and I can also see that that service may well simply get assimilated into the Global–Cable–TV unicorn over time, making that unicorn's service the TV and radio app … or something like that!

OK, enough crystal ball gazing for now. Let's look at some of the models that failed.

6.3   Failure Cases

While it is all well and good to learn from the success of others, it is also probably *more* important to learn from the mistakes and failures. By maintaining an understanding of what hasn't worked before, it improves design simply by avoiding the mistakes.

In the online content world, some of those mistakes have been technical design issues, while others have more often than not solved key technical problems, but inadvertently (or not) blundered into a viper's nest of business and commercial problems. In fact, if an online service is particularly successful in terms of its scalability, it becomes even more torn apart by the regulators and government agencies that see it either as a good opportunity to throw some incredible legal fees about, making lawyers rich and rarely rewarding anyone but the legal backers shareholders in the long term. We see this issue spanning both technical and artistic intellectual property rights. Patents, once the principle of opening ideas and protecting small independents, have now become an environment where smaller disruptive upstarts are suppressed by the weight of corporate legal funds that "troll" patents while *not* bringing products that they protect to market for protectionist purposes.

But at the same time, against this potential firestorm, those smaller design solutions that do "get away" with managing the intellectual property rights around the commercial model properly have a clear path to become the next unicorn players in their sector, as we have discussed among the success cases above.

6.3.1   Scour.net

For my personal first-hand experience when I missed registering "mp3.com" by a couple of weeks, and instead registered "m3u.com," I spent quite some time, funded by a pioneering VC Incubator, exploring opportunities to exploit the domain, on the shirt tails of mp3.com's resounding success.

One incarnation of our model was to create a robot to walk webpages searching for *.mp3, and where it found those with a complete http://*.mp3 sequence, we would index it and present it for immediate play on m3u.com.

While we were in the middle of exploring this between 1997 and 1999, I met the Scour team.

Scour had more or less had the same idea. Their model was not about sharing content, it was about sharing metadata *about* the content. Like Scour, I was of the view that copyright was focusing on the units of fixation or, in the digital world, the "ephemeral fixation of content in an mp3."

Neither group wanted to be reproached for storing and distributing illegal copies, so we simply directed users to go and get the files themselves. For reference, while Scour would provide download links, the niche that m3u.com offered was that the links we provided would progressively download, and start playing instantly.

What happened in practice was the RIAA amassed a massive legal war chest from its members, and launched a very targeted attach on Scour. Despite having some key studio-savvy founding investors, Scour was targeted as a warning shot to others. It rapidly filed for bankruptcy protection, foreseeing that its entire capital would be tied up defending the core model, with little or no resources left to expand the business. This starvation tactic is now quite typical between corporates. At the time it seemed luddite of the RIAA, and in the event all the RIAA members took a further five or six years to actually realize that the Internet had permanently disrupted their traditional "record fixation" based business, and to then move to adapt.

Indeed Scour was just the first of a series of ongoing p2p "shutdown" cases.

6.3.2 mp3.com

While Scour was in the laser sites of the RIAA, so too was mp3.com. It had grown rapidly by serving only independent music released directly through its platform, and I was increasingly focusing on launching my.mp3.com as a sub-service within that platform. The model was that you could prove to the system (through a variety of means) that you had a copy of a particular CD and then use a "locker" on mp3.com where you could access the music you had proved to have original copies of.

While mp3.com did not allow sharing of the music between users proactively, each user would technically have had access to a shared copy of the original mp3, giving mp3.com efficiency to scale (since it didn't have to store multiple copies of the mp3, one for each "locker").

The RIAA didn't see things the same way – they saw the service as providing access to unlicensed copies of the original works – and the case was eventually settled out of court for an amount of money that effectively put mp3.com on the scrap heap overnight, having only two years earlier being the largest of the dot-com IPOs.

6.3.3 Napster

While Scour and mp3.com were in their way relatively high-profile news, neither caught the zeitgeist of the issue more than Napster. Still to this day most people have heard of the Napster case.

There are a number of reasons for this. First, Sean Parker – a key partner at the founding stages of Napster – went on to become president of Facebook, and his ongoing presence in the IT world has continued way beyond Napster.

Second, Napster burned extremely brightly. The adverse, unintended consequence of the RIAA's suit against Napster was that it was extremely divisive, with arguments about individual rights facing directly up to corporate interests. Everyone had a view. The news media picked up on the story globally. While this was a lot of heat for those involved, it also promoted Napster to a global market. It exploded. Everyone downloaded it, and then software engineers cloned it or reverse-engineered it and released myriad me-too versions, fully decentralized and unstoppable without fundamentally changing Internet governance.

This caused a huge swelling tide of illegal file sharers. Mums, Dads, kids, and grandparents all joined in, confident that the probability of being made an example of as a pirate was rather nonexistent. By the time Napster essentially collapsed in on itself, file sharing was the norm for Internet users, and I remember many ISP conferences I attended or spoke at where the topic of the day was "nearly half our traffic is P2P." Today, that is changed to "nearly half our traffic is video," with a surprising amount of that being premium or "legally distributed" content.

There is no doubt from both Napster and Netflix that the consumer wants easy access. That is *the* most valuable thing. The key demarcation for success, though, is keeping the rights owners on their side.

It is often said that "content is king." My own take is that the "audience is king" and that the "content rights owners are law" – we in the distribution sector are something of the king makers – with the ability to create systems that ignore or satisfy the king, and run circles around the law, or indeed comply with the law regardless of what the king wants. Ultimately, where we find success together, the three will end up in a moving consensus.

6.3.4 Broadcast.com

Broadcast.com was an interesting failure case. Some may even say it wasn't a failure because Marc Cuban and Todd Wagner – the co-founders – were personally instantly made billionaires as the company made its explosive IPO. Broadcast.com was very early in the game, and was arguably the first online aggregator of live and on-demand audio and video content.

So why, today, does www.broadcast.com take you to www.yahoo.com and not the hub of all things multimedia online?

While we could absorb ourselves almost endlessly in a character analysis of Marc Cuban, and his opportunistic deal with Yahoo when he sold broadcast. com to them for $5.7bn, for the purposes of this book it is more relevant to explore a little of what Yahoo might have seen as the opportunity in those heady days of the dot-com bubble, and why they met with a variety of factors that ultimately meant they never really saw broadcast.com's value become what, presumably, they had invested in.

The story of broadcast.com is a story not only of entrepreneurial opportunism but an inability of a large corporate to capitalize on a visceral sense of market moving because of its sheer size and lack of agility. It is my take that those who enabled the massive acquisition to happen from within Yahoo were absolutely right about the market that broadcast.com could see was emerging.

Today, the OTT infrastructure market is worth in the order of $20bn to $30bn. Had broadcast.com given Yahoo controlling access to that market, then the $5.7bn investment looks fairly sane.

However, at the time, in part because of the drawing of breath that the content industry as a whole took while Scour, mp3.com, and Napster were under pressure, the market did not mature as quickly as Yahoo was hoping it would. Indeed broadcast.com had limited revenues and Yahoo was still massively loss making. Both had liquidity from their stock valuations in the absolute height of the dot-com bubble. They were both all about "taking position early."

That was where the synergy lay. Yahoo saw itself as a granddaddy of search. This was before Google had emerged when Yahoo was at the pinnacle of its growth. Broadcast.com was positioned as the granddaddy of video and audio. It was able to try to take the strongest position possible.

However, by moving early, they "scared the horses." The broadcast industry, which had significant rights-monetization systems established, was simply not happy with the idea that the likes of Yahoo thought it could replace them, and to hold back on licensing, used its "existing business" leverage on the rights holders that were essentially a continuation of the broadcasters.

Yes, "low quality" and "it's not ready for prime time" were often shouted by the broadcasters, but if "prime time" is what all your audience is doing most of, then that was increasingly surfing the net, and not "watching TV," then those who believed in online saw that putting TV on the net was inevitable if you wanted to reach the audience at all.

So Yahoo actually definitely got it right in terms of a visceral feel for where the net was going to take broadcasting.

But what happened next was influenced by two key factors:

- Yahoo was on an acquisition spree, and its leadership had focus issues with regard to the specific success of broadcast.com.
- The lack of rapid influx of "rights-cleared" content stalled the evolution of the sector, and accordingly media sales didn't transpire as quickly as expected.

To this last point the online advertising market had revenues in the order of $2bn to $4bn, with the OTT Infrastructure market essentially being a fraction of that. Broadcast.com had revenues of around $7m.[3]

Without focus and rights deals to bring audiences, the advertisers were not interested enough, so the market didn't jump start as the acquiring team at Yahoo must have hoped. And today, broadcast.com doesn't even exist beyond Yahoo's front page.

6.3.5 The "Yacht Projects"

There is one last failure case that I want to cover. Actually this is more of a category of failures. Often I have worked with streaming engineers, and there is a term (or variations similar) that appears every now and then, and that is to describe a streaming project that is clearly more about the investors' vanity than about making a sustainable platform. We call them "yacht projects." They are usually the result of someone wealthy, and with too much time on their hands, who doesn't get the TV industry and wants instead to own a "small" TV station, which is actually a webcasting business.

There are dozens of them out there.

They are the worst kind of customer. They almost invariably take up a lot of sales and business development time up front, wanting you to share the excitement of their vanity-publishing platform (which is incidentally extremely easy to sell into – just tell them "you love the idea"), but then get cold feet when they discover they have to both find and earn an audience, you can't just "buy one."

There were many years when niche channels would start up, and create a lot of noise, and then simply go out of business overnight. This so-called dot-tv boom (in part because of the.tv domain suffix being made available at the time) drew a large number of skilled, but unemployed, people across the streaming sector and changed some of the dynamics from the human resource aspects of the sector.

Platforms like YouTube Live now soak up most of these "yacht projects" at the start up stage, and they soon lose interest when they realize they have to produce *good* content for a sustained period to really build an audience that they can monetize. If they get through the YouTube stage and want to grow further, then they start to become interesting clients with some specific problems to help them engineer solutions for. Also they will have some sustainability.

The good thing is that some of the "yacht projects" are quite interesting in their own right. The niches that people want to create video workflows around

---

3 http://www.gurufocus.com/news/138012/mark-cuban-and-broadcastcom-the-multibillion-dollar-coup

are as varied as there are people. As an engineer, if you can find a critical mass of clients to work for, and can help solve their problems, then some of those yachts are nice places to spend some time.

Also yachts tend to get people talking. They are generally more interesting to the individuals in the market than building one mega-platform for a global broadcaster. Small events and projects, enabling individuals and small groups to communicate better is extremely good acumen. I still occasionally help friends out for free with webcasts if they are going to look good on my company blog or other such PR.

Yet, looking for those opportunities has a relatively high cost of sale, and often depends almost entirely on relationships.

But I digress. Yachts are more about how you do your business than about content delivery network design. Let's get back to the premium models.

6.4 General Commentary on Commercial Models

In this section I borrow strongly from a series of talks I gave at Sussex University as a "primer" on the niche within the computer engineering space focusing on content delivery. Among other things, during the presentations I took a close look at a very simplified model of the premium content delivery chain. Figure 6.1 shows the basic model I used.

The model is laid out referencing the key domains of influence that various key Telco operator groups have in delivering Internet content OTT to a consumer. That consumer may be connected to a last mile ISP on DOCSIS or via DSL or Telco (including obviously radio telecoms and WiFi). The solid lines show where an operator has the physical network under its own controlled SLA. So for DSL Telco ISP operators such as AT&T or BT the scope of influence over which they can offer an SLA is almost all the way from peering

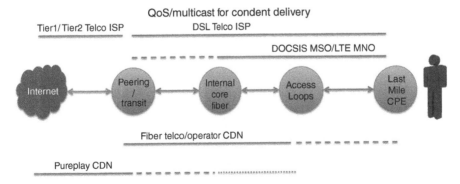

Figure 6.1 Basic reference model for premium and commercial content delivery.

to consumer. This continuity of connectivity, as we will see in a moment, means they can readily offer IPTV type services.

Varying slightly, the cable provider (DOCSIS MSO) may have its own last mile and internal network, but it will start to need to buy from upstream Fibre Telcos to reach the peering points. Moreover, while commercially they will have a contract – one that is part of underwriting an SLA to the consumer and publisher – they will be less likely have direct control of the peering network, although it will depend on each operator as to how much they retain that control.

Coming from the other end, we can see that a Pureplay CDN with a managed network may get as far (on its own networking) as the peering point. Without other commercial agreements the Pureplay's ability to directly and hands-on offer oversight to underpin an SLA deep into the operator network is limited (the increasingly dashed line labelled Pureplay CDN).

As we move content from the left of the model to the consumer on the right, we can see that we need to jump from solid line to solid line, and if the customer is paying to directly access any particular entry point, they will generally have to subcontract some order of telecoms to reach the consumer for the contribution feed, meaning that the SLA is subcontracted out too. This in turn can compromise premium-licensing deals.

Let's now add a few content and revenue flows to my model.

6.4.1 Cable TV

In the cable model of Figure 6.1 we now add a shaded arrow showing the flow of content, as in Figure 6.2. Content enters the network directly (contribution is shown as a vertical line). From the internal core fiber entry points (for

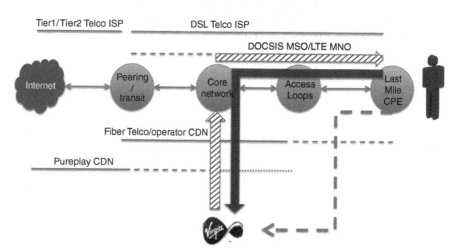

Figure 6.2 Cable TV's content (shaded arrow) and revenue (solid arrow) flows.

example, "head-ends" in the MSO cable terminology), the content is delivered entirely over the cable MSO's network to the consumer.

Conversely, the subscriber revenue is paid directly to the cable operators (the dashed arrow) – usually some form of monthly direct debit. Accounting data and usage data flow back up the system (solid arrow) varying with usage, and that is collected along with the subscription. This is an on-net model: the operator accounts and bills for use of network services.

6.4.2 IPTV

The IPTV model can be offered by potentially any last mile operator as shown in Figure 6.3. The key thing about IPTV services is that they guarantee SLA end to end, and so offer just as high a standard of quality delivery as a cable TV network, enabling a Telco to offer the same service as a cable operator.

Our royalty premiums (or at least the SLA QoS measurement and accounting data for them) has to pass through the fiber Telco environment to the source. This is much the same as how a super head-end (SHE) would talk to regional head ends in the traditional MSO model, but now the last mile can also be addressed by copper and fiber last mile operators.

There is little to stop a mobile or wireless operator from offering their customers an IPTV service too, but SLA claims will get muddied by the fact that the last mile will have a variable QoS depending on the local radio link. Accordingly expectation management could become a significant overhead. However, with OTT services now being the norm, even mobile operators can consider in-house IPTV as a service offering to their customers, if the operators themselves have the aptitude to negotiate suitable rights deals.

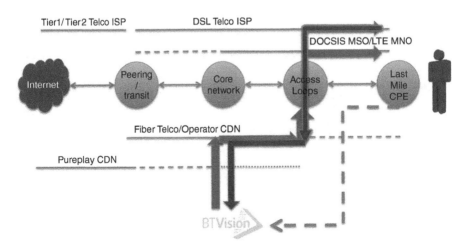

Figure 6.3 IPTV model's content and revenue flows.

6.4.3 OTT Pureplay + Operator CDN

First, for reference, a quick view of OTT Pureplay (here iTunes) on its own is presented in Figure 6.4.

This is probably the simplest diagram to follow. Content is delivered directly to the end user and the return path for content flows in reverse along the same path. There may be some element of monthly subscription too.

Critically the Pureplay operator can only offer an SLA as far as the peering/transit connection, and relies on the regional Telco and ISP to provide good enough service to the end user to underpin the premium charged.

As Figure 6.5 shows, the key difference between IPTV and OTT is to do with the placement of the paywall. If the paywall is within the last mile operator's network, where the operator might have its own internal CDN (an operator CDN) to manage content delivery across its own "owned" network, then the model is essentially IPTV.

If you simply move the paywall outside of the operator's network, so that the end user has to have a subscription to the operator network for access to the network, and then a payment relationship with the content provider for accessing the content, the model is known as an over-the-top model.

If an OTT provider is large enough, it may use a Pureplay CDN to deliver content to the operator CDN, and the operator CDN may be able to offer a CDN service to the OTT provider under commercial terms. At this point the OTT provider would have contiguous SLA agreements in place from source to delivery of the content. Netflix is a great example of this hybrid model. To form the operator CDN relationship, there may be a revenue stream that the operator CDN receives from each use of the content within the CDN. This

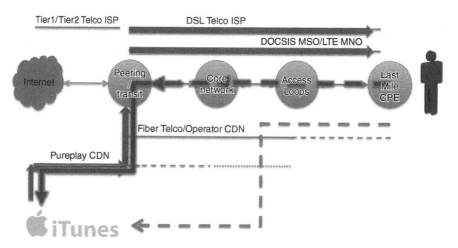

Figure 6.4 OTT Pureplay (iTunes).

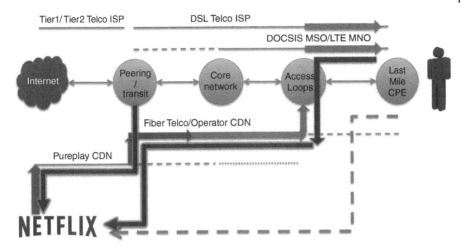

Figure 6.5 OTT and operator CDN models.

incentivizes the operator to maintain premium service and together Netflix and the operator are well aligned to deliver an excellent premium experience to the end users.

Pure OTT models typically do not provide a commercial incentive to the operator, and accordingly OTT providers may find that they do not have the leverage to ensure a high SLA in the content delivery.

6.4.4 Fog Distribution

Traditional server warehousing has become highly centralized as public cloud models and virtualization in data centers has taken off.

A Fog is a trendy new term for highly distributed computing models. Often coupled with the term "microservices," the principle is that you move all the computing to the data that you want to process.

As mentioned in many places in this text, there is now a trend to virtualize common network functions and to deploy them in a very lightweight way deeper into the network. These functions can – when targeting specific business problems – be very sophisticated, or at least specialized for certain functional models. They can increasingly deal with all the payment and security issues along with all the transcoding and packaging issues that a media network may require.

The next generations of live/linear CDNs will acquire content in a "mezzanine" format from a single multicast or broadcast feed, and will process the content for protection, device type and even delayed or on-demand playback from the very edge of the last mile network.

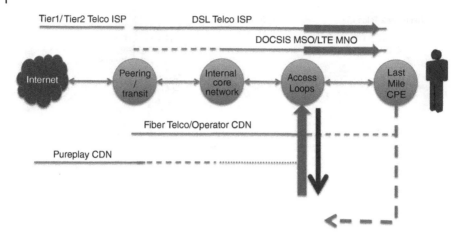

Figure 6.6 FOG distribution.

Over time we will see CDN edges appearing in mobile radio access networks (RANs) or in DSLAMs in Telco networks, or even in DOCSIS FTTC cabinets, as shown in Figure 6.6.

In fact, taking these virtualized models to the extreme edge, the customer's premises equipment (CPE) will eventually host microservices that transcode mezzanine content for each device type in the house. This way the household will need to only receive a single stream, even if multiple formats and bitrates are needed in the home network.

Such networks will require central orchestration, but very little of the video will travel from the hub to the edges of the spokes of the network; rather, it will be delivered by more efficient means, and prepared in the last stages of delivery for specific use.

6.4.5 Variation from Live Linear to VOD, and Everything in Between

As the various premium delivery systems evolve, the traditional modes of delivery have become blurred. It used to be that a broadcasting DTT over-the-air network, or a QAM cable broadcaster used to allocate some frequency for live/linear transmission, plug in the source and leave it broadcasting. Access to the channels was controlled via a separate "conditional access" control system. If you wanted to add video on demand, then it was likely that you needed to add a completely new technology overlay to the platform. It may share some of the common network links, although the video on-demand service would almost entirely signal over that network in a different way to the broadcast live/linear feeds.

Fast-forward to modern IP-based delivery networks, and there is barely any difference between live/linear workflows and on-demand workflows. This may or may not be true for the contribution feeds for the origination of the content, but this almost universally stands true in the distribution side of things. Once video moved away from session-based streaming protocols to adaptive bitrate, it has become incredibly difficult to separate the two, with just a few key indicators helping a network operator separate the two. The first is that the live/linear sessions typically run for longer than even the longest on-demand sessions, and the second is that the live/linear streams need to manage concurrent contention (demand) for service. Indeed an on-demand system has more flexibility because the contribution feed is coming from a memory storage system rather than from a network pipe.

Even "pause and rewind live" models essentially jump the consumer from the "most recently available fragment of video" to one that was cached within the last few minutes (etc.) – nothing else changes in the entire IP delivery. The same player technology decodes the content, and the same request router routes the user to the right fragment. The fragment's index number (or sequence number, etc.) may change as the user seeks the desired fragment, but the same edges, servers, and network pipes will be delivering the content.

This blurring of lines between live/linear/pausing live/start-over and catchup/on-demand services has provided premium operators with a number of innovative ways to repackage the commercial propositions to the consumer, with minimum reinvestment into the network.

Largely these services are all available to operators once they have the two extremes of live and an on-demand capability in place. The nuanced service models of catch-up/T-VOD/S-VOD, etc., can be introduced as soon as the KPI metrics about the consumers' usage can be accounted and inserted into the billing system and portals promoting the services.

As networks migrate more toward microservices and FOG architectures, we might expect to see more and more variations on these themes. Creative accounting around how they are propositioned to market makes them all possible so long as the rights owners see the right level of royalty benefit, and that they ultimately enhance the revenue generated by a particular event or title.

6.4.6 DRM

We touched on rights issues in Section 6.1. The tradition in IPR law was relatively intransient, having spent the hundred years or so before the Internet was invented and necessitated a global structure for protecting intellectual property rights. WIPO's history – particularly since the Berne convention – assumed that the natural friction in the distribution system was the cost of the mechanics to copy material, or the cost of the raw materials, or the physical network infrastructure. The model could not have foreseen a global distribution network that was more or less available to occasional or independent publishers if not for free then at least pay as you go.

The resulting change was that the pirate could set up a stall, relatively openly in terms of market discovery, and could reproduce someone else's intellectual property at virtually no cost, and entirely in response to paying demand.

With Information services unregulated from 1988 and exploding through the 1990s the IPR law was crippled by having a sudden influx of claims, but little or no precedent law cases to draw on to guide them in making useful policy.

Conditional access was considered a viable way to control access to rights – particularly by cable and satellite premium service operators.

In simple terms conditional access allows you, for the duration it is granted, access to all content secured within the network. The content within the network has little or no protection itself, other than the fact you can't find it unless you are allowed access. Once you have access you can just copy it.

So conditional access is typically simply a secure encrypted network connection.

When you are trapped behind a closed network terminated in a Set-Top Box, at a digital copy level you are – as a layperson – trapped behind a layer of security that ties the box to the network. You can't simply open the link, plug in your laptop with FTP, and copy the files in perfect/highest quality.

Obviously you can simply re-record the video output to the TV screen. And the quality loss is likely to be minimal. And indeed this is how the majority of live sports piracy is conducted today. For years the important message between network operators and rights owners has been "we will put in absolutely all the protection we can, but we won't guarantee any of it because a paying/legitimate customer can become the next pirate."

With the network secured, the "all the protection we can" focus was then directed at file encryption. The aim being that files were, in theory, always rights controlled – at every use. So digital rights management was incepted. Instead of locking the door to the library, the principle was that every book needed a key to open, and would only open for a limited time.

Again, a single paying-customer–turned-pirate foils the video DRM systems in an instant by screen grabbing a copy of the content he or she has legally paid for and making a digital copy. Despite that, there are numerous DRM systems in use in the commercial content distribution networks today. Most have become successful in SVOD and TVOD models, and are almost invariably used for premium live webcasts. They are, however, viewed more as a "compliance" technology rather than an "effective" technology.

These are the common DRMs:

- PlayReady – by Microsoft – has been largely adopted by the Hollywood studios for the best part of the last decade and is arguably the most widely used in premium content delivery. It relies on relatively simple public/private key encryption handled by app-layer plug-ins for various media players that have subscribed to the Microsoft relevant licensing.

- Widevine – now by Google – works on a wide range of platforms both Google's own and with integration to many third party software platforms by virtue of a license-free integration.
- Apple Fairplay – Apple's device centric (more to the point QuickTime) specific DRM platform naturally works with HLS.
- Adobe Primetime – Since Adobe was once the leading video distribution platform, it was natural that they eventually introduced a DRM system. And naturally it targets Adobe's AIR and Flash Media Player platforms. While Apple, Google, and PlayReady also have OS deployments, Adobe are an add on that the user needs to opt in to before being able to access Adobe DRM'd content, and while they still have very significant reach, in rights negotiations, that slightly smaller reach and access to market, compared to Microsoft, Apple, and Google, is probably why they renamed it Primetime from "Access."
- Marlin – Created as an open standard, Marlin has so far had limited deployments, notably in hybrid TV systems including HbbTV and the Playstation. Sony was one of the founding members of the consortium that set the standard in motion. The other founders are also all electronic manufacturing giants, including Panasonic and Samsung.[4] There has been much talk about it for some time, and in my gut I sense that it will become a significant DRM over the next few years.

DRM is a wonderful pub debate, or one for a long drive. It is clear that publishers, contractually and for compliance reasons, have to have a DRM strategy. It simply "looks bad" if you just give away the content without trying to protect it as far as possible.

However, the expectation is not that there will be no piracy. As iTunes prove, and Netflix followed with, the trick to making the content valuable is making it easy to discover and access.

Undeniably DRM makes that more difficult for the legitimate user, but for the pirates feeding off their backs with an infinite supply of rips and digital dubs, DRM is essentially an anathema to them, so (strangely some may say) they simply don't use it.

As a CDN architect, expect to support it. Just quietly raise an eyebrow, and if you are specifically asked, *never* promise it will make the CDN impervious to piracy!

6.4.7 Watermarking

Watermarking has been around since pre-digital days. The process of embossing, through a vaguely complex method, a secondary validation of the authenticity of a fixation of content has certainly had successes. Notable is paper cash.

---

4 https://en.wikipedia.org/wiki/MarlinMarlin_(DRM)

However, particularly in the digital world, one of the problems with watermarking is that it can be relatively simply removed. While this may be as simple as overwriting the channel ID bug with a black square, if the watermark is applied invisibly using steganography, then it can be placed anywhere in the video. To remove it, you would, broadly speaking, degrade the video quality. Depending on how the steganography is applied that may only be a small degeneration.

A bigger problem is that applying watermarks at scale is a complex task. For broadcast signals, sometimes a code has been burned in between the integrated receiver decoder (IRD) element of the receiver, and the video-rendering system. However, that pipeline can be relatively simply hacked. If you want to make your content hacker proof, then there is no point delivering him a clear signal in the first place …

… so watermarking has traditionally struggled because all content bears the same watermark. It ultimately only proves that it was that watermarked version that was pirated:

> Shameless plug here: At id3as we came up with a watermarking system that actually delivered each viewer a uniquely watermarked (through any watermark application model you want to plug in) stream at every distribution. This means that if the file is redistributed (which we think is unpreventable by force) the pirate copy can be traced back to the initial authorised user directly. If it is tampered with using other video of the same source, and if that second video is also from our network, then we will simply end up with a fingerprint of both pirates.
>
> We think that this model places the responsibility for antipiracy response clearly at the door of the rights holders: it presents them with the data to act. Critically this in turn frees up the distribution networks from having to bear the cost of this reaction (think ISP "take down notices") in order to fundamentally secure the business revenue strategy of a separate party – the rights holders.
>
> Sadly disruptive technologies are not always welcome, and while I do dream our watermarking technology could create a new tactic that while it doesn't prevent piracy, it does empower rights owners, who can isolate entities who are systematically pirating and target them with direct legal action, where today you largely have to prosecute vicariously "via the ISP and Telco because of privacy law" since only the last mile networks can tie IP addresses with residencies, and they are tied up with a great deal of regulation about releasing that. Our model allows the rights owner to examine a sample of "pirated" content and directly look up who they licensed it to who's copy was allowed to be pirated without needing to go through the ISP. From a technology point of view it works for DRM free content, simplifying issues such as targeting a universal HTML5 video renderer.

Some of this will be given more context in Chapter 7.

As a final comment very few CDN architects will ultimately have to do anything with Watermarks. The rights owners take a view that the 'DRM suffices, so lets focus on discovery' way forward is the best and has been so for some years.

Watermarking could be a disruptor in the right time, but for now the market – and in particular, the lawyers and accountants – are finding some working models with DRM, and is resistant to further major disruption.

Be ready to add a transparent "bug" if you ever have to capture video. But other than that, watermarking is, sadly, unlikely to become a widespread, and more important, a key accounting function in monetizing music or content online in the next few years. I do, however, expect it to emerge in the next 8 to 10 years as an increasingly interesting way to enforce rights – particularly of high-value premium live events.

7

Competition and the Regulatory Environment

In the preceding chapter I touched on several fairly sensitive aspects of the handling of content. In particular, DRM conversations can be fraught with strong opinions. But the topic is much broader than that. To really understand some of the historic evolution of the regulations that streaming and online content delivery engineers have to understand, one has to take a very encompassing view.

When I started webcasting, it was immediately apparent that I was entering a brave new world. There was a complete and utter sense of pioneering. The people who were interested and focusing on the technology were few and far between, and in terms of any regulation we were it. The only real regulation was one of our peers looking at what we were broadcasting or how we were using technology and sucking a tooth. The "policy" was highly opinionated and fell to each individual.

At the time the advertising standards bodies, the music licensing, the pornography "monitors" ... none of them had a strategy. Webcasts were open to tobacco funding, to running adult content 24/7, to streaming betting services from overseas, etc.

Sadly, I am not that "bad boy" – but I know so many groups and individuals who suddenly had unregulated businesses with access to vast new markets.

Particularly with porn, but also with betting and other content genres, the problem everywhere was that the companies were unable to prevent their competition taking market share from them. The porn industry had become so crowded that only occasional aggressive aggregators could rise up on the tide for their 15 minutes of "fame" but then loose out to the endless tide of unregulated competition.

So in the basic supply and demand economics, certainly as far as a content rights owner, or someone who monetizes rights, the digital age blew open the doors on not only the ability to deliver to the demand but also to the supply as it became relatively cheap to use a CDN.

The fairly regionalized regulators are still struggling to manage the content regulation, but that is, to me, no surprise. There is no "global" regulator beyond

Content Delivery Networks: Fundamentals, Design, and Evolution, First Edition. Dom Robinson.
© 2017 by John Wiley & Sons, Inc. Published 2017 by John Wiley & Sons, Inc.

WIPO, and they are ultimately part of the UN. In the next sections I will talk a little about how various key players are acting out a larger strategy than simple content and copyright.

I see all the supply–demand economics of the copyright content delivery models as existing in the "application layer" – in tech terms, layer 4.

Back at layer 3, we are trying to create an interoperable network framework, so we can easily provide access to our content inter-region.

But it is at layer 2 and below where the regulators are able to take some control over the very delivery networks themselves. This is where the content models that aspire to "go global" online need to develop more understanding, since we all have a strong but incorrect picture that the Internet is so decentralized that it is indestructible. That is how the Internet has developed a reputation as unregulated space for so long.

That could be changed though. To understand it, I need to take you back through some central parts of an Internet Governance Diploma sponsored by ISOC that I was privileged to take part in some years ago.

7.1   ISOC, ITU, and WSIS

Let me start with a little orientation.

ISOC is short for the Internet Society. I have been a member since the mid-1990s.

Here is ISOC's brief history in its own words[1]:

> The Internet Society and Internet History
>
> The Internet Society was formed in 1992 by Vint Cerf and Bob Kahn, two of the "Fathers of the Internet." The Internet Society's history and values reflect this founding lineage. Among its leadership and membership one can find many of the Internet's technical pioneers, innovators, and global connectors. Its mission—to promote the open development, evolution, and use of the Internet for the benefit of all people throughout the world—mirrors the guiding principles that gave rise to and enabled the propagation of our era's defining technology.
>
> For more than 20 years, the Internet Society has also played an important role in informing and creating the history of the Internet. The Internet Society's foundational pillars – Outreach, Technology, and Policy – have found expression in initiatives that have helped

---

1 http://www.internetsociety.org/history

to connect the world, supported the development of fundamental Internet technology, and promoted transparency and a multistakeholder, bottom-up approach in addressing global Internet governance issues.

Believing that "the Internet is for everyone," the Internet Society has worked since its founding to make that goal a reality.

ISOC ultimately could be viewed as a group of elders who help oversee the ethics of Internet Governance by guiding a collective of (originally US founded) independent bodies that collectively oversees components that "make the Internet" – such as standards. This puts ISOC in the firing line when representing "the Internet" in globally regionalized legal debates.

The typical interface the public may think of is Vint Cerf talking about net neutrality before the US Congress or a similar political enquiry.

ISOC is a product of the Internet. However, the Internet itself, while ultimately a coming together of many things, was underpinned by a single key change in regulation that occurred in 1988 in the Telecoms market.

At the time the ARPA net had been switched off for four years, and the Internet was becoming the de facto way for academic institutions to Inter-Network. It was far from a mass market technology.

However, the Telecoms market was under pressure to open up. The ITU updated the International Telecommunications Regulations (ITRs) in 1988. For various reasons it was decided that Information Services would be left unregulated as a trade-off for maintaining more regulation on the lucrative, but increasingly competitive, "minutes" business that Telcos traded in. More governance helped the bigger ITU members protect their interests. They didn't see information services as being a particularly lucrative side of their business for another decade. By which time they started a lobby to try to get the Internet back under governance by the ITU, claiming that the Internet was a communications tool, not an "information service."

That took a further 10 to 15 years to get back to the table, by which point the explosion of the Internet in Russia, China, India, and Brazil had changed scale completely, not to mention the political impact the Internet could have and with very little governance or control. These were previously disinterested members of the Internet's multistakeholder governance model, who now felt that they should have the right – as governments – to be able to impose governance. Ultimately The World Congress of Information Technology (WCIT-12) was chosen to create an agreement that ITU members would amend the ITRs to include the Internet as part of the ITU's remit for regulation. However no consensus on the amendment was finally reached.[2] Notably the BRIC countries were strongly in favor, and

---

2 https://www.asil.org/insights/volume/17/issue/6/internet-governance-and-international-law-controversy-concerning-revision

US and European countries were dominantly against, the amendments. It was clear that there has emerged divided thinking on the subject.

Some countries were ultimately motivated because the historic founding organizations that oversaw the coming together of the Internet were dominantly US based. Those countries – particularly BRIC countries – were thinking that it would be better to now annex that regulation clearly into UN oversight, and to exercise this by bringing Internet Governance under ITU authority.

As an interim point, note that each country has always had sovereign rights to govern its own regional Internet policy, although it was up to them to provide the resource to enforce such policy. Here in the UK there is a general self-governance policy, with a few overarching laws of the land such as copyright and those protecting minors that do in fact now regulate the Internet landscape in parts.

In China, famously, their perimeter IP is all "firewalled" and heavily regulated within that "Great Wall."

There is though, no central governance of the Internet today. There is no global ban that can be placed on a user, and no particular inter-regional laws that can enforce firewall or prioritization – at the moment such technical interfaces are purely down to the agreements between the connecting operators. Within a region the local operator might have to adhere to the law of the land in terms of what to allow into the country / region, etc., but the frontiers are currently unchecked by any bilateral oversight.

Anecdotally – purely because I cannot find a public record of something I recall strongly – governments that are driving toward this central regulatory ability have been accused of "mercantilism" by various key heads of policy in the ISP community. I think this is a very good way to view this. In a world where the Internet has disrupted the typical government's ability to control its propaganda, and to fiercely enforce tight borders, the Internet age has challenged not just the music and content industry but many industries. Those that are change resistant and conservative – as most governments tend to be – are wary of this, and feel the erosion of their ability to maintain a sovereign territory border within which and across which they can enforce duty and taxation through self-determination and regulation.

With other disruptions coming from Internet technologies such as bitcoin and social media, the traditional government models are fighting to adapt to this post-Internet era, and sometimes they simply weigh in with their protectionist boots on the ground and create government policy to highlight what grasp they do retain.

The ITU and WSIS position and thinking relating to overall Internet Governance is likely to go on for a good while. Indeed, if it doesn't find a new way to frame the debate, it is likely that the stalemate will deepen and ultimately balkanize the Internet into at least two or more regions.

It is clear that in terms of the Inter-Operator, inter-continental, and inter-regional networking, the traditional Tier-1 networks are really those Telcos that would be most faced with compliance changes if regulation does move to the ITU.

There are only around 18 Tier-1 networks with global presence.[3] All but one of them (Tata) currently has headquarters in Europe or the US. Tata is the only BRIC country headquartered Tier-1 Telco. Notionally I could see the other 17 of the 18 simply washing their hands of the ITU and leaving.

7.2   Policy – Net Neutrality

Among all the various Internet governance and policy debates is one topic guaranteed to inflame any debate: that of net neutrality.

I have, over the years, written a good deal about net neutrality. I have also learned that the term very much symbolizes a number of relatively unrelated topics, which become interchangeably linked, and this causes an incredible amount of confusion.

As ISOC summarize on their webpage on net neutrality[4]:

The Internet Society works on a range of issues that fall under the umbrella of net neutrality, including:

* Allowing the freedom of expression
* Supporting user choice
* Preventing discrimination

We also work with local and global businesses to develop solutions around things like:

* Network traffic management
* Pricing
* Business models

Call me an engineer, but just the scope of the list itself tells me that net neutrality has just become a policy "bucket" for policy makers to raise when they want to create a lot of debate, and look participant in a range of issues, while ensuring that there can barely be one policy that covers the range of issues required.

For me, the net neutrality debate struggles most with one underlying problem: the Internet doesn't actually exist(!). I am sure if it did then it *would* be neutral, but the term "Internet" is an abstract platonic ideal or even a collective

---

3 https://en.wikipedia.org/wiki/Tier_1_network
4 http://www.internetsociety.org/net-neutrality

noun describing in a singular way what in practice is a network of heterogeneous networks, each different, and each interconnected in a different way.

The ability for a poorly connected hosting farm with a single server, and located at the leaf of a sprawling remote network, to deliver a good quantity of content – such as a video stream – to a large user audience in another country is, in principle, much less likely than if those users are served by hundreds of servers located in a data hosting center co-located with their ISP. Even if all traffic on both systems is treated with neutrality, it is clear that one service will be better than the other.

With some of the slowest devices online still running at 9.6kbps, one way to ensure network neutrality would be to slow the net down to the lowest common denominator. But obviously that idea is mad. Forcing all networks to interface equally to achieve a neutral state is a ridiculous idea.

Another problem that some of the net neutrality debaters have is with competition. They see the ability to afford access to a CDN as a competition issue: smaller organizations often cannot afford access to their target market through a CDN, so those that do have something of a competitive advantage when guaranteeing SLA of premium content delivery. Some of these debates also talk about ISPs' "throttling" back services that may compete with other closer partners' services. Of course, all this leads to a fear that the likes of Netflix will tie up deals on various ISP networks, where it is essentially the only watchable platform.

In practice, throttling is only possible in areas where the traditional telecoms regulation has left the landscape uncompetitive. If a BT customer has a sense that channel1.tv (for example) was throttled on BT's service to the detriment of the users' experience, then the users may switch to Virgin or another ISP. However, in some areas only cable broadband is available, so it may not be that (for example) a Comcast customer can switch. This would indeed make it difficult if Comcast did throttle channel1.tv, perhaps in favor of comcastchannel1. tv. In reality, there is very little evidence for such anticompetitive service throttling. Most of the examples given have subsequently been proved to be traffic shaped by other events or by simply wrongly interpreted data. It is not without possibility, though, and some more intensive oversight may lessen throttling on a region-by-region basis. It is clear that in broad terms competition at many levels is fundamentally manageable through regional policy to ensure that companies play fair. However, any sense that the Internet can be transformed into a perfect scheme, with every service is equally deployed, is fantastical in the extreme.

For this reason CDNs will increasingly form a natural part of the network architecture landscape, and individuals will increasingly be able to use services such as those provided by public cloud operators like AWS to launch cheap, scalable, and well-connected service models, starting from bootstrap and growing with them to become global operators. Indeed that wonderfully woolly term "cloud" in some ways is taking the heat out of policy debates about the much more woolly term "net neutrality."

As a final comment, most people – at least those I know – believe that from an individual or even a company's point of view, equal access (to your competition) to given services is something of a right to demand. However, the practical reality is that commercial forces and technical evolution construct something of a postcode lottery about what service level can "actually" be accessed. That is not because you are being discriminated against; it is much more down to an almost chaotic number of service-affecting variables that are introduced for the delivery of any given Internet connection.

7.3   Value Chain Alignment with QoS and SLA Propositions

I see a very clear relationship between QoS guarantee / service level agreement and the confidence that network operators have in offering premium services. Ultimately content delivery without SLA makes a premium proposition difficult.

I also see that the closer to the subscriber edge that the rights deals can be made, and the content directly acquired to the remaining QoS-enabled network segments, the higher is the premium. Cable TV and IPTV services in these models are higher quality and therefore command higher premiums than OTT services with lower SLA structures. As end-to-end SLAs do become introduced more comprehensively, even for OTT services, more globally centralized premium rights models will become possible.

The regulation focused on advertised speeds by ISPs through the late 1990s and most of the first decade of this millennium ensured that 512Mbps was at least generally possible on a 512k line. I can see a similar situation arising in the policy and regulatory space where content publishers that offer a commercial service will increasingly be pressured to guarantee a minimum service level or return some of the service fees. While I believe that some OTT operators do try to offer this type of SLA, presently I am unaware of any regulation enforcing this. So I do expect, where there is commercial success, to swiftly see regulators take an interest in interfering.

7.4   Layer-2 Workaround?

One of the areas that policy such as net neutrality will cause some pressure is where limited content pathways can be opened up to deep edges, offering high SLA – for example, an operator CDN model or a multicast network – but (because the capacity of the specific service is limited) it may only become available to specific customers. Within end-to-end IP-only architectures that type of service layout may open up debates around net neutrality.

Many operators are realizing that by using hybrid models, they can, if not bypass, at least compound the complications around arguing that their service is not net neutral. To see this, say a DTT signal is acquired off a traditional broadcast transmission mux remotely at various data center edges and delivered into the IP infrastructure at the edge, without having to traverse the same IP routes as other video signals available at that edge. Then, because the broadcast network is not broadcasting in IP, it cannot be argued that the service was conflicting with net neutrality, even if the DTT broadcast signal was delivered to the data center with a completely different SLA model to the all IP broadcast.

By dropping out of IP into a lower layer-2 telecoms network protocol, it is quite possible that any net neutrality regulations that are introduced may just be worked around by the engineering teams and leave the publisher and end user with unequal service delivery models without actually affecting net neutrality …

… only time will tell. But expect eMBMS / LTE-broadcast services to be scrutinized for this exact situation as soon as the first commercial ones become available.

8

Cultural Change

8.1   Traditional Broadcasters

Cultural resistance to change is a central issue to manage when designing and deploying a CDN. There are many stakeholders who are affected by a CDN deployment, and despite best intentions, not all of them will see the benefits. I aim to provide a little of my view on the psyche of some of the players in the various stakeholder groups.

In most recent conferences over the past two or three years there has evolved a sense that most technical challenges faced by CDNs can be addressed. However, there is a universal sentiment that the biggest challenge facing CDN and IP video platforms is in cultural resistance to change.

I still see some companies proclaiming the imminent "death of SDI." Having myself spent 20 years delivering IP video, I had to go back to learn about this legacy technology, and yet there are many tens, if not hundreds of thousands, of TV broadcast companies that still run their operations with SDI as the backbone network technology. Those operators are, understandably set in their ways, working typically to a mantra of "it ain't broke, why fix it."

The intransience of others can be excruciating to live with, once you have yourself taken the mental step into the IP delivery paradigm. Even more so once you have gotten the service velocity advantages of microservices and the NFV models (which I discussed in detail in Chapter 7 above).

In my practical experience trying to proactively help traditional broadcast operators into the brave new world of IP is rarely easy. Patience is ultimately the best approach, but that also means setting that expectation in others. The traditional broadcaster is essentially used to a circuit-based private network. We are going to have to change that broadcaster's expectation to the service models offered by "best-effort" IP. Boadcasters will nit-pick over quality, since they are from an age where one expensive appliance produced one highly specified/restricted type of video, and if it wasn't compatible with the rest of the workflow, the workflow simply wouldn't work until either the vendor had

Content Delivery Networks: Fundamentals, Design, and Evolution, First Edition. Dom Robinson.
© 2017 by John Wiley & Sons, Inc. Published 2017 by John Wiley & Sons, Inc.

issued an upgrade or the unit was swapped for that of a different vendor. Such mistakes were costly, and network rollout was a complex waterfall business with huge associated costs.

It is a Herculean challenge to change the traditional broadcast culture to align with what Google, Apple, Facebook, Amazon (GAFA), and other IP centric companies (let alone the thousands of smaller companies who are operating that way) call DevOps or "agile" development.

The idea of continuous development within an infrastructure whose owners are used to the environment being closed, invariant, and homogeneous is a whole worldview change.

The TV boomers who now form the senior executive management of most infrastructures can see their kids and grandchildren occupied with smart devices, but they themselves still maintain that "it will never catch on" in some form of (to be honest slightly worrying) denial.

We are several generations of human resourcing in the streaming sector. Arguably we have rolled out more complex models in the short 10 to 15 years we have existed than the TV and broadcast networks have rolled out in 80 years. And that pace is accelerating. Through this we learn quickly. We fix quickly. The technology provides economic advantages and reaches the audience demanding the content.

Most broadcasters run 5- to 10-year strategy cycles. IP-based companies can afford to be more reactive to the markets, and those markets are driven by an increasing end user audience who are demanding new and different technologies all the time. Long technology cycles in the IP space are three to five years. Most changes are almost annual. Meeting that type of customer is not what the traditional broadcaster is used to.

There are huge parallels with the story of the music industry 15 years ago. There are protectionists who really want it to "all go away" and to return to a world where only TV broadcasters operated broadcast video, and they could dictate how it would be received and consumed. Today, the consumer decides the device and format for the content delivery, and the place and time. With so many technical service platforms now able to step up and meet that demand, the traditional models are simply too inflexible to remain relevant.

But the traditional broadcasters are big lumbering, and powerful dinosaurs, and they provide significant revenue to the rights holders and content providers. This is making rights deals for online operators difficult to obtain. The traditional networks simply have a lot of historic leverage. However that leverage is inexorably diminishing as independents like Netflix and iTunes show that there is huge potential value in online rights licensing.

While statistics may always interpret the situation favorably for one side or the other, the very evident fact is that as the present generation ages, it is moving toward IP for its connectivity and content consumption. Any broadcaster who denies that should look back at the music industry (covered in depth in Section 2.3.4).

The music industry used to comprise the recording industry along with the music rights owners. Now the reproduction industry is a poor ex-girlfriend of the music publishers who are doing licensing deals with online portals and seeing unprecedented revenue.

Today, the traditional TV industry is at an earlier stage of the same cycle. It is struggling to make that separation of infrastructure from rights aggregation. As commercial models prove the viability, shareholders will take interest and more focus will be placed on doing the online deals. We have already reached critical mass. In the past three or four years we have finally seen the rights holders start to seriously embrace online models, and if not openly, then by their actions they have admitted that IP is the future.

8.2 The Millenial Subscriber

Rather than try to bring in to the discussion a wide range of statistics on the millennial subscriber, statistics that invariably support the main sponsors worldview and defend their strategies, I am going to write here about the millennial from my own viewpoint.

I am an early adopter. I was online before the web was invented, and I was conversant with most of the device technologies as they emerged. So I am a digital native, although right at the very front of that wave, and I have a complete understanding of what came before. My parents, and to some extent my wife, had to learn how to use the web and email (etc.) rather than evolving with mail clients and browsers as they emerged from first principles. For me, this is mother tongue stuff rather than an acquired skill.

For nearly everyone younger than me, by the time they had access to a computer, it was online. That's what computers do isn't it? They provide access to the Internet?

However, for some of my peers and all of the generation before me, the Internet was something that you might consider adding to your computer. The computer was a glorified typewriter, with a few other bells and whistles.

Now I look at my daughter, born just when the iPad and Netflix were, and my son, who was born entirely into a smart TV chord-cut "connected" home, and I cannot imagine their general routine without hopping devices connected to what they want to be connected to.

It took longer to explain why they couldn't carry on streaming films to the iPad when we took it in the car, and away from WiFi, than it did for them to learn to use the device. This expectation is native to them. I fear a little for what they would do if the Internet simply weren't there. But we could say the same for currency, police, and roads, so we simply all normalize to it.

So I struggle with the (fortunately) increasingly few people who somehow think that the millennial will take out subscriptions to content packages, and to infrastructure services that tie them to a specific location. I honestly think that my daughter will be confused, as she moves into her student halls or first home (probably in a decade's time I hasten to add!) and she is approached for a fixed-line broadband service, and a cable or satellite service attached to the wall. In fact I am so sure her generation will not take out traditional cable or satellite (CabSat) services that I have a public bet with the head of the UK Digital Terrestrial Television Group, Richard Lindsay-Davis, that I will *eat* a cable or satellite Set-Top Box if my daughter has one installed in her home as an adult!

Obviously this anecdote is intended to amuse. But I also want to make the traditional operators think. While their annual growth of subscribers has traditionally been tied to factors such as new homeowners, students moving into the housing/rental market, in just a few years, all those new homeowners and students will most likely have a 4g or 5g mobile service and a couple of OTT subscriptions. They will be using technology like Apple's Airplay to forward the streams to specific larger displays.

This will cause a complete collapse in growth for the traditional networks, and as the older customers churn the operators will need to move to the OTT world with them, or face diminishing returns, or worse, collapse.

I have heard very strongly traditional broadcast consultancies try to brush off the millennial as "just a small trend" or "still insignificant." In polite company I would call that view optimistic. The reality is that impact will hit very hard as the first millennial school leavers come of age and take up their homes over the next three to five years, literally shelving the growth rates for these traditional subscriber networks.

The good news for streaming and CDN architects is that this means our technology will finally come of age.

8.3 ISP and Content Providers

When residential ISPs started up in the early and mid-1990s, they were, more or less entirely, focused on generating revenue from dial up users. The last mile Telco and the ISP were both aligned in that the longer you spent on the phone the more you paid the ISPs. They didn't care about what you actually did online, so long as you didn't call them for support. And that was basically it. Life was good for the ISPs.

Gradually they moved from minutes to always-on services with monthly billing, and the relationship with the last mile Telco changed. The ISP was essentially wholesale reselling "extra" always-on copper phone connections. However, given install quality/availability and service varied, the ISPs started to shop around much more, and eventually the last mile operators opened up their own direct-to-market/retail ISP services too.

As the music industry (in particular) started to struggle with its transition to online, they explored a numerous legal opportunities to attack the ISPs, squarely blaming them for the decline of their record revenues. Here in the UK the Electronic Commerce Directive brought in, and embodied in law, the general principle that the ISPs had self-regulated under, for the years up to that point, "mere-conduit."[1]

Mere-conduit states that operators will have no legal liability for the consequences of traffic passing through their network. By and large the ISP has been indemnified from liabilities caused by its customers.

As part of granting this mere-conduit status, the ISPs did have to agree to act swiftly if served a notice (called a "take down notice") of illegal activity on their networks. There have been cases where extreme piracy or extreme political or abuse websites have been blocked within territories and within specific AS network footprints. Generally, this has been brought about through laws relating to copyright or to public obscenities, and had the same action been carried out using paper, then the paper distributors would have been also forced to stop.

The "take down" approach was adopted between the music industry and the ISP community, and indeed other publishers, such as YouTube, have systems that can effect "take down" expediently and reasonably automatically on requests from trusted/known parties such as music rights holders.

The ISPs did push back on some of the proposed measures, not least to limit exposure to the cost of issuing "take down notices," not only in terms of execution but in terms of brand too.

Generally, though, the ISPs now have working processes in place, and essentially this has created some form of framework for the various parties to at least form a working arrangement.

Where I expect ISPs to start changing is that soon they will start to look for ways to upsell their subscriber value, and as content is becoming more available for online models, I predict more ISPs will start to offer IPTV services on their internal operator CDNs, and upsell high-quality video and VR as a "walled garden" service for on-net customers. As these models open up, it is doubtless that ISPs, which ultimately have direct relationships with subscribers – always of interest to those monetizing content – will start to find traction in the types of "IPTV walled garden" models offering premium content with billing for access to that content integrated with the ISP service billing. Models like this were tried 10 to 15 years ago online (think AOL Time-Warner), but this was long before there was any content available for such online models, and more important, before there was an ability to offer IP-based SLAs in an acceptable commercial way.

---

1 http://www.legislation.gov.uk/uksi/2002/2013/regulation/17/made

8.4   Telco and Telecoms

The Telco sector has historically remained aloof from the emerging online content delivery models, taking a more "mere-conduit" position than even the ISPs. As outlined in the comments in Chapter 7, Section 7.1, the Telcos in some ways gated themselves out of being able to competitively monetize content based on its type (other than voice minutes) through regulations that pre-dated the World Wide Web.

Once it became obvious that the vast majority of telecommunications-based businesses would be Internet based over time, the Telcos culturally shifted, and where IP used to be a part of a mixture of network service types, alongside frame-relay, ATM, and other such technologies, Telcos are today almost singular in their drive to focus on IP.

That is not to say they entirely "get it" – which is, in some ways, odd given that IP and the Internet exist within the Telcos. But much like a sports hall owner may not understand all the sports played in his hall, Telcos have typically been cautious with their own direct-to-market retail ISPs, waiting for their wholesale customers to pave the way and demonstrate how to deliver IP to markets, and then copying them.

Today's operator ISPs are now much better placed than they were and are starting to enter into premium rights negotiations already. BT Vision has been vying with Sky for premiership Ffootball rights for the past few years. Slowly but with acceleration this landscape is transforming.

8.5   Content Providers

In 1996 Bill Gates published a hard to find paper called "Content is King," coining a powerful phrase and concept that both endeared content providers to Microsoft (presumably its initial intention) and also, I would argue, dropped the content providers defenses (intentionally or not), opening up the IT industries' ensuing disruption of their sector.

I have enjoyed some raging debates on this topic. There are strong arguments that "infrastructure" or "consumer" is king, and not "content." My own position is that it is like saying "supply is king" when looking at the economic law of supply and demand that arose in the eighteenth century. They are different facets on a complete system that define each other by coexistence. Remove one, and the other becomes meaningless.

That said, rights law, as it has emerged under the auspices of WIPO in the recent decades, definitely gives content providers the ability to curtail distributions of content in purely legal ways, arguably a "king's choice." By comparison, the consumer is provided options – generally, a limited Hobson's choice of options – that is carefully controlled by the content rights holder and somewhere in the middle the infrastructure is purely the enabler. At least this is the case for "legal" content distribution.

What happened, as the Internet opened up, was that it became easy to provide consumers with access to pirate content. Piracy had traditionally been tied to costly manufacturing of fixations. Be they illegal paper-printed bibles, or cassettes, or DVDs, the pirate had to take some significant capital risk in preparing stock to then sell to market. To some extent this limited piracy in the pre-digital age.

That all changed when digital piracy made it possible to easily and freely redistribute perfect copies of content, in direct reaction to the individual consumer's demand for that material.

At first the exploding Internet and World Wide Web were perceived to be bringing about a vast demand for content into a market that the content providers had monopolized for decades (if not centuries). This anticipation of vast demand for a hitherto limited supply brought about the underpinnings of the dot-com bubble. What emerged, in reality, was that the supply of competing options to feed that demand was also unlimited. As this sunk in, the dot-com bubble burst.

Even in terms of nonpirate content production small "independent" producers ("Indies") could reach the Internet market with the same cost as "Majors" (here we are talking about TV, music, or film, although the same will apply to most content sectors). This massive change in supply left the consumers with an almost infinite option, and so competition made it extremely difficult to maintain price.

As I discussed earlier in Chapter 2, Section 2.3.8, by the mid-2000s content providers were learning that the key to unlocking the portentous value of these vast audiences was not in trying to protect the fixations of the items of content using DRM or conditional access specifically but in offering well-curated and easy-to-use discovery. While the web itself was an amazingly versatile tool for searching for content, filtering out all the fake links, dead URLs, or simply badly indexed content from the content the user wanted was painstaking.

This content discovery has been very much a two way street: not only has it worked for consumers, but also critically, content providers themselves have "discovered their audiences" amid the vast noise of the Internet.

This change in culture has been key to the success that is now making the online content provider market the multibillion dollar industry it has become in just a little over a decade.

9

Preparing for Change in Your Design

9.1 Preface and Philosophy

In these last chapters I am going to turn back to explain more fully why the
title of the book, and to think a little about why you picked up the book to read
it. I will try to guess what it was you sought from these pages and, admittedly,
be making a few obvious assumptions about those things. I am also going to
try to offer some thoughts on "how to lay the foundations for a good CDN
implementation" and all the work that entails, while writing from as generic a
perspective as possible to meet the many different expectations of the readers
this book may reach.

This commentary should be viewed purely as an insight into my way of doing
things. It is certainly not a "how to" guide for best practice. There are many
engineering consultants who can almost certainly offer a more disciplined
approach, and indeed 25 years ago I spent studying systems engineering – in
particular "decision support" systems – as I was developing computer telephony integration (CTI) for some early call centers I ashamedly built (and I have
never quite lived down the guilt!). The analytical design process is fascinating
in its own right and can provide a great resource in certain contexts.

In practice, however, I have come to my own conclusion that such disciplined models, if overly enforced, solve the problem that they were designed
to solve, but not the particular problem that the client in front of you requires
a solution for.

As I moved into the entirely new field of CDN and streaming media, one of
the things that attracted me was the utter lack of convention. The sector is
young enough that it is still very results focused.

I have no MBA or indeed many other qualifications in the sector. In many
ways I am a tradesperson, not a professional with portable skills. I am accus-
tomed to practice in an area where everything is new and has no formal process.
So as far as streaming media infrastructure goes, I am no great believer in best
practice. For me, it is imperative to pay attention to the problem I am trying to

Content Delivery Networks: Fundamentals, Design, and Evolution, First Edition. Dom Robinson.
© 2017 by John Wiley & Sons, Inc. Published 2017 by John Wiley & Sons, Inc.

solve with the CDN design. If that problem is interoperability, then I design for that. But if that problem is cost, or performance, or unique features (etc.), then I design solutions for that problem.

Yes, of course, there exist myriad common problems – and sometimes these are so common that it makes sense to create a common product as a solution. However, once the product defines the problem space, many vendors have to work with their clients to engineer expensive problems to then sell expensive solutions.

At id3as we specialize in "tailored" solutions. We do not offer off-the-peg models, and for this reason we talk of approach and capability rather than methodology and feature-set.

When designing with a client, I believe that it is essential to not be afraid to ask basic questions. As my colleague Adrian Roe says, "In a workflow running from a to b to c to d, why don't we just engineer from a to d directly?" Thinking around the problem laterally can make dramatic differences – even if they render some of the existing workflow redundant. Simplicity is invariably easier to deliver and support.

With this approach you can simplify vast, seemingly complex infrastructures into much smaller components. Indeed CDNs are invariably "macros" of many moving parts that end up working in concert to perform a relatively limited set of overall functions for the wider system that they deliver to. The inputs are fairly well defined, and the outputs are invariably well defined, since that is usually why the CDN is considered to be a solution in the first place.

Internally the design should always remain simple. Visio diagrams that seem to architect the Star-Ship Enterprise in atomic detail may look impressive, and may look like you have over delivered, but in practice, you are more than likely to be including complexity, and complexity is bad, not clever.

So ask stupid questions, listen to the client really define the problem their company is trying to solve, and not just the specific problem the client has brought you in to solve. Solve the fundamental problem – critically – and don't disempower the client on the way! Ask questions that provide context, and understand the context, for in the context you will find the core business objectives for the CDN and the real constraints, or at least the perceived "real" constraints, and perhaps your design will not overwhelm the client but will show a simpler and arguably "better" path where the constraints as they were simply become irrelevant.

And one final comment is on taking a position: Always make sure the client takes "ownership." As you do the design, once you make that critical leap yourself, do not present it as your "fait accompli" – instead help your client discover that along with you – so take your own cap in your hand and congratulate the client for the brilliant idea. In that capacity you will develop the longest relationship and have the best alignment for what is actually your design.

9.2 Models, Diagrams, and Schematics

I cannot emphasize enough how essential it is to be able to draw simple diagrams to present your strategy. Learn to diagram before you learn to write, and do both before you start to speak. However abstract the term "design" has become in vernacular use, there is still a sense that designers can "draw" anything. If you are designing a CDN, then deliver on this one expectation.

From these diagrams comes common terminology, and that must be ingrained into the language of the wider stakeholders in the CDN design.

For this reason create simple top-level models. If your design is good, it will remain constant throughout the lifecycle of the project. It will doubtless be versioned many times. But if the most recent design is vastly different from the first, then it is likely the business objectives have changed, or, if they haven't changed, then the system has lost sight of its objectives.

In the imaginary CDN team office that design should be on a whiteboard above the office fireplace! The network operations center's walls should still contain the essence of your diagram in the oversight and monitoring systems.

When developing the design models, focus on all the objectives at all times. Every diagram should be "complete" and not just show isolated "subcomponents." This is key to maintaining purpose. Even when you are focusing on a specific subprocess, ensure that all the inputs and outputs are still represented, even if cursorily.

9.3 How to do a Good Diagram?

First make sure you start on a freehand drawing tool! In the same way you would use bullet points to start a narrative, use a pen and paper, or a whiteboard, or even better a digital whiteboard (so you can digitize the initial drawings – where arguably some of the most creative thoughts are captured) to quickly frame the basic model. And keep all these early sketches – however wrong you think they were, it will save you from having to recall why you think they are wrong.

One of the systems engineering building blocks I tend to use often is as follows: Start with a blank sheet. Draw a circle. That which is inside the circle is in my scope of responsibility, and that which is outside is the responsibility of others. That circle defines the worldview from the designer's perspective. In German, this translates as *Weltanschauung,* and this terms crops up often in some schools of systems architecture. It greatly helps define roles, responsibilities, and interfaces. I find the more common term "scope" a little limiting in its general interpretation; it does not allow for variation in the surrounding influences. Worldview modeling is very useful. The wide contextualization it forces de-risks things, not only for the client, but for the designer too.

While I like the worldview modeling, I differ with many of these systems methodologies in one key aspect. These suggest including "constraints" as an input at the outset of the design. I don't – not for first pass. I prefer to design models for the ideal ("unconstrained") solution to the problem. I know that a million factors may constrain it. That is natural. I always let the model become constrained by all the stakeholders, and not my own assumptions.

However, if you start with the unconstrained model, and present that up front as a "what I would do if it was possible," and then "throw it away" in front of the client and turn to the constrained model, the client will immediately have both strategy to plan forward with, and yet a sense that you have empathy for the practical reality of the situation, despite the frustrations the client might have to deal with, and this will help begin to move everything toward the "ideal" design now the client will have conviction (with your support) that strategic aims are at least technically feasible. Sometimes it is simply valuable to demonstrate the "art of the possible."

Once you have your basic worldview model of the system in place, then add schematic overlays showing workflows. Scenario plan the workflows thinking "up and down the entire network stack and storage pyramid" at every stage both mid-process and inter-process. It may be useful to keep referring back to both Figure 2.1 (classic live streaming workflow) and to Figure 3.5 (storage model).

Again, on one level this all seems so incredibly crude, but if you develop principles, and constantly refer back to underlying related models like these, then your architecture will have some solidity in its foundations, and "feel" familiar to those stakeholders who need to buy into the design.

Briefly and just for interest (and because it seems odd to talk so much about diagrams without including one!) I have included Figure 9.1 showing the CDN design template I occasionally use. Notice how quickly it can be used to overlay workflows and start to map out everything from layer 1 to layer 4.

9.4 Scenario Planning

When you have a full ideal schematic model in place, then it's time to think about production realities.

Not by any means a rule, but I like to think about design from four approaches:

- Political – Manage disruptive change gently.
- Success – Who defines success? What does success look like?
- Constraints – Keep the worldview model in hand all the time.
- Delivery – What are the key deliverables and when are they promised. No more than high-level milestones needed.

And always be prepared to throw away yesterday's "best idea ever" and replace it with today's "even better idea!"

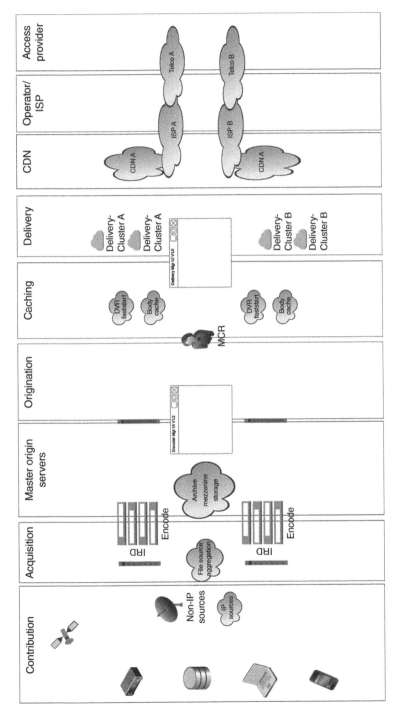

Figure 9.1 CDN design template I have used on occasion.

9.5 Risk, Responsibility, and Reassurance

Make sure the client's expectations are pragmatic. IP is generally provided in a shared network environment, and its service is best effort. While SLAs may guarantee nine-nines availability, if that 2 seconds of annual outage happens in the middle of the 100 m final, then the rest of the uptime means nothing to the end users and client. Your clients have to understand that risk!

As the number of eyeballs consuming content from your distribution network grows, the heat from those 2 seconds of outage grows in the actual event of that failure happening.

As a CDN designer you need your clients to be judicious and to understand that risk, and that they cannot pass that ultimate liability on to you! So you must build trust, and ensure that they know you are aligned in reducing that risk, but that it is ultimately their risk, not yours.

However, rather than phrase it in those terms, ensure that the client is clear about what "good enough" will be from the outset, and put 80% of your effort into that, and only 20% into the nice-to-have extra features.

Only once you have a good enough system live, and a happy client, then you might consider starting to test new technologies in a DevOps fashion, constantly rolling out new features to small groups and expanding the availability of that new capability to larger actual audiences.

By evolving the system this way, you can quickly find the Heisenbugs[1] that are almost impossible to find in any other form of testing. This type of pragmatic evolution of the design is a tricky concept to introduce to a traditional broadcaster. The benefit of virtualization is counterintuitive for those who have themselves evolved their legacy networks in a very different mode. But there is almost no doubt in my mind that it leads more quickly to a better deployment than any other model I have had first-hand witness to.

9.6 Optimization and Upsell

If the initial goals are met to good enough levels, then anything more is a bonus, and that bonus can be offered as an upsell as it becomes tested and viable. By implementing a good enough approach, you will acquire customers that won't hesitate to buy more in the context of a working reliable and good enough solution. So long as the system is scaled correctly to its top-level demand – something increasingly possible with cloud models – the entire value chain aligns for growth.

---

1 https://en.wikipedia.org/wiki/Heisenbug

Most CDN designs can readily offer a good enough service models. The most important value proposition to the consumer isn't then how well the video is delivered but what the content is. If the content is well placed, easy to discover, and the distribution is good enough, then the "delivery" will be a success. If the distribution is much more than good enough, then you will see diminishing returns for the investment in the "excess" capabilities. Sometimes these returns will have other strategic benefits to the business owner/CDN customer, and these should be captured at design time as pressures, but while the "latest" feature may turn a niche of heads, nothing turns everyone's head the other way if the core service proposition of a CDN – delivering content – fails.

9.7 Value Creation/Agility

A well-designed network may both be extremely lean and tuned to its purpose, but a well-designed network will also be able to adapt to changes. Many technology stacks are built to embrace all the current options and leave the customer to configure all the required changes. That is tantamount to providing someone with a limited coding language and telling them to get learning.

Immediate value can be created when you can deliver clients what they need in a simple form, but in a way that can be put into service quickly. Long-term value can be created when that system is agile and can evolve with the clients' requirements and the end users demands.

9.8 Expectation Management

The customer requiring a CDN is often quite confused about what it wants the CDN to do – if you explore the client's requirement in detail. Some clients do think they have a detailed and clear requirement definition, but most will try to describe a detailed solution for an ill-defined problem.

While they will often tell you they need a range of specific key performance indicators, or features, they have almost always lost sight of the fact that what they *really* want is a good clean end user experience. Understanding and, more important, managing the audience's expectations are paramount.

It is worth noting this as a reason that the industry has generally responded well to a move toward a focus on "quality of experience" and away from SLA and KPI as I touched on earlier.

Returning to "good enough is good enough" all the time will ensure that there is a focus on first and foremost delivering a working and usable solution. Most customers think they want all the latest bells and whistles, but often they overlook the fact that something less racy will actually be more reliable and help them succeed in delivering the content better than the very latest technology.

Expectation management starts on day one. Any CDN that promises anything more than it can certainly deliver will fail on the slightest detailed performance measurement.

With so many variables in action within the typical CDN, it is important to make sure that the client remains aware that the "simple effect" of delivering media to a device is, behind the scenes, immense and complex.

To be sure, if expectations are managed properly, everyone is happy. This may be a little bitter sounding final note, but the most emotionally difficult-to-deal-with result of all the effort of delivering a CDN platform is that when it works it is a thankless task, yet should it fail, the problem is often very high profile.

10

Multicast – the Sleeping Giant

It has been said, by more than a few of my close friends, that I can talk endlessly about IP multicast. It has fascinated me since I first heard of it back in the mid-1990s. My exposure has been pretty deep.

In the early pages of this book – Section 1.2 to be exact – I touched on some of the early factors that piqued my interest. But I want to take a voyage into multicast and, looking into the crystal ball, more specifically focus around what I think IP multicast can bring, and how tantalizingly near with the technology, yet so far culturally we are from bringing that to be possible.

10.1 Multicast Recap

Multicast came about when Steve Deering – lead designer of IPv6 – postulated IP multicast extensions in the IETF RFC966.[1]

This is not the right book for a detailed breakdown of IP and IP classes, so I will either assume you know or can otherwise research this elsewhere. Here I want to try to create a simple picture of multicast and, more important, the challenges it faces in technical deployment for a CDN.

10.1.1 Basics

IP multicast aims to deliver the same packet to multiple receivers. That is essentially it. In its early days it was termed "selective broadcast" because the model was to open a selective path through the IP network – rather than open the entire network for a "broadcast" (which would congest networks where the data wasn't wanted) – and to then transmit the packet once on the wire, but at a point where all those nodes that did want to receive the packet were listening and received the transmission "as if" it had been broadcast. This essentially meant that you could indefinitely increase the receiver numbers until the

---

1 https://tools.ietf.org/html/rfc966

Content Delivery Networks: Fundamentals, Design, and Evolution, First Edition. Dom Robinson.
© 2017 by John Wiley & Sons, Inc. Published 2017 by John Wiley & Sons, Inc.

unlikely time (on the Internet at least) that all nodes wanted to receive that transmission, at which point the multicast would "be" a broadcast.

One of the challenges is that not all packet forwarding in IP networks is carried out in the same way at all points.

Between nodes on a LAN, where computers are directly connected to each other through a local switch or hub, multicasting very much is possible. Since the packets are not being routed – but simply switched – a receiver simply registers with the switch by listening to it, and when the multicast sender transmits, then – without any extra effort – the switch will allow all listeners to receive that transmitted packet.

Routers connect different network segments together, such as LANs to LANs or LANs to ISPs.

Once the multicast LAN segment connects to a router, that router has to make a routing decision, acting as an "agent" for any upstream receivers, to join the multicast or not. The intelligence has to be introduced, allowing the router to know when to forward the packet on to another network segment.

10.1.2 Routing Protocols

This "intelligence" is called a Multicast Routing Protocol. Somewhere upstream the remote receiver that wants to join the multicast on the original LAN needs to signal back to the router that it wishes the router to join the multicast on its behalf, acquire the multicast packet from the transmitting LAN, and forward it to the remote receiver.

In order to achieve scale, the router should also only need to do this once for all receivers connected on the upstream networks. If there is a public Internet connection somewhere between the original router and the "rest of the Internet," it may be that that the router at that public connection (while not strictly accurate in all models, let's call this a "peering" router) has requests from multiple peer networks, and the peering router will need to forward that packet just once over each of its own interfaces to its peered networks.

The deployment of a suitable Multicast Routing Protocol is what people typically talk about when exploring if a network is "multicast enabled." It is generally true to say that unless a security policy has actively prevented multicast on a LAN segment, all LANs are already multicast enabled (some engineers talk about "multicast aware").

However, if the routers cannot negotiate which interfaces to forward a multicast to, nor where to actively join the original transmission on behalf of its downstream connections, then the multicast is not enabled and cannot flow from the transmitter to the receivers on the rest of the Internet.

In practice, very few ISPs allow their end users to send IP multicast upstream past their customer premises equipment (CPE). The CPE may even offer a variant of IGMP (the Internet Group Management Protocol that allows users to forward requests to join multicasts, and is used to store "active subscriptions") for given multicasts on a given router. However, the IGMPv2 requests are rarely forwarded to the ISP's peering router, and extremely rarely forwarded over the public peerings and transit connections between ISPs.

10.1.3 Flood, Prune, Storms, and a Bad Taste

In part conservatism toward multicast is a security approach (human decision/ by design), but in part this is because of the history of multicast discovery. When multicast was first introduced in the mid-1990s, the models all assumed that end users would be remote, and not necessarily have a two-way connected session anywhere. In fact such a two-way connected session was "the enemy" in the design principle, and so new subscribers were "discovered" by periodically "flooding" an announcement to all parts of the networks connected to the transmitting router, allowing would-be subscribers to receive a detailed guide of the available multicasts, and then to listen for further specific floods of packets, or to, in theory, "prune" themselves out of the listening network, until the flood processed checked in again.

The problem was that these floods themselves had a technical issue: they would sometimes find a secondary path back to the originating network, causing a phenomenon termed "broadcast storms." A simple analogy to understand these by is to think about "audio feedback" when you hear your local pub band set up. That screeching noise when the singer's microphone starts to amplify the PA system and a deafening runaway cycle of sound knocks your hearing out for a minute or two. While there are some technical ways (TTL is worth exploring) to solve broadcast storms, in the mid-1990s, when the first flood-and-prune protocol-based multicast tests were occurring, these unexpected storms knocked out entire ISPs, filling their networks with noise and clogging up all available routes. The network essentially needed a reset to quell the traffic. A major outage scenario!

Rapidly multicast was stained with this legacy. The problem with a Heisenbug when it causes a major outage of a large network is that the fear of it happening again reduces the confidence in the new technology, and its ability to migrate from the developer's desk is limited – if not forever, then for a very long time.

By the end of the decade a new generation of multicast protocols was emerging that relied on the two-way nature of the Internet to allow would-be recipients to "explicitly join" a multicast tree emerged. The problem of the broadcast storm was firmly solved. Yet by then the topic of IP multicast had been tarnished so badly that ISP's CTO were reluctant to give it another go.

10.1.4 Commercial Outcome

There was a commercial issue that arose at this time too. CTOs like to have tools in their arsenal to use to optimize their network. The issue with multicast has been that the candidate applications for multicast have never been given the opportunities to mature to the point where they can commercially make enough difference to justify implementation.

As I mentioned in Section 1.2 when talking of my CDN, Global-MIX, the incentive to reduce 20Gbps of traffic on a 40Tbps overall volume was arguably worth doing for one of our peering partners. However, in doing so, our buying power in the general data market decreased, so our unicast purchasing costs (still 80% of the overall traffic) went down, in turn inflating the price of our on-demand delivery services and compromising our wider business. It became commercially inefficient to be efficient.

It was much the same for ISPs. Video online was in its infancy, and the "risk" of multicast combined with the relatively small commercial benefits did not inspire the ISPs and Telcos to simply turn it on. The only time this model works is when you launch a service that can only scale with multicast, such as IPTV where the operator is commercially involved with the market, and as a result aligned with optimization, quality, and value.

Today, this is where we stand. IP multicast capability is nearly ubiquitous but crippled to the LAN. IP multicast services are easily made available. There are some variations on how it can be done, and this means there needs to be some coordination, and while this could be driven by standards bodies, it can also be driven by functional requirements underpinning wider strategies such as IPTV and operator CDNs have in those larger Telcos seeking content revenue.

10.2   What Happens Now?

All is not lost, however. IPv6 multicast is baked into its functionality and the routing protocols are better coordinated. This is not least because Steve Deering – inceptor of multicast – also led the IPv6 protocol definition. Logically we ultimately should see a full migration of all IP network services to IPv6. This has dramatically accelerated since IPv4 address block registrations were all allocated.

Indeed most established ISPs are in the process of delivering IPv6 to the end user, and most IP core networks are already operating on IPv6.

As users churn their devices and their CPE, IPv6 is becoming widespread. Developing nations will be deploying new network infrastructure and will go straight to IPv6.

Multicast is a prerequisite on the LAN for IPv6, and not simply a "nice to have" as it was for IPv4. Service discovery, which IPv4 conducted through "broadcast" (effectively flood and prune, but limited to the local LAN segment) is now conducted by IPv6 using multicast.

While this approach doesn't magically solve the Multicast Routing Protocol issue, there is also a new approach to deployment of the multicast protocol (to which I have made a tiny contribution about use cases myself[2]) that is being championed by my friend Greg Shepherd, Cisco fellow and thought leader in the space.

It is called "bit indexed explicit replication (BIER)." One of the key issues with Multicast Routing Protocols, as they have historically existed, is that they needed to ask every router on the multicast spanning tree to hold "state" – a list of all the downstream listeners and upstream sources of each multicast. That itself was a scaling issue, particularly between the routers of large operator CDNs.

BIER follows a common trend that has evolved with IPv6, which is to move state from the network to the packets of data that are being forwarded. By doing this, the router has become simpler and doesn't require memory to store state, so each packet can be dealt with independently, without referring to a "master list" – saving processing cycles.

BIER is fast becoming a working and available technology. As it (or something similar) does, it enables LAN-to-LAN "routed multicast" to proliferate, and makes inter-domain and inter-AS multicasting more attainable as a "normal" capability of the Internet.

Similarly it is likely at layer-1 all consumer devices will become dominantly mobile, and mobile ISPs have good IPv6 deployment. They additionally bring some layer-2 solutions that are essentially capable to extend some IP multicast models (particularly one-to-many) to the handset (such as LTE-broadcast/ eMBMS – see Section 7.4).

Any device should be able to directly deliver a live stream to all the viewers who wish to connect to that stream. As this happens, it will open up the TV models, although (particularly for mobile) these will not instantly open to the general public (there are still general spectrum and front-haul capacity limitations to overcome). There will most likely be a gradual, controlled, and phased introduction of such services to carefully limit supply for the most demanded models (TV?) and maximize profit by maintaining price, enabling the operator to negotiate with content providers even better.

Over time, as such models commoditize, it seems that there will be a tipping point where the layer-2 limitations are worked out, and these IP networks open up to the idea of many–many multicast. This could ultimately mean that any Internet connection could transmit a live video picture to (notionally) all other users with minimum network impact, entirely by routing, and with not a server, edge, or proxy in sight.

---

2 https://datatracker.ietf.org/doc/draft-ietf-bier-use-cases/

10.3 To Singularity and Beyond

While one-to-many streaming may be very interesting to ensure scale for live and linear online TV-like services, for me, looking a little beyond that, the really exciting thing is that with multicast comes the option to develop many–many multicast models.

So far, because the capability isn't really set up on many networks at all, there are very few real-world examples of a many–many multicast-based applications anywhere.

But, if developers were given the opportunity to innovate in this area, there are numerous possibilities I believe that scaling multicast to many–many models could potentially bring.

There is a widely spoken notion of "technological singularity" – that we are, as a civilization, nearing the point where our technology overtakes us. The Wikipedia definition is robust[3]:

> The technological singularity (also, simply, the singularity) is the hypothesis that the invention of artificial superintelligence will abruptly trigger runaway technological growth, resulting in unfathomable changes to human civilization. According to this hypothesis, an upgradable intelligent agent (such as a computer running software-based artificial general intelligence) would enter a "runaway reaction" of self-improvement cycles, with each new and more intelligent generation appearing more and more rapidly, causing an intelligence explosion and resulting in a powerful superintelligence that would, qualitatively, far surpass all human intelligence.

Artificial intelligence (AI), upon which the notion of singularity is predicated, is really a layer-4 challenge rather than something obviously related to IP multicast in layers 2 and 3. Yet, an entire evolution of application design (such as "singularity" would require) in layer-4 may itself be predicated by a change in available capabilities provided by the network on which the application can be run.

In the constraints of today's general networking, we typically have applications that are either unicasting data point to point, and when there are many end points to serve, we do this in a (broadly/simplistically speaking) "round robin" unicast way. TCP can service many clients in this way, and indeed today's HTTP and streaming infrastructures – the ones that have been at the center of this book – are able to scale significantly.

---

3 https://en.wikipedia.org/wiki/Technological_singularity

Indeed breaking headline news video is, today, one of the most significant "scaling" challenges we face in the CDN space. And much of this book has been underpinned by that thinking, as it is broadly where we are as a streaming and CDN industry today. The obvious candidate for scaling live TV is clearly IP multicast, which is well known to be technically possible but is caught up behind a number of challenges concerning disruption of the cultures of production, network operator commercials, and rights. The technology is there but the will to adopt it is in transition, and not entirely "there" yet.

Sad though it may sound, I often lay awake at night trying to re-scope my own sense of scale for content delivery and push myself to think of applications that may require orders of magnitude more scale than live TV. I ponder what other industries may benefit from IP multicast, and not only in a one–many model but also in a many–many model?

In order to try to scale out further I lack real-world applications to model against. This is in part because I haven't yet conceived/discovered/realized or even understood the problems I can solve with technology. So I am unable to articulate them, let alone define models and solutions to those problems.

In my gut I feel the most immediate candidates for next-generation application design, which may benefit from IP multicast becoming more widely available, are video conferencing and virtual reality. Potentially significant bidirectional data flows helping large groups "meet" in VR space. These begin to suit a many–many IP multicast paradigm.

Once data can flow from all points of the network to all other points concurrently (rather than round robin) and also follow the end-to-end principle[4] (and so reducing complexity) with technologies like BIER, new – and importantly low-latency models like these can be considered.

Massive multiplayer online (MMO) gaming platforms today largely rely on predistributing the graphic content, and they share metadata about the players' deltas from a previous known state. They share only tiny amounts of "change-data" and reflect the change on the other players' machines as a "local copy" of the region of the MMO.

As IP multicast models arrive, the MMO could become a more truly "shared" space, streamed from a core where the game world is created and the end user viewpoints are streaming "windows" on that world. This could change the distribution models at one level. At another level it may change the entire game design.

Another model that I feel could emerge is in discovery and learning.

When a kid in a school hears others question the teacher, he gains from hearing the answer even without having asked the question himself.

---

4 https://en.wikipedia.org/wiki/End-to-end_principle

Today, when I search Google, I "ask it a question" and "it replies" directly to me. There is no opportunity for any third party to benefit from that interaction (apart perhaps from Google itself).

With a properly scaled up IP multicast model, there is no reason why I couldn't set up a model where if questions are asked online about a particular topic, and if a response is returned, that response could be sent to multiple subscribed end points. If I wanted to subscribe to the responses for all searches that included "BIER" in real time, I could just watch my screen and learn as the entire community develops the construct and searches for contributions to that process.

In a human context this seems a bit limited, and indeed bulletin boards, Twitter, RSS feeds, and the like, may at first appear to offer something of this type of capability. But typically they are limited to small chunks of data, so applications that may use this type of messaging are sharing data in a very limited way.

But, if the model is extrapolated somewhat, I could imagine machine-to-machine (M2M) communications benefiting from this type of data-sharing model extensively.

In a "superintelligent" system, for example, "context" and "awareness" of all points on the network could be constantly communicated to all other points by IP multicast (in a way that neither unicast nor broadcast could offer in terms of scale), allowing the system to include a far wider and, to a human, seemingly chaotic amount of influences on every decision.

In some-ways at id3as, we already use this thinking to manage our virtual workflows and optimize deployment and traffic. Yet, the possibilities of this capability are, almost by definition, a generation beyond our own ability to design applications. Still I can see humans delivering this framework, and the developers in layer 4 beginning to leverage such capability in AI systems.

So as a parting thought this is why I think that any realization of the technological singularity is predicated by the ubiquitous deployment of IP multicast as a "native" capability of the Internet.

11

Deep-Dives (Case Studies)

This section contains two articles that look in depth at some infrastructures I have been closely involved in designing and deploying. The first is look at a hybrid TV platform extensively used in the UK, and the second focuses on NASDAQ's Market Disclosure platform – one of the largest and most used platforms I have designed and deployed. From a commercial perspective these are both very much live platforms, and so I am relatively tied about getting free reign to talk about too many specifics. However, some time ago I cleared the two texts through their PR departments as part of a publication in *StreamingMedia* magazine I was asked to contribute. While they first appeared in 2014, they are still, at the point of writing, absolutely relevant.

11.1   Hitting the TV Screen – IPTV/Hybrid TV and OTT

(This section was first published as an article in www.streamingmedia.com *in 2014[1])*

The term "OTT" is used for many types of video delivery. Here are the different OTT workflow models, and the various ways they bring videos to viewers.

"Over the top" (OTT) is one of the most overused and ambiguous buzzwords in our industry.

In order to understand linear video delivery in OTT models, first, you have to look at what OTT means outside of video. To mobile operators, OTT is a scary proposition. Calls, text messaging, and image messaging had been entirely within operators' control until now, and therefore presented an opportunity for revenue. For those operators, OTT services are an almost unavoidable symptom of smartphones requiring open Internet access, and bring with them many services that compete with operators' traditional revenue models. King of all these is Skype, and it provides a clear example of what "top" the

---

[1] http://www.streamingmedia.com/Articles/ReadArticle.aspx?ArticleID=97565&PageNum=1

Content Delivery Networks: Fundamentals, Design, and Evolution, First Edition. Dom Robinson.
© 2017 by John Wiley & Sons, Inc. Published 2017 by John Wiley & Sons, Inc.

service comes "over" to earn the moniker OTT: namely the pay wall that is the per-minute billing system of the mobile operator.

In exactly the same way I often dogmatically emphasize that "cloud" is an economic term defining the move of CAPEX to OPEX when building IT infrastructure, OTT is also an economic term first and foremost. At best, it means that the operators are able to derive data transit and bandwidth-oriented revenues for the delivery of network service on behalf of providers that otherwise charge much higher premiums to end users or sponsors. At worst, operators are loss-leading that data transit to encourage subscribers to stay with them rather than take their business to other operators. All the while, OTT services are taking revenue from network operators' subscribers and not (necessarily) sharing any of that revenue with the network operator.

However, with this economic common denominator noted, in any specific technical context the term OTT has a range of implementation models that ensure that the cost of this data transit and bandwidth delivery itself is as profitable as possible for the network operator, whether profit is measured in operator CDN revenues or in terms of subscriber retention.

Therefore one group of operator-focused broadcast OTT models for the increasingly connected TV market typically uses subscriber ISPs to deliver OTT services. For this community, OTT evokes a tight coupling of application control, typically embedded securely in smart TVs or Set-Top Boxes, with a primary content origination strategy.

This typically results in a streaming video-based workflow connecting content publishing sources with points of distribution in some form of content management system. This in turn is synchronized with the applications in the end user premises, and presented as some form of electronic program guide or other user interface on their device.

Broadcast OTT providers work closely with operator CDNs to ensure quality of service across well-managed IP networks, and they will work in regions. This is result of these operator CDN relationships, as well as the market-shaping caused by the existing TV content rights models.

For example, in the UK, we see the BBC (iPlayer), Sky (SkyNOW), and BT (BTSport/BT Vision) as leading examples of common OTT propositions. While the content originates in a form that is delivered directly to the Internet for general-purpose access through a device of the consumer's choosing, each of these publishers also works very hard to also deliver their own services well to connected TVs and Set-Top Boxes. This results in, for example, Freeview, YouView, BT Vision, and Virgin Media Set-Top Boxes in the UK, with Internet connections, that can access BBC iPlayer, or Sky Now, and these services typically appear alongside other OTT providers such as YouTube, Netflix, and Vimeo.

There is a key separation between simple streaming applications that the device can browse and the broadcast OTT providers – the broadcast OTT provider's services will appear "integrated" with traditional broadcast TV, where services such as YouTube and Netflix will be entirely separate applications.

An example: A typical user might see TV, YouTube, and Netflix options on her main connected TV menu, but might not see BBC iPlayer as a stand-alone menu application. However, the traditional BBC1 linear TV broadcast might include extended features, such as red button, network DVR, pause and rewind live, or extended on-demand viewing catalogs, perhaps related to the current broadcast. All of these are made possible by the tight integration of the BBC with the broadcast OTT provider's app that is in effect native on the end device.

This native capability is brought about by the device manufacturers' adoption of various "standard" OTT models that have formed within different schools and layers of the broadcast industry as it has worked out how to adopt IP in its distribution workflow.

Some examples of this are the UK Digital Television Group's D-Book standard, and YouView's and HbbTV's initiatives as well as the Open IPTV Forum. Each lays out parameters for how devices should respond to applications that are delivered over the air, giving those who are able to deliver such applications an exclusive reach and capability to derive additional revenue or value.

In the D-Book/Freeview Plus model, an MHEG (Multimedia and Hypermedia Experts Group) application is broadcast along with the digital television signal, and is received and decoded by the device, which in turn responds to any streaming content requests made by the user by using the device's Internet connection to acquire and play the stream back. Because the application is only available to those in the broadcast footprint, the users of the service are limited to that footprint too.

This means that an ISP covering the same footprint becomes a great candidate for a broadcast OTT provider's content delivery network, and a direct connection from the broadcast OTT provider's content aggregation and origination point effectively means that the broadcast OTT provider is delivering content directly to the end user. Again, partnerships between broadcast OTT platforms and particular network operators are common, if not imperative.

YouTube and Netflix, by contrast, are user-activated applications. These need to be specifically coded against the device's native middleware and may simply be extensions of the device's Internet browsing capability. The content is delivered from the YouTube or Netflix CDN to the end user through the end user's ISP. While this simplifies publishing for YouTube and Netflix (they don't need to establish a new delivery workflow for each operator), the lack of tight integration with the end device limits them from offering certain broadcast-friendly premium features, such as the red button services overlaid on the broadcast services.

So this application "paywall" still exists and draws a protective boundary for the broadcasters to add value and maintain their subscriber revenues.

11.1.1 The Taxonomy of OTT Video

As you can see, the definition of OTT really depends on where the service is charged, rather than on any specific technical strategy.

While Netflix and YouTube are often cited as typical OTT services, they actually represent only one type: "Pureplay OTT" for the purposes of this article, to distinguish them from the more tightly workflow-integrated broadcast OTT models discussed above.

Going further, we could loosely group the different models like this:

11.1.1.1 Digital Terrestrial Television (DTT)/Direct to Home (DTH) Satellite Operators

The operators may use a DTT or DTH system to provide traditional broadcast services. They may or may not use IP on these privately managed networks, and will require specific consumer devices/ Set-Top Boxes to connect to these networks. The OTT application control (MHEG/ EPG data, etc.) needs to be transmitted over the (usually non-IP) broadcast network as part of the broadcast transmission. (The red button trigger is sent in the broadcast stream.)

11.1.1.2 IPTV Operators

These are, in effect, ISPs with QoS controlled subscriber circuits, managed IP end to end. The consumer would have to subscribe to her network services to receive the IPTV packages, which come with a specific Set-Top Box and a specific access circuit to the home.

11.1.1.3 Broadcast OTT Operators

These are analogous to the traditional DTT/DTH multiple service operators, although they work entirely in the IP domain, and they hand off the delivery responsibility to either their own operator CDN and access network or third party ISP subscriber networks. They target specific devices and often tightly integrate with the existing DTT/DTH and Telco services to provide the OTT services as value added extensions of the existing DTT/DTH broadcasts. While the paywall may reside with the broadcast OTT operator, the partner DTT/ DTH and Telco networks often have a direct commercial relationship, even if that only extends to providing access to the Set-Top Boxes with EPG and UI support (although it may extend to a near-IPTV like distribution model too).

11.1.1.4 Pureplay OTT Operators

These are completely distinct from the access networks and the application layer delivery. In reality the very large players such as YouTube and Netflix will work closely with connected TV and Set-Top Box vendors to provide native optimized applications closer to the broadcast OTT model, although there are many PC-based Set-Top Boxes on the market that can access Netflix and

YouTube APIs and display the content in their local browsers as if there was a native application. Pureplay OTT operators might not develop relationships with the broadcast network operators, leaving the content distribution to partner Pureplay CDNs. One thing they do share, and which defines them as Pureplay OTT operators, is that they do not have end-to-end QoS guarantees. In that respect they are technically indistinguishable from traditional streaming services found online throughout the web today.

These models are all shown on the topology schematic of Figure 11.1.

I would like to highlight a few key things that I have tried to represent in this diagram.

The circle to the right shows the physical broadcast access networks that reach the end user. A subscriber who is connected to this wired physical network layer (which may well not be IP based) can connect through that physical layer to the cable TV broadcast signals. Consumers with IP access are able to reach the operator CDN, the IPTV services, and potentially third party Pureplay OTT services.

The circle in the middle outlines the broadcast operator's operational networks, where the content is prepared and distributed to the physical access networks.

The small circle shows a third party telecoms (or cable) network that provides the end user with Internet access through an ISP that is neither involved in the OTT services nor in the broadcast services.

Note that in the top-right corner the DTT and DTH broadcasters can use broadcast networks that are not physically connected to the end users. Broadcast models such as this provide no native return path, which is critical for IP-based OTT services. For DTT and DTH this means that a separate Internet connection must be provided to the end user, typically by ADSL or FTTH, and this may or may not be bundled with the OTT service subscription.

Within and between the right and the middle circles, operators can control QoS, and the perimeters of these circles show the boundaries where that control ends.

The circle to the left represents the Internet, where, for example, a Pureplay CDN might operate. The edges of that CDN network might offer public Internet peering (shown as the - - - route) or private peering and transit connectivity (the —— route), and this direct connection to the broadcast operator's physical IP network could provide a QoS managed environment from the CDN hand-off forward to the end user.

This topology does not allow for guaranteed end-to-end QoS, since the CDN only offers a best-effort SLA. In turn the Pureplay OTT provider can only pass on "improved" QoS to the broadcaster. The typical approach to the non-QoS regions between the CDN and the ISPs or operator networks is to provision significant extra capacity in interconnects and peering and cross their fingers – and to be honest, this model works very well.

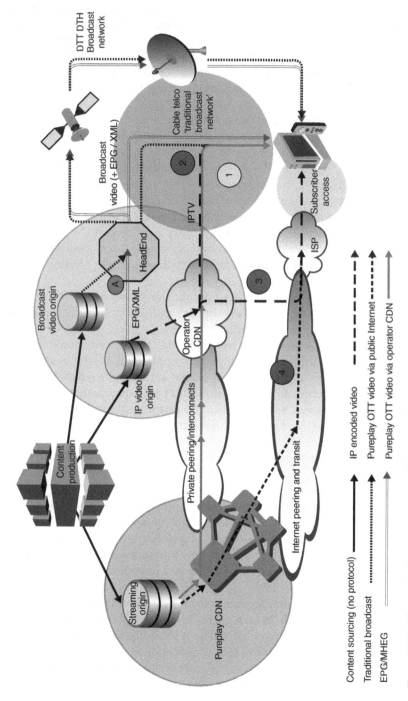

Figure 11.1 Schematic of premium content delivery platforms.

Content sourcing (no protocol) ———

Traditional broadcast ·············

EPG/MHEG ————

IP encoded video ———

Pureplay OTT video via public Internet ············

Pureplay OTT video via operator CDN ———

DTT DTH Broadcast network

Broadcast video (+ EPG / XML)

Cable telco 'traditional broadcast network'

IPTV

Broadcast video origin

HeadEnd

A

EPG/XML

IP video origin

Content production

Operator CDN

Private peering/interconnects

Streaming origin

Pureplay CDN

Internet peering and transit

ISP

Subscriber access

1

2

3

4

That approach, however, is not usually viewed positively when commercial contracts are put in place. Therefore private links between the operator and the content provider are usually created for accountability reasons rather than technical ones. This can lead to certain OTT providers working closely with the broadcast operators, such as Netflix arranged with Comcast in the US.

This model is shown as the (——) line. It represents a service such as Netflix as an augmented service to IPTV generated inside Virgin Media and delivered over their network with QoS guaranteed end to end, or even simply to the traditional cable, DTT, or DTH service with little operational overhead for the broadcast operator, beyond charging Netflix for the regional operator CDN distribution as an incremental revenue to their core broadcast subscriptions. In this model, end users may subscribe directly to Netflix as an extra expense on top of their basic broadcast package subscription.

Of course, free content such as YouTube or BBC iPlayer carries no premium subscription from the end users. In these circumstances the operator CDN costs may be perceived to be simply a loss leader for the OTT providers, so YouTube or BBC may simply opt to extend its web-facing streaming content to the Virgin Media Set-Top Box audience through the public Internet model. With this approach the user avoids becoming dependent on the operator CDN.

This tends to create a more level co-dependent playing field for both parties: the operator CDN might opt to internally bear the cost of bringing the content to the EPG, so that the Pureplay OTT services can be browsed. This can be as straightforward as supporting the OTT services in the Set-Top Box's browser. The broadcast OTT provider would have to make an investment to do this, but the Pureplay OTT providers' content is a must-have that they cannot exclude from their package without losing subscribers.

In this case the cost of network transit between the Pureplay OTT providers' CDN edge and the end user is free to the broadcast network if it is delivered by the Pureplay OTT operator and distributed through the end user's chosen ISP. This is the lowest QoS SLA and accordingly the cheapest OTT model, but it is also usually good enough for most consumers.

At the other end of the spectrum, the (– –) IP-encoded video can be delivered directly from the operator network to the broadcast access network and, so long as the end user is "on net," then QoS can be guaranteed. This would classify the IP delivered video as being IPTV; it is interesting to note that the same video delivered via a third party ISP would change the terminology from IPTV to OTT, and this QoS differential is often (questionably) cited as the wall that we have gone over when defining OTT, leading many to think that OTT is of worse quality than IPTV or broadcast.

Finally, point A shows a critical interface where the MHEG app, or similar EPG details that announce the existence of any OTT content over the traditional broadcast network, is established.

This thin ══ line (seen by marker A in the head end) represents metadata and small application data that is distributed over the broadcast network to facilitate access to the broadcaster OTT content. It is exclusively available as part of those traditional broadcasts, and this couples these services to relationships between the broadcast network operators, the broadcast OTT operators, and the content providers. This closeness creates commercial control and is driving revenue for all these parties, something that Pureplay OTT services often do not do.

Arqiva, which delivers the Freeview Plus services in the UK, calls this version of broadcast OTT architecture "hybrid TV" with their particular product known as "Connect TV."

At an encoding and content preparation level, the only difference between OTT networks and typical web streaming workflows comes down to the encoding profiles for targeting the connected TVs and OTT Set-Top Box decoders.

At the network layer there are several models that vary cost, quality of service, and control of the paywall, and each provides different value to the various stakeholders.

To sum up, OTT has many topologies and workflows, but all share the common theme that the revenues they drive are typically, at least in part, earned by third parties external to the broadcast and ISP access networks used by the end users and subscribers.

11.1.2 Arqiva Connect and Freeview Plus

The Arqiva Connect TV hybrid platform is designed to provide OTT content to the DTT service Freeview Plus (available to around 6.6 million homes in the UK). My company, id3as, provided some of the core software components.

In Figure 11.2 is a schematic showing the technical layout of the workflow.

Since Q1 2013 the id3as microservice and virtualization strategy has provided Arqiva with 100% availability (at the point of writing!). It is an ever-evolving and dynamic model by design (much is effectively located in a private cloud internally at Arqiva). The core workflow is optimized as shown in Figure 11.2.

Working left to right, a variety of content is contributed in broadcast video formats to Arqiva's facility, from which Arqiva can select various signals and route them though an acquisition process into diverse IP sources.

Once in IP, the signal is then made available to our encoding cloud where id3as' software manages the live and archive content generation, ready for the end users' connected TVs, devices, and Set-Top Boxes.

In parallel to the technology platform shown here, the clients then receive a signal via their DTT broadcast transmissions that, through the device's electronic program guide, notify the user of the available OTT content.

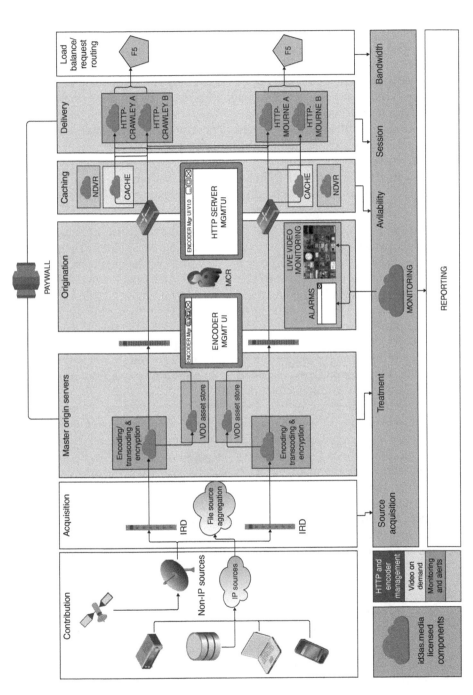

Figure 11.2 Schematic of id3as' Arqiva workflow for hybrid TV.

Once selected, the OTT MHEG application launches. At this stage, functions such as payment and security can be completed using the device's Internet connection, and the user can access the online content management system and content distribution network.

As you can see, there are several options in the delivery, load-balancing, and CDN layers, and these can be dynamically adjusted to manage any variation in the service orchestration.

Supervision, control, and reporting are all centralized in the master control room, giving complete oversight in a condensed and responsive way to Arqiva's operations teams.

Osman Sen-Chadun, head of technology and operations for hybrid TV at Arqiva, has this to say about his company's OTT strategy:

> Arqiva provides mission critical communications and media infrastructure, and so it is natural for us to be adapting our capabilities to help our many existing clients, who are at the very heart of the broadcast sector, to extend their reach into emerging digital TV markets – many of which are being delivered online or at least using IP.
>
> We have a reputation among those clients for offering the very best operational supervision and continuity of service for their extremely valuable business. Venturing into the OTT space is not something we have undertaken lightly. For an industry used to ASICs and very high grade, tested appliances, considering "commodity servers" in our core has taken some cultural adjustment.
>
> While the demand for "TV Everywhere" is growing rapidly we have had to ensure that we have sufficient control and resilience over the technology we operate for our clients. We guarantee to deliver the best possible service ourselves, and that the experience for our customers is consistent with the many other broadcast services that we already provide to them.
>
> The multi-site private cloud model we have adopted gives us the ability to meet this level of operational oversight of the physical computers, but also to dynamically reallocate resources between the varied demands for the various tasks of encoding, transcoding, security, and distribution (and so on).
>
> id3as, our software partner, has provided a tailor-made technology stack, which is ideally suited to this dynamic OTT workflow, and integrates tightly with our wider working processes. This includes one of the widest device compatibilities of any comparable provider, and that is largely down to our ability to be flexible and add box-by-box support as new configurations come out – something that would be much more complex in our traditional environment.

These changes to the core of how broadcast can be delivered are in turn precipitating new propositions for end users. We are seeing the economics disrupted, meaning that, for example, some broadcasters can offer several more focused niche OTT channels in the place of a second broadcast channel.

Internet-delivered services are a fantastic partner for a long-term technical joint strategy, and that is what OTT represents to Arqiva. It is a way to bring together the inherent advantages of reliability and confidence that the discipline of traditional broadcast carries, with the diversity of application and innovation that IP delivered technology can support.

And this IP connectedness also brings unprecedented audience understanding – we have a discrete "return path" from each user, and every day we learn more and more about audiences. This helps optimize every aspect of the broadcast media workflow in a way that has, in the broadcast sector at least, always been extremely valuable.

11.2 Creating Nasdaq's Cloud-Based Virtual Workflow

(This section appeared as an article in the August/September 2013 issue of StreamingMedia *magazine as "NASDAQ's Cloud-Based Virtual Workflow")*

Before I get into the meat of this article, I need to preface with a couple of comments. First, this is a case study about my own company's solution for one of our major clients. I rarely write in these pages about my own clients and solutions, but when I learned that this edition was focusing on cloud-based workflows, I wanted to break my own tradition. The story I am about to tell you has been one of the most interesting voyages I have undertaken in this industry, and it has direct relevance to this edition of the magazine.

Second, I wanted to comment on the term "cloud." I appreciate that in the mass market the term "cloud" has become a generic buzzword for anything that works on the Internet. At the same time, in the "innovators" circles, it is trendy at the moment to decry the word, opting instead for more specialized terms and definitions. I too have my own definition and understanding of the term. At the outset of this story, I thought cloud was a technical description. At the end of the three years this story spans, I have learned that cloud is *really* about the service and economic advantage that the chosen architecture can offer its eventual owners.

Now let me provide some backdrop. Webcasting is an evolved technology that has found traction in the financial markets since it first emerged. While most financial institutions are quite conservative and deliberate about their technology spends, the spend made by their marketing and public relations (PR) teams on their own IT to manage their corporate communications has typically been more autonomous; it is seen as something that operates outside of the corporate firewall, at least up to the point that the chair's annual report is broadcast into the enterprise network infrastructure. This internal tension between the typical public company's IT directors and the marketing directors has often led to debates over who has the right to use the corporate network, as well as for what reasons. The in-house AV teams are often thrown the ball to sort the problem out, and they often opt to outsource the webcast production service to their PR agencies, who subcontract professional webcast service providers.

No company has positioned itself so strongly in the middle of this pool of webcast service providers for the financial markets as NASDAQ OMX Corporate Solutions. In 2013 NASDAQ OMX acquired the Investor Relations, Public Relations and Multimedia businesses of Thomson Reuters, including the webcasting unit to whom my company provides extensive technologies). With tens of thousands of live events held annually, NASDAQ OMX Corporate Solutions is the 800-pound gorilla in the financial service webcast sector that provides fair disclosure and investor relations services to its many Fortune 500 (and other) clients.

11.2.1 The Genesis of a Virtual Workflow

Some years ago, I was engaged in a late-night conversation at a Streaming Media Europe event with Andreas Heidoetting, global head of webcast technology, who has a range of responsibilities for the NASDAQ OMX Corporate Solutions webcasting infrastructure. We were discussing the various workflow aspects of operating its four global broadcast network operation centres, through which NASDAQ ran all its online events. We were thinking outside the box and focused on removing expensive, heavily manual third party encoding call capture vendors – on which a great dependency had developed largely as a legacy from the acquisition of Corporate Communications Broadcast Network (CCBN) several years before. Such a change could yield a potentially significant efficiency saving if we could deliver it.

Essentially, the workflow was scaled to meet a peak demand, which NASDAQ hit on each quarterly reporting round, at which time there may be many hundreds of live events running across the platform. However, generally, the systems were running an average load nearly an order of magnitude lower. For a year this meant a whole lot of expensive kits on standby and skilled operators that needed occupying.

The brainstorming session developed into an initial consulting project where we isolated the key technologies that could not be emulated in software, which were relatively few, and started talking about developing an entirely virtual workflow. This had appeal, since you could launch such a workflow on a virtual platform, use it when you needed it, and then destroy it (getting rid of any maintenance and hosting cost).

Afterward, with my team at id3as (a professional services consultancy for streaming media), we put together a working proof of concept for NASDAQ OMX Corporate Solutions that removed the reliance on the audio capture interfaces that were historically deployed to dial into analyst briefing calls – the lion's share of their webcasts. With this removed, we had a workflow with Internet protocol (IP) in and IP out; everything else was software based.

We deployed this proof of concept on Amazon Elastic Compute Cloud (Amazon EC2), and while it was crude – inasmuch as the entire process was manually driven via remote desktop – it proved that we could build a workflow to complete the same task as the tens of thousands of audio-only analyst briefings that were operated from within its existing network operations center (NOC), without any requirement for physical servers, phone lines, or encoders.

Andreas had introduced Simon Ball, global head of webcast operations, NASDAQ OMX Corporate Solutions, who was very engaged by this stage. Ultimately there were a number of seeds germinating, and it was clear that by the time they came to fruition, the opportunity here would be to decommission the NOCs and pay only for the compute time that they used, with little or no underutilization.

We ran some spreadsheets, and the business case looked extremely attractive. While it would be inappropriate for me to discuss my client's inner financials in this article, the cost savings were predicted in orders of magnitude.

Having hundreds of encoders and management computers running in multiple webcast operations centers – ready and waiting for peak usage, and yet normally operating at a small fraction of that capacity – meant underutilization was an expensive business. We subsequently changed that dynamic so that the only time any infrastructure was up, operating, and costing money was when it was directly in use for client delivery and directly earning money.

Regardless of how it was done – I will look at some key aspects of the technology later – this "cloud" of intangible systems is brought into action as soon as required, and it is destroyed (at least as far as any cost of ownership is concerned) the moment it is no longer directly making the business money. For me, this is what the cloud is all about: the cloud should really refer to dynamic economic and service models and not to anything technical at all. It's all about what it offers, not how it does it. Anyone who leads with any technical advantage the cloud delivers misses the point if he or she doesn't offer an economic/ service advantage first and foremost. Now that I have labored that point, let us look at the relevant technology involved.

11.2.2 The Technology Behind the Workflow

Those of you who are managing workflow infrastructures such as the ones that the NASDAQ OMX Corporate Solutions teams operate, and who are considering the cloud as a way forward, are probably itching to ask a few questions. While I can't predict all of them and must be mindful of my client's confidentialities, here are a few of the questions we have been asked at some of the Amazon developer and Streaming Media conference presentations we gave last year. I'll use these as a base to dig a bit deeper into the infrastructure architecture that my company, id3as, delivered.

11.2.3   Why Amazon EC2?

In 2010, when we tested out the various public cloud operators that we were hoping to use, we had a mandate to ensure that the entire solution would be vendor independent. The first important thing this meant was that we were limited to cloud providers offering Infrastructure as a Service (IaaS). In IaaS compute models, you pay for a virtual computer by the minute or hour and that's it; it's up to you to configure it to whatever application you require. This differs from what Platform as a Service (PaaS) offerings such as OVPs may offer, where you buy access to a range of applications that are all preconfigured and you fit into their workflow. IaaS also differs from Software as a Service (SaaS) platforms such as CDNs in general, or perhaps Amazon's CloudFront or simple storage service (S3) networks, which perform specific software functions that you can integrate into your own applications.

Many people view content delivery networks (CDNs) as SaaS clouds – and thus they are seen as some of the first commercially available clouds. You are not, for example, buying time on a computer to run your own media servers. Instead, you are buying just the software service of (for example) real time messaging protocol (RTMP) Flash streaming.

At the time, only three operators had significant IaaS infrastructure available for global services, and we really struggled with another well-known provider. While the company touted its cloud proposition, the reality was that its offering was more of a virtual hosting environment. Its control API was limited – certainly compared to Amazon EC2's – and while the pricing per hour of compute time was competitive, we had many occasions where the servers we ordered through its system were taking not seconds or minutes to provision and become available; they were sometimes taking hours and even days! To be fair, I would imagine the other vendor has addressed this issue by now – we did provide an extensive debug for its staffers to work against at the time – but the lack of confidence was already instilled in our client's mind, and we were left with only one option: to build an Amazon–Amazon resilience. Essentially this means that we always launch the workflow in two totally separate regions and availability zones and are ready to instantly deploy a third workflow in a third region within a few seconds.

To summarize and answer the question directly, the key reason we use Amazon EC2 is that we had no real option at the time. We are still open to vendor diversification, and, to be fair, we will review other vendors during the next 12 months. However, the reality is that for IaaS, Amazon EC2 is an extraordinary platform – way ahead of the pack as far as public IaaS – and has proved to be extremely reliable and cost-effective, as well as truly global.

A still (Figure 11.3) from an animated model representing actual activity in the cloud shows Amazon East (light gray) and Amazon Ireland (black background) scaling up to meet demand during peak usage. The black and grey boxes represent the 24/7 central management systems.

This data model (Figure 11.4) shows the 24/7 central management systems during quiet times; the Amazon nodes have been spun down to save money.

Figure 11.3 Operating at scale.

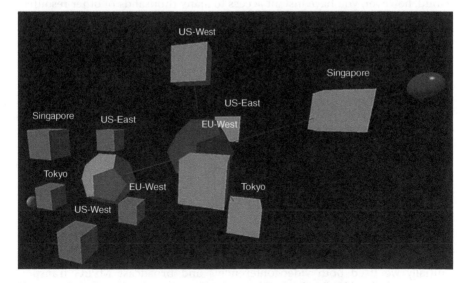

Figure 11.4 Scaling down in quiet times (where public cloud *really* adds value).

11.2.4 What Sort of Scaling Issues did You Face?

The NASDAQ OMX Corporate Solutions platform has extremely volatile usage patterns. At the end of the financial year, we may see thousands of companies reporting at pretty much the same time; this requires, along with several management and reporting servers, at least double that number of encoders to deliver. This level of spikiness is an outlier even for a company the size of Amazon EC2, so we had to negotiate specific permission to create such large demands on its infrastructure on short notice.

One thing that was crucial was the ability to move encoders from one availability zone to an alternative in the circumstances that the initial target zone didn't have capacity. Our technology completely abstracts NASDAQ OMX Corporate Solutions' working processes from all that underlying complexity.

11.2.5 How about SLA?

Amazon EC2 offers at least 99.95% (aws.amazon.com/ec2-sla) availability. This translates to a target of 4.38 hours annually that the entire service may be unavailable. Our application always runs in at least two regions all the time. Broadly speaking, this means we end up with an overall service-level agreement (SLA) for our application of $(100 - (0.05\% \times 0.05\%)) = 99.9975\%$. The key to maintaining this availability is the autonomy of the different regions and the applications. The chances of something going wrong on a server in a public cloud data center are hardly different from the odds of something going wrong on a machine you own and host in your own location. In the case of an IaaS public cloud, however, you have instant access to many thousands of other resources to use in place, and you can – and should – be using multiple systems for redundancy all the time.

I have written before about people who claim Amazon EC2 is not reliable after famous Reddit and Netflix outages. Amazon EC2 is usually operating well within its SLA; the issue was that Reddit and Netflix did not code their applications well to respect outages or failures. In contrast, the platform we delivered to NASDAQ OMX Corporate Solutions is automatically operating hundreds of servers in multiple regions of Amazon EC2, and we only knew that the previously mentioned outages had had any effect on our delivery by inspecting our logs. Our applications simply fail between machines (in a single frame of video or audio), the downstream origination, and the upstream CDNs, and the clients would have been unaware.

11.2.6 What about Signal Acquisition?

In simple terms, signal acquisition into Amazon EC2 has to be facilitated on IP. Initially we used both videoconferencing and broadcast MPEG transport stream video sources to contribute signals into the infrastructures directly from events. Likewise we used voice over IP (VoIP) for audio-only signal acquisition.

Today, we have delivered a "field encoder" image – our Out-Side Kit (OSK) – that combines a simple web GUI on top of a minimum configurable encoding engine to avoid engineering issues in the field. The cloud–core system configures each remote OSK for each job. The OSK uses GRIT (our multipath channel-bonding protocol) to aggregate available IP into a single logical pipe, and can encode from low bitrate audio to 4k. Each OSK contributes to multiple points in the Amazon network, and we also have a virtual telephony bridge that acquires a backup audio stream from the "normal" analysts' conference bridge in case the IP fails all together. This can be muxed into the video streams or simply delivered as its own audio stream to the web users.

The Amazon web services data centers are all extremely well connected, so contribution issues have usually been down to remote connectivity at the origin (on-site at the event). We have, at times, experienced network splits within the Amazon infrastructure, emphasizing the importance of being able to automatically select alternative zones for encoders on-the-fly.

11.2.7 What about OS Choices and Stacks?

The initial implementation was built using Windows, as it made use of several Windows-only third party tools, such as Windows and Flash Media encoders. Once it was live, we found that almost all of the operational challenges we faced arose from these third party tools. Over time id3as developed its own end-to-end suite of technologies (id3as.media) capable of replacing all these third party tools (apart from codecs) and doing so in a platform-agnostic way. This has allowed us to greatly improve platform stability and significantly reduce IaaS costs by moving from Windows to Linux, which is considerably cheaper by the hour.

11.2.8 How Is the System Controlled?

Agents in a NASDAQ OMX Corporate Solutions operations center based in Manila, The Philippines, and Leipzig, Germany, supervise the entire system, although there are disaster recovery capabilities across the world, since the management layer is entirely web based. Schedules for events are delivered by the NASDAQ OMX Corporate Solutions management systems into a resilient and distributed (cloud-based) database. These management systems are in multiple availability zones, and they receive instructions about when to fire up encoders for various events. Notification is presented on the web GUI to the supervisors.

This same web GUI allows the operator full control over the events, including cutting and editing on-the-fly (using DVR-like techniques to mark up the edit decision list) to ultimately produce on-demand files within moments of the live event finishing. The GUI also alerts the operator to any signal confidence failures and enables a single operator to supervise multiple events at the same time, greatly increasing the productiveness of the call center team. The id3as.media management and control subsystem is all written in Erlang, a language designed specifically to produce very large-scale, extremely available/reliable distributed systems.

11.2.9   How Does it Report?

As the id3as.media software replaced all the third party technologies in the workflow, it provided an opportunity to consolidate reporting into a clean, clear, and dynamic reporting model using graph-like output. This means that id3as can drill into any issue in the workflow in a graphical way, with an almost unlimited amount of detail available. This ensures that stand-alone, real-time monitoring is possible out of the box; it's also tightly integrated into NASDAQ OMX Corporate Solutions' own management and reporting systems.

To summarize – and I have said it before – the IT craze for all things "cloud" would, at first, seem to be all about technology, but it's not. It is really a broad term for dynamic economic models that are underpinned by a variety of technologies.

Yes, you can generally (technically) do in the cloud what you would do on private dedicated equipment, but the key advantage should be cost and flexibility. It should, as with the example in this article, be driven by the real value proposition to the customer and not clouded with trendy buzzwords.

12

Wrap Up

So here we are in the final pages. I won't keep you much longer! I hope that the contents of the book has given you plenty to come and have a chat about should we intersect at a conference, and indeed hopefully a few reasons to have a robust debate and perhaps change both of our thinking for the better!

I also hope that through the narrative to have provided something a little unusual in terms of technical reference and thought provoking insight when considering all the facets involved in designing and delivering a CDN of any type.

Before we go it's probably worth a recap of some of the chapters and some of the things I hope you will take away having read this book.

Early on we looked at both my perception and experience of the sector. It is a sector that I feel has grown up around me more than one that I have grown within (although obviously both are true!) While I'm proud of my career and I had some amazing experiences, it is by no means unique. There are many people I have met on my voyages who have had equally (if not more) interesting experiences and can offer deeper insight into many different aspects of this exciting and emerging industry. It is a vibrant sector for sure.

As I return to the day-to-day duties of business development and innovation at id3as, I am reminded how lucky I am with my job to spend my time playing with both impossibly large hard and soft constructs and at the same time trying to pay attention to impossibly tiny atomic detail.

We looked at some of the commercial successes and failures that I have both undergone myself and have seen others around me undergo as online video streaming and CDN's have emerged.

I hope by seeing some of the failures you're now better armed to avoid repeating the mistakes of others. While many academic books focus on current best practice, I am confident in my conviction that there has been a place in the market for a text that can contextualize the CDN designer not just to build the best network for today but also to provide themselves architectural advantages that will allow them to ensure that their design is agile enough to keep up with the pace not change coming not only "tomorrow" but more than likely "today."

Content Delivery Networks: Fundamentals, Design, and Evolution, First Edition. Dom Robinson.
© 2017 by John Wiley & Sons, Inc. Published 2017 by John Wiley & Sons, Inc.

Virtualization has to be central to your strategy. Without a doubt, the biggest problem my early CDN Global-MIX faced was our inflexibility and inability to adapt to the changing marketplace as it became driven by the consumer.

Today, I understand architects who believe that virtualization doesn't bring anything to network that is always doing the same thing. But while I do understand them, I think this view is shortsighted, and reflects inexperience. If nothing else my 20-year purview does offer some "experience," and I know that every CDN needs to change constantly to reflect its target markets demands. Virtualization is the first step toward that, but critically even in periods where there is no change happening, virtualization brings higher availability and greater service velocity to meet traffic demands and the localization of services.

We took some time to look at the ownership of various technology models. Patents and their "trolls" have even had a look in! At the time of writing this wrap up, news has just been announced the Nokia has launched a patent attack on Apple and notably Acacia who were the subject of our focus on patent trolls in Section 2.4.2 are the partner of Nokia in their suit against Apple. Apple interestingly are countersuing on the grounds that they are simply being trolled.

For people new to the sector, my hope is that by becoming more aware of these types of behaviors and cycles in the industry, they can better prepare themselves as they select their technology and strategy within their designs.

By my own admission, throughout this book I have taken a very live TV centric approach to CDN. I have only cursorily touched on dynamic site acceleration, web object, and other such aspects of the CDN market, so I would encourage you to read widely and to explore deeply these models. While they tend to "assume" more from the underlying network, and require less-specific expertise in networking and telecoms than the challenge of live TV or live webcasting online, they address many other problems in an extremely closely related area. A good understanding of both is key.

If you picked up this book expecting more about general content delivery architecture than I have delivered, I can only apologize and encourage you to reach out to me so that either I can help or I can put you in touch with some of the leading thinkers in those specific areas.

On reflection, we spent lots of time exploring a wide range of topics that must have at times seemed wildly off course when searching for insight on the pure computer science of CDN architecture. However, a CDN is invariably a complex beast servicing many people's expectations, and to try to deliver into those expectations as the CDN's designer, you must think as big as possible, as broadly as possible, and as laterally as possible, and must also master the depth of detail in all these contributing elements as they influence your design.

To this end, conversations about the regulatory environment, content rights, the commercial aspirations of network operators and content providers, and the pragmatic reality of the consumer (and so on) must ALL always be taken into account at design time.

Obviously for a small CDN being built between two or three locations, much of this may not seem pertinent. But in practice, if you take a moment to think about the issues explored in this book and consider them in your design, you will find that your design is improved by such broad contextual consideration.

You will have noticed that I've purposefully tried hard not to be too specific about particular vendors and to talk generically about technology types. Those I have highlighted have been mentioned to clarify a topic, rather than to overly praise or scathingly put down. In the same way, while I have mentioned a few details about my own commercial ventures, I have tried not to labor these explorations unnecessarily for fear of the text becoming boring!

There will be plenty of time for that at the conference bar when we meet.

For now I hope reading this book has been fun, thought provoking, and stimulating, but most important, I look forward to seeing and hearing from you over the next years about how these words have impacted your work on real-world content delivery network fundamentals, design, and evolution.

dom@id3as.co.uk

Index

Content Delivery Networks: Fundamentals, Design, and Evolution, First Edition. Dom Robinson.
© 2017 by John Wiley & Sons, Inc. Published 2017 by John Wiley & Sons, Inc.